Parting from Phantoms

➤➤ ◄◄

CHRISTA WOLF

➤➤ ◄◄

PARTING *from*
PHANTOMS

SELECTED WRITINGS, 1990—1994

➤➤ ◄◄

Translated and Annotated by Jan van Heurck

THE UNIVERSITY OF CHICAGO PRESS ✦ CHICAGO & LONDON

CHRISTA WOLF is the most prominent writer of the former German Democratic Republic. Among her works that have appeared in English translation are two novels, *The Quest for Christa T* and *Cassandra*; *"What Remains" and Other Stories*; and *The Author's Dimension: Selected Essays* (the latter translated by Jan van Heurck, the translator of the present work).

The University of Chicago Press, Chicago 60637
The University of Chicago Press Ltd., London
© 1997 by The University of Chicago
All rights reserved. Published 1997
Printed in the United States of America
05 04 03 02 01 00 99 98 97   1 2 3 4 5

ISBN 0-226-90496-2

First published as *Auf dem Weg nach Tabou. Texte 1990–1994* by Verlag Kiepenheuer & Witsch, Cologne. © Luchterhand Literaturverlag GmbH. Munich

Library of Congress Cataloging-in-Publication Data

Wolf, Christa.
   [Auf dem Weg nach Tabou.   English]
   Parting from phantoms : selected writings, 1990–1994 / Christa Wolf ; translated and annotated by Jan van Heurck.
      p.   cm.
   Includes bibliographical references and index.
   ISBN 0-226-90496-2 (alk. paper)
   I. Heurck, Jan van.   II. Title.
PT2685.O36A613   1997
833'.914—dc21   97-8799
                                                         CIP

Contents

✥✥ ✥✥

CONTENTS

Translator's Foreword

→→ ←←

Seeing clearly is important to Christa Wolf. A central noun in her fiction, as in her literary criticism, is *der Blick*, "look, gaze," and her protagonists are would-be clairvoyants, from her alter ego Nelly in *Patterns of Childhood*, who learns to see through the lies of Nazism, to Günderrode in *No Place on Earth*, working "to rend asunder the web of deceit which hides her from herself," and Cassandra, who stands on the wall "to watch the light for the last time" in her Troy where she "had never seen anything more unreal."[1] Christa Wolf has spent much of her life trying to "part from phantoms" inside and outside herself.

Parting from Phantoms, Wolf's first major essay collection since German unification, documents the newest stage in her ongoing and always half-failing struggle against what she calls the "loss of reality." The opening piece explicitly asks readers to collaborate in the process of seeing: to collect the fragments she offers and from them to compose their own picture. The fragments are, for the most part, views of Germany after the Wall, of our world after the Wall, sometimes from the vantage point of other writers—Günter Grass, Jürgen Habermas, Volker Braun—whose letters Wolf includes side

---

1. *Patterns of Childhood* (*Kindheitsmuster*, 1976; English translation 1980), *No Place on Earth* (*Kein Ort. Nirgends*, 1979; English translation 1982, p. 73), *Cassandra* (1983; English translation 1984, pp. 137, 135).

by side with her own; sometimes in the work of artists whom others may not have looked at as carefully as she (Nuria Quevedo, Otl Aicher, Anna Seghers, Paul Parin); sometimes in stylistic experiments on the borderline between essay and fiction or poetry ("Trial by Nail," "Mood Fit," "Reply to a Letter from Volker Braun"); sometimes in her journal entries, recorded at one-year intervals from shifting places and perspectives (Wolf's family home in the East German countryside, her working center in Berlin, and Santa Monica, California). The pieces reveal hidden corners of the self, the ambiguities of motivation, and the difficulty of separating oneself from the phantoms of public and private history. Perhaps no moment in this volume is more characteristic than the lit-up vision near the beginning of the journal entry "Berlin, Monday, September 27, 1993," when Wolf sees her kitchen table shine briefly with the shapes of all the people who have gathered there over the years, tracking the history of the GDR along with her, including the many who are unable to see, and the deliberate spies and deceivers. "We gazed at each other over time out of many pairs of eyes."

Telling us what she can see from her series of vantage points, Wolf does not hide her own propensity to self-deception. Peter Demetz pointed out in *After the Fires* that the struggle Wolf underwent to free herself of the Nazi illusions that made up her childhood gave her a deep commitment to antifascism, which made it more difficult for her later to separate herself from the lies of GDR ideology. To be a loyal Marxist was a kind of expiation.[2] But now, struggling to wake up from the dream of the GDR, she sees the rest of the West deeply enmeshed in falsehood too, as mendacious Greece was in its war with deceitful Troy. In this book she is still the bewildered survivor trying to pick her way among the hordes of phantoms that surround her, trying to cure herself of them one by one if possible, seeming not to arrive at clarity but unwilling to accept the clouded truths that others may come to about her, even if she respects or trusts them as much as she does Grass or Habermas.

My one face-to-face meeting with Christa Wolf occurred after I had already translated three of her books into English, when I attended a conference of her translators near Cologne two years

2. Cf. Peter Demetz, *After the Fires: Recent Writing in the Germanies, Austria, and Switzerland* (New York: Harcourt Brace Jovanovich, 1986), p. 143.

after the Wall came down. At that time she was still under heavy attack from Western critics who, no longer able to make political capital out of citing her as a part-time GDR dissident, now resented her failure to embrace the Western alternative. She was holding out for some other country that lay neither in the West nor in the East, neither in Greece nor in Troy, but somewhere that didn't exist yet, "on the road to Tabou" (as this volume was originally entitled).

"I always pictured you tall and blond, a California type," was the first thing she said to me, having never actually seen me before. There I was, another image in the mind that had to be dispelled. She was leaving for California soon, she said, to spend a year there—the year as a visiting scholar at the Getty Center that she describes in this volume—and she wondered if I would be in the area, because "friendly presences were always welcome." She was going to look back at her country from the faraway United States, thinking she might see it more clearly.

I stammered something to her about the loss of alternatives in my own country and the difficulty of letting the voices of other peoples be heard within the United States. The disappearance of the GDR, whatever its flaws, meant the loss of another space where something different could have been tried in human history, where people could have experimented with their new insights like the citizens of the caves in Cassandra's Troy just before it fell. So I felt at the time, and so I believe did Christa Wolf.

But I was shy about expressing sympathy over the recent press attacks on Wolf and her sudden drop from literary favor. I did not believe she would want anyone to gloss over her mistakes and confusions, and the essays in this book confirm it. In her Berlin journal entry she describes an evening when, addressing her lecture audience, she finds herself wondering if she really thinks what she is saying or has only read it. It is "one of the increasing number of subjects about which I have no definite opinion." She warns against any form of "GDR nostalgia." And in reply to a question from her audience, she rejects as "typically German" the notion that the Stasi files can represent the conscience of her country. Written documents are no substitute for conscience, which requires a living being who is struggling to see clearly at those moments in history when "the Wild Hunt is over the land" and, as Wolf describes the scene at the end of "Trial by Nail," we turn around to look at our pursuers and glimpse our own faces, which we did not want to recognize.

Wolf's ideal of writing, as she states it in the opening piece "Self-Indictment," would show the person "without disguise but not stripped bare, the gaze stricken but not clouded by the residue of unclarified resentments, not cold but involved, as unsentimental as possible, and thus meriting unbiased attention." As a translator I simply want to point to Wolf's language of seeing, to her call for collaboration from the reader in the work of separating from phantoms, and to her claim for unbiased attention. Her work characteristically has the tone of elegy; it speaks of universal delusions and universal human loss behind what newspaper stories may celebrate as victories. It is the speech of those on the losing side who see.

A word about the footnotes: all are by me except notes 4 and 9 to "Rummelplatz, the Eleventh Plenum . . . ," which belong to the German original, and most of the notes to "Cancer and Society," which were prepared for the German edition by Rainer-M. E. Jacobi. The German Democratic Republic is abbreviated as GDR, and the Federal Republic of Germany as FRG.

The only changes to the original German text were to omit the essays on Max Frisch and Friederike Mayröcker, and to add Wolf's television interview with West German journalist Günter Gaus, which was taken from Hermann Vinke's compilation of materials surrounding the question of Wolf's involvement with the GDR's state police.

Jan van Heurck
October 1996

Self-Indictment

→→ ←←

My ideal of writing would be a sort of collaboration. A pen would follow life's traces as exactly as possible; the hand holding it would be my hand and yet not mine. Many people and things would write along with me; what is most subjective would knit inseparably with what is most objective, "just as in real life." A person would be shown without distortion but not stripped bare, the gaze stricken yet unclouded by the residue of unclarified resentments; not cold but involved, as unsentimental as possible, and thus meriting our unbiased attention.

What am I talking about? Today and here, where it is impossible to write with a steady hand, and where the craving for scandals in public life threatens to stifle critical sympathy?

But life continues to leave its mark, and the writings I have collected here bear witness to life, its frustrations and convictions, the disquiet of self-questioning and self-doubt. I have not lost my zest for a challenge. The instruments that time uses against us are sharper than the pen we may use to defend ourselves, to stand our ground. I have tried not to get out of practice. And I am happy to talk about fellow wayfarers on this road, the people I talk with, those who remain and those who are newly discovered, companions essential to my life. Some of their letters show that we are engaged in a permanent dialogue.

So this is a collection of pieces, of fragments that correspond with each other, question each other, even call each other into question. At times, fissures open up between them that I cannot heal, or not yet. These writings do not simulate harmony where none exists or can. They are a mosaic from which observers may compose their own picture if they choose. Texts that often seem to contradict each other, flying high one moment, deep in doldrums the next. But that's how it is. Not portraying contradiction but living it—this experience can be conveyed only in fragments.

A "road to Tabou"?[1] Perhaps only a path, and anyway what does it mean to "move on"? Tabou, or taboo—a welcome ambiguity. That place we never reach, whether it lies in Africa or somewhere else. The way includes backtracking and detours. Observations, notes, that I feel compelled and obligated to record. I am grateful to the people, books, images that prompted me to do so, and to those who demanded it of me.

January 1994

1. A play on the German title of this book, *Auf dem Weg nach Tabou* (see "On the Road to Tabou" below).

The Language of the Turning Point

→→ ←←

E very revolutionary movement liberates language, too. What before was so hard to express suddenly trips off our tongues. We
are amazed to hear what we have been thinking, evidently for a
long time, and now we shout it out to each other: "Democracy—
now or never!" What we mean is rule by the people. We remember
the earlier initiatives in our history that broke down or were blood-
ily suppressed, and we do not want to sleep away once again the
opportunity offered by this crisis, which has awakened all our productive energies. But neither do we wish to spoil it by rashness, or by
turning around our enemy-images to face in the opposite direction.

The word "turning point" is one I have problems with. It
makes me picture a sailboat when the wind turns. The captain calls
out a warning and the crew duck down while the boom sweeps
across the deck. Is this an accurate picture of what is happening?
Does it apply to us, in this situation which every day moves on to
something new?

Speech given in East Berlin on November 4, 1989, the day of the largest mass demonstration in the GDR, which led directly to the collapse of the Honecker government.
The German text was first published in Christa Wolf, *Im Dialog. Aktuelle Texte* (Frank-
furt/Main: Luchterhand Literaturverlag, 1990), and the English text in Christa Wolf,
The Author's Dimension: Selected Essays, translated by Jan van Heurck (New York: Farrar, Straus & Giroux, 1993), 316–18. This essay © 1993 by The University of Chicago;
all rights reserved.

I would like to speak in terms of a "revolutionary revival." Revolutions start at the bottom. "Bottom" and "top" are changing places in our system of values, and this change is turning socialist society upside down. Great social movements are under way. Never has so much talking been done in our country as in the past few weeks; never have we talked so much with each other, never with so much passion, with so much anger and sorrow, and with so much hope. We want to put each day to good use. We don't sleep, or we sleep only a little. We are making friends with people we never met, and having painful quarrels with others. We call this "dialogue." We asked for it, but by now we have become almost deaf to the word, although we have not yet learned what it means. We stare suspiciously at many of the hands people suddenly hold out to us, at many faces that used to be stiff and unsmiling. "Suspicion is good; keeping watch is even better." So we twist around old slogans, slogans that once oppressed and hurt us, and "return to sender." We are afraid of being used. We are afraid, too, of rejecting a proposal that is meant sincerely. The whole country is ambivalent. We know we must practice the art of not letting the ambivalence degenerate into confrontation. These weeks, these opportunities are a gift we will be given only once—a gift we have given to ourselves.

Puzzled, we watch those resourceful individuals popularly known as "weathervanes" who, according to the dictionary definition, "adapt rapidly and easily to a given situation, handle themselves well, and understand how to use it to advantage." These people are the main obstacles to the credibility of the new politics. We have not yet reached the point where we can regard them with humor—although in other cases we are already managing to see the funny side. On banners I read, "If you can't get off the running board, then get off the tram." And demonstrators call out to the police: "Change your uniform and join our army!"—a generous offer, by the way. We also think about being thrifty: "Good laws save money on enforcement." We are even ready to make basic sacrifices. "Hey, people, turn the tube off and join the parade!" Language is shedding the officialese and journalese which swaddled it, and is remembering the words for feelings. One of them is "dream." We are dreaming wide awake.

Picture this: Socialism arrives and no one goes away! Instead, we see pictures of those who are still leaving the country, and we ask: What can we do? We hear the answering echo: "*Do something!*" And that is what is beginning to happen, as demands turn into rights and obligations. Commissions of inquiry, constitutional law, administrative reform. So much to do, on top of our regular work. Not to mention reading the newspapers!

We have no more time now for parades to show our allegiance, for government-staged rallies. No, this is a "demo," legal, nonviolent. If it stays that way right to the end, we will have learned something more about what we are capable of, and stand up for that in the future.

I have a suggestion for how to celebrate May 1:

Government leaders are paraded past the people for inspection. Unbelievable transformations. The "East German people" go out onto the streets—so as to see that they *are* a people. For me this is the most important sentence of the past few weeks—a cry uttered by a thousand throats: "*We—are—the—people!*"

A simple statement of fact. Let's not forget it.

November 4, 1989

➤ 1 9 9 0 ⤙

By resisting you also combat your own
impatience and laziness, man's deadly sins.
You do this by remembering.

HANS MAYER
Ein Deutscher auf Widerruf, 1984

Momentary Interruption

→→ ←←

I am sure you will believe me when I say that academic honors are not what I have on my mind these days. Nine months ago, when you kindly and cordially insisted that I accept an honorary doctorate, I was living in a different age, and so was everyone else in my country. The enormity of what we have experienced in the past four months threatens now to cut us off from observers outside our borders, however well intentioned they may be, and even from West Germans. I have grown wary of predicting the future. But it could be that this process of estrangement will continue to grow below the surface, beneath the outer layer of brotherliness and rapprochement. This could happen if, in the rapid annexation of the GDR by the German Federal Republic—an Anschluss that is being described as a "unification" or even a "reunification"—East Germany's history is publicly suppressed, once our nation ceases to exist, and is driven back inside the people who made, experienced, and endured it. This could happen if East Germans self-sacrificially devote themselves to trying to fit in, while West Germans act out feelings of superiority and victory. Oughtn't we rather to concentrate

Speech given on January 31, 1990, when Wolf was awarded an honorary doctorate by the University of Hildesheim. The German text was first published in Wolf, *Im Dialog*, and English text in Wolf, *The Author's Dimension* (see footnote, p. 3 above). This essay © 1993 by The University of Chicago. All rights reserved.

on a mutual exchange of information—not just about politics, economics, finance, science, and the destruction of the environment, but about our inner state and feelings, too?

So, although I owe you my thanks and render them gladly, please allow me not to clothe them in a ceremonial speech but rather to express some groping, hesitant thoughts that at least suggest the problems we in the GDR are confronting today.

November 4, 1989, in Alexander Square in East Berlin was the moment when artists, intellectuals, and other groups in our society came together and achieved the greatest possible unanimity. That moment was by no means just a fortunate accident, as amazed Western reporters interpreted it. It was the end product and climax of a long process in which literary and theater people, peace groups, and other groups had been coming together under the aegis of the Church to meet and share talk from which each learned the urges, thoughts, and language of the others, and drew encouragement for action. For years we had been addressing certain tasks in what we intended to be our opposition literature: to name the conflicts which for a long time were expressed nowhere else, and thus to generate or strengthen a critical attitude in readers; to encourage them to resist lies, hypocrisy, and surrender of self; to keep alive our language and the other traditions of German literature and history from which attempts were made to cut us off; and, last but not least, to defend moral values that in the dominant ideology were cynically earmarked for sacrifice. Later generations, who perhaps will live in less troubled circumstances, will decide which of our efforts were superficial, inconsequential, or timid, and conserve what has enduring value as literature. In any case, these efforts were needed, as were the people who made them, and for a time we appeared justified in our belief that the fall of the old regime, achieved by the masses, would lead to the revolutionary revival of our country.

We seem to have been mistaken. Our uprising appears to have come years too late. The damage to many people and to the country runs too deep. The unbridled abuse of power has discredited and undermined the values in whose name the abuse occurred. In a period of a few weeks we have seen our chances to make a new start at an alternative society vanish before our eyes, and seen the very existence of our nation vanish with them. A defeat does not become less painful because you are able to explain the reasons for it; nor less disturbing, if it is a repetition of the past. Is this left-wing nostalgia? In recent weeks I have been reading with very sober eyes the writings of Hölderlin, Büchner, Tucholsky. And I have checked over the names of allies who have fought for the same things for years: Heinrich Böll, Erich Fried, Peter Weiss, Günter Grass, Walter Jens . . . not a few of them Jews, not a few of them in exile. A "unification" founded on radical democratic thinking, which I would have no fear of joining.

The people out on our streets now are no longer the same ones who achieved the revolution of a few weeks ago—not as far as I can tell. The lightning disintegration of almost all our social institutions is leaving the field open to embittered advocates of partisan economic and political interests, before our society has had time to develop new mechanisms and safeguards to integrate all its different elements, or to develop an immunity against the economic slogans of Western nations. Many East Germans are disoriented and are sinking into depression. Others throw fits of hatred and revenge to evade their understandable feelings of rage and disappointment, fear, humiliation, and unacknowledged shame and self-contempt. And what will happen to that group which is very vocal right now which hopes to see its situation improve rapidly once it lets itself be swiftly and unconditionally annexed by that other Germany which is great, wealthy, powerful, and fully functional? What political direction will they take if they find their expectations disappointed again? This perhaps is a question for farseeing politicians in both the Germanys to consider, even in the middle of an election campaign. We have not been granted any pause for thought. While still in a state of extreme emotional upset, we must make decisions about a future we have not been allowed to contemplate. Does all this mean that what we began in autumn of 1989 has already failed? I hesitate to say that; I refuse to give in to that suggestion. I want to remember the conditions that we decided were no longer acceptable. I want to remember the almost unbelievable levelheadedness of the masses of people who changed those conditions, essentially without the use of violence to this very day. I want to remember the spirit of generosity toward all, which fundamentally transformed people's attitudes, especially the young people's, and nowhere as clearly as in Berlin. But I especially want us to look at the thousands of people—there are only thousands, not millions—who regard the freedom they have earned by their own efforts as a chance to take responsible action. In hordes of citizens' groups, in residential districts, town councils, and committees, they are uncovering the evils of the past, breaking up the structures that caused those evils, working tenaciously on useful projects, and designing concrete blueprints for specific sectors of society. They are grass-roots democracy in action. Incidentally, we writers can learn invaluable lessons by associating with groups like these.

But, in the midst of all the turmoil, what has happened to art? The post it occupied so long is now vacant. Too much was laid on its shoulders, and it is a relief to be free of that long-term strain. At the same time I see sources of friction. Literature is no longer forced to do the work of the press. Many books that met with opposition only a few months ago are now passé because radical social criticism is coming directly from the public. The theaters are half empty. Even productions which a short while ago were besieged by audiences who used them to shore up their own protest actions seem deserted now. Sometimes people's feelings of inadequacy lead to a hostile attitude toward art and artists, of a kind which in the past had to be fostered artificially by state and Party machines bent on a deliberate policy of creating scapegoats. We have not yet shed the patterns that German history has spawned in this century. I think it is a mistake for artists to give way to moaning and self-pity. We need to ask ourselves if we have really been released from our public responsibility, and, if not, what our future role should be—assuming that it will be more marginal than in the past.

I wonder what will become of East Germany's forty years of history? A history that is not a phantom, after all, although when it is gone, it will leave a phantom pain. Who will continue to express openly the grief, shame, and remorse I read in many people's letters and see in their eyes—once everyone is busy trying to improve our material conditions? Who will still oppose the negative effects of an economic system whose blessings most people understandably desire? There is another possibility, too, though I hardly dare mention it so soon. We may see the gradual return of a need for utopian thinking, evolving out of everyday experience rather than out of theory.

In short, literature will be called on to perform the same task it must perform in all times and places: to investigate the blind spots in our past, and to accompany us into our changing future. Any attempt on our part to deny who we are would destroy our creativity at its roots. My plea to you is to give us your sympathetic but critical attention. That is something we should be able to agree on so that we may gradually get rid of the old estrangements and let no new ones emerge to take their place.

I thank you for the opportunity to talk with you about this.

A German You Can Contradict

Hans Mayer

➤➤ ◄◄

H ans Mayer, I feel that your presence here today is a noble gesture from a man who has always attached great importance to loyalty and friendship. For me it is a symbolic moment to meet you on this podium at this point in history.[1]

Of course, thinking about Germany can also mean thinking about Germans. Walter Benjamin gave us a concrete example of this in 1936 when, using the pseudonym Detlef Holz, he published in Switzerland a collection of letters called *Deutsche Menschen* (German people) and so supplied true-to-life portraits of Germans who had displayed actively humanitarian attitudes, in sharp contrast to the foaming rage that was now coming out of the "Reich" and that Benjamin, as an émigré, could still hear and feel from his place of exile in Paris.[2] Like Benjamin, Hans Mayer had gone into exile in

Wolf's introduction to the speech by German literary historian Hans Mayer (born 1907) in the lecture series "Thinking about Germany," held in Berlin at the Staatsoper unter den Linden, November 11, 1991.

1. The second anniversary of the uprising that brought down the GDR government and ended in unification.

2. Walter Benjamin, 1892–1940, was a German writer and critic who committed suicide when he believed himself about to be recaptured by the Nazis.

Paris; the two men knew each other. The letters Benjamin published were drawn almost entirely from the "great century" of German literature from 1750 to 1850, in other words from Lessing to Heine—the same period that Hans Mayer later made his special study.

So, Hans Mayer is an exemplary figure, what he called a "test-model German."[3]

The title Hans Mayer gave to his collection of writings about the authors of Germany's great century was "The Unhappy Mentality" (*Das unglückliche Bewußtsein*), a phrase he took from Hegel, who said that an "unhappy mentality comes from a broken reality." Personal experience compels me to agree with all my heart. But what does this statement mean at different moments in history?

The self-image of the middle-class German—a mentality that has been unhappy from the start—is a symptom (Hans Mayer says) of the fateful division in Germany between the *citoyen* and the *bourgeois*, but it was the bourgeois who most often triumphed in concrete social struggles.[4] All the great writers from Lessing to Heine knew and described this split as a "mental and psychological wound of the Germans that refuses to heal."

Hans Mayer made it his job to put his finger on the wound and to show, in the fates of the poets, what it has cost Germans to try to rid themselves of this wound, to free themselves from this defect. Such a job calls for some qualifications, among which I would mention a personal stake in the issue; an unusually refined sense of how emotional and social influences combine to affect a person's actions and writing; and dauntless courage, because we Germans are not too keen on tracing the German malady back to its roots.

Hans Mayer was bound to feel personally involved because of his own life history as a middle-class German Jew who was con-

3. A play on the title of Mayer's 1982 book *Ein Deutscher auf Widerruf* ("A German subject to recall" or "Test-model German"). The German title of Wolf's essay, "Ein Deutscher auf Widerspruch," means something like "a German who tolerates or courts contradiction."

4. As described by Hans Mayer in his discussion of Ernst Bloch in chapter 1 of *Außenseiter* (translated by Denis Sweet as *Outsiders: A Study in Life and Letters* [Cambridge, MA: MIT Press, 1982]), the *citoyen* is the bourgeois citizen who remains faithful to his roots in the bourgeois revolution, that is, to the principle of utopianism, and remains "a permanent Jacobin."

fronted early in life by the especially strict rules of behavior within a Jewish enclave struggling both to maintain its identity and to gain the respect of the outside world. As a young man searching for an alternative to this destructive double life, he discovered "history and Marxist thought" at the end of the twenties through his study of Kurt Tucholsky and the *Weltbühne,* Carl von Ossietzsky, Ernst Bloch, and Georg Lukács, and joined a Marxist student group.[5] He tried in his own life to close the rift between progressive thinking and political action that kept producing an unhappy mentality in German middle-class writers. For example, he worked in his socialist student group, "the first community that enclosed my life," and as editor of the *Roter Kämpfer,* a Marxist workers' newspaper in which, rereading it many decades later, he found a hint of what would have been needed to stop the Third Reich. "We all knew from the outset that we would lose." It is remarkable how much more keenly aware I was of parallels this time, the third time I read Hans Mayer's two-volume autobiography. I did not yet see or did not want to acknowledge the final meaning of these parallels back in March 1987, when I had the privilege of giving a speech at the West Berlin Academy of Arts to congratulate Professor Mayer, my teacher during my university days in Leipzig, on the occasion of his eightieth birthday.[6] We who belonged to later generations had to relearn, at the end of the fifties and on into the sixties—some forty years too late for the critical period in German history—to "distrust belief in saviors" and to see that "humanization must be an immanent process within society." It has been clear to me for a long time now what tragic results ensued when realizations like these

5. Kurt Tucholsky, 1890–1935, was an antifascist journalist and author whose writings were banned by the Nazis and who committed suicide in exile in Sweden; he had frequently contributed articles to the liberal periodical *Die Weltbühne* run by his friend Carl von Ossietzky, 1889–1938, a journalist and pacifist awarded the Nobel Peace Prize in 1936 who died in a Nazi concentration camp. Ernst Bloch, 1885–1977, was a Marxist philosopher of the "principle of hope" (*Prinzip Hoffnung*) whose attempts to reform Marxist thought led to the suppression of his writings in the GDR and his defection to the FRG in 1961. Georg (György) Lukács, 1885–1971, was an influential Hungarian philosopher and Marxist literary theorist, author of *The Destruction of Reason,* for which see "The Leftover Baggage of German History: Correspondence with Jürgen Habermas," below.

6. See Wolf's essay "For Hans Mayer, on His Eightieth Birthday," in *The Author's Dimension* (see footnote, p. 3 above).

were not passed on directly to the next generation as would have been natural, but were blocked by the invasion of National Socialism with its barbaric dehumanization of education and thought. In any case, there were plenty of reasons why Hans Mayer had to leave Germany very fast in 1933, quite apart from his Jewish origins. For decades he carried with him Marx's "little gray volume on historical materialism" and the Insel-Verlag edition of Büchner.[7] This meager literary luggage could hardly have been more significant for his future. The first book that Hans Meyer wrote as an émigré in Geneva during the period 1935–37 was called *Georg Büchner und seine Zeit* (Georg Büchner and his times). (Mayer, far from sporting the "professorial Germanics of professors of German," was a lawyer.) He had to wait eight years to see the manuscript published. A war intervened, which for him brought internment, starvation, humiliation, inactivity. The aberrations of history are no easier to bear because you yourself warned against them. An unhappy mentality may of course be an accurate mentality, and the unhappiness of perennial minorities is not brightened a whit if the majority meanwhile are wallowing in the awareness of well-being—which of course raises the question of whether the pleasurable rush that comes from going along with the crowd can still be called a mentality at all.

The "dialectic of enlightenment" reveals this contradiction, Hans Mayer tells us.[8] Absolutely true. He also accurately observes the "unresolved contradiction between the humanization of thought and emotion on the one hand, and the increasing dehumanization of societal practice on the other." In a sentence like this we feel he is describing our experience too, if only in part. But now that we have been through the same old mill again—though the process of German unification is definitely not just a "return of the same"—we have to ask ourselves very urgently if we shouldn't be

7. Georg Büchner, 1813–37, was a German dramatist who had to flee to avoid arrest after publishing the revolutionary pamphlet *Der hessische Landbote* and died in exile in Switzerland.

8. The "dialectic of enlightenment" is a term coined by Max Horkheimer and Theodor Adorno during World War II when they wrote, while in California, a social-cultural analysis called *Dialektik der Aufklärung: Philosophische Fragmente* (new edition, Frankfurt: Suhrkamp, 1969), translated into English as *Dialectic of Enlightenment* (New York: Herder and Herder, 1972).

focusing on the trend toward practical reason in the European Enlightenment rather than on ideology and the faith in saviors, and
doing all we can to support it in the future, even in its embryonic
forms and those which may lack "majority appeal"? A number of
writers in the GDR have worked for a long time—and largely
alone, at least in the beginning—producing novels, plays, films, essays, poems, and songs to help create a critical mentality, even
though these efforts of ours are now being disparaged or denied for
obvious reasons and with obvious aims, and in fact our work is even
presented as the opposite of what it was. For a number of years, books
had the powerful effect of actions here. They were the sustenance and
the method of the citizens' groups that sprang up in the eighties and
that produced a series of completely novel organizations last autumn
which suggest the face and form of a free, humane, social society
growing like a chrysalis under the armorplate of the old state. Having
witnessed and participated in this process is an experience never to
be forgotten. I know that you, Hans Mayer, shared our hopes of that
time a year ago. You said so in a book dedication you wrote in December 1989, which moved me very much.

Was it foreglow or afterglow?

Our hopes could not be fulfilled. The sensation of defeat has
been with me since 1965, but I have seldom felt it more strongly
than on that Sunday morning in early summer of this year when
we stood by the desecrated graves of Bert Brecht and his wife, He-
lene Weigel. I couldn't help feeling I was in a time warp. The words
"Jew pig" were there once again. Back in the early fifties, when you
were a professor in Leipzig and I was a student, no one could have
convinced us that this would happen. To think that we could not
prevent even this. The horror, the shame, the pain of knowing how
rare it has been in history to be German and humane at the same
time, and how finally the two parted company in a frenzy of destruction and self-destruction that could never be put right. This
shocking realization was the main reason for our commitment in
the postwar years. Brecht, whose grave was now being despoiled
forty years later, once reflectively observed: "We who meant to lay
the groundwork for friendship could not manage to be friendly ourselves." I have thought and thought about that sentence. Now I must
reexamine it.

I believe we lack a screen on which to view our experience. It is so important now to ask the right questions and to ask them, as far as possible, in the right way—which rarely happens. I will not hide my fear that that unknown creature, the GDR, is being demonized, in part intentionally and in part through a lack of information, in the vacuum produced by our loss of direction. This demonization is now going forward at full tilt. Part of it is the freak show of former GDR citizens being paraded through the media. Events have occurred in such profusion that they have overrun our capacity to draw distinctions. We must insist on concreteness and ensure that the life that we really led is not taken from us and replaced by a distorted phantom. The chapters on the GDR in Hans Mayer's autobiography supply considerable material for dissolving legends, so I am eagerly awaiting his new book, which is subtitled *Erinnerung an eine deutsche Demokratische Republik* (Memory of a German Democratic Republic).

Where was I? I was talking about Hans Mayer's book about Büchner. When he was writing this book, he began to perceive another side of his own nature, probably the most important side. He started to realize that he was a writer, even if he did not call himself one until much later. "Finding himself," "becoming recognizable," developing "identity" after an "awakening"—these recurring phrases in his work describe not a scholar but a writer, admittedly one who expresses himself through a certain subject matter, poets as paradigms of human fate, and through the fictional characters they create, compressing into them the contradictions, sufferings and struggles of their time. Hans Mayer seeks a setting for his own deeply problematic existence, which is often challenged by self-doubt and threatened by external perils, and he finds this setting in the exemplary lives of others, by which he measures his own, but without forcing them into any mold in the process. Hans Mayer, I hope you will forgive me if today I make use of your method in my own search for self-command, by comparing my struggles and difficulties to yours, which we can now say you came through successfully. Indeed, you must have noticed some time ago that I am tracing parallels between us.

For example, Hans Mayer writes a sentence about an early discovery of his that I had assumed was an original, if belated, thought of my own: "Identity is possible only through attachment." What he does not say in so many words but knows from experience is that identity is forged by resisting intolerable conditions, which means that we must not allow attachments to deteriorate into dependency but must be able to dissolve them again if the case demands it. In all of Hans Mayer's books you learn a lot about this field of permanent tension between loyalty, commitment, willingness to compromise, and strict defense of your innermost zone of freedom. Whatever he may have been forced to do or to be in his life as a "test-model German," a "German subject to recall," Hans Mayer developed an irrevocable loyalty to his convictions. (Since "identity" has become a key concept in the debate about former GDR citizens, I must say that those who held their ground and resisted inside the country have a quite recognizable identity. People who never resist, wherever they are, are alike in every country and system in the world, and differ only in their standard of living and particular style.)

To give you an example of resistance, here before me is a manuscript on poor-quality copy paper, very yellowed at the edges. The author is Professor Hans Mayer, the title *Zur Gegenwartslage unserer Literatur* (The current state of our literature). Hans Mayer, you remember what it is about: On November 28, 1956, four weeks after the suppression of the rebellion in Hungary, you wanted to broadcast over German radio something about the "crises," the "diseased condition" of our literature; to contrast it with the abundance and diversity of German literature in the twenties; to let GDR writers know that they had lost contact with the modern techniques and forms of world literature and were depicting reality in a schematic way. Moreover—you actually begin a particularly bold sentence with "moreover"—"Moreover, many administrative and bureaucratic obstacles must be eliminated if things in our literary life are to take a turn for the better." You say that we must put an end to the "rubbish" of sectarianism, which you expressly relate to the cult of personality. You really lay it on the line.

I knew about your plan to broadcast this statement over the radio because my husband, who was the arts editor at Deutschlandsender[9] had received and approved your manuscript, and on top of

9. Deutschlandsender was the government-run radio of the GDR.

that had sent telegrams to important figures like Heinrich Böll telling them the date of your talk. I don't know if we ever told you how we spent the evening of the broadcast. We planned to celebrate it with a meal at the Press Club in the Friedrichstraße. But then the poet Peter Huchel came over to our table; he was furious and accused my husband of having broadcast a different text, a trite and hackneyed one, instead of yours. I remember that my husband was dismayed and went to make a phone call, and after that our mood changed completely. A censor higher up in the ranks had intervened and broadcast his own commentary. No doubt you are right in thinking that a breakdown occurred in the mechanism of censorship, which allowed your talk to be printed several days later in *Sonntag*—I have this article too with me now—and it triggered a well-orchestrated simulated debate, in the course of which you were accused of having "insulted not only German but foreign authors" in your remarks.

This same pattern was repeated over and over to block the efforts of the older generation of writers, and then of the rising younger generation as well, in a way almost incomprehensible to people today.

But even you had to undergo the painful experience of defeat again in 1963, after fifteen years in Leipzig, and not for the last time in your life. Looking back, you neither deny nor disparage those fifteen years; on the contrary, you refer to Lecture Room 40 in the old Leipzig University as "my place." You had scrupulously investigated whatever signs you could find in this second German nation that might point the way to "the future possibilities of the strange creature who walks upright." Among these signs was the "down-to-earth attitude" that you found in students of the Workers' and Peasants' Faculty. (It would be worthwhile to follow up the life histories of these worker and peasant students today, as an exercise in how to write concrete history.)[10]

"The great and unshakable memory of my Leipzig years is something I can only define as the experience of life without what the Jewish utopian socialist Ludwig Börne called the 'poisonous

10. Workers' and Peasants' Faculties were established at GDR universities to prepare students for entry, preference being given to students of working-class background who often needed special preparation. The faculties were closed down in the 1960s.

money-based economy.'" So wrote Hans Mayer in 1984. Nevertheless he could not stay in Leipzig. "One academic opinion too many," was the verdict passed on him in the Leipzig student newspaper, the verdict which broke the pact he had entered into and drove him out of the country.

Another case of "coming home by going away."

And was it another defeat? Something else I have learned from Hans Mayer's life is how to put the term "defeat" into perspective. The playwright Peter Weiss was quite right when he said that "the gods despise losers"—and of course people despise them too. But often the defeated can see more than a victor, and perhaps can see what is essential, if they are clearheaded, without self-pity and self-indulgence, and are capable of learning. Hans Mayer's great books—about the poets, about the "outsiders," about himself—were all written in the past twenty-five years, the period in which the author became "recognizable" in all his possibilities, as I understand it. Commenting on his great essay *Aussenseiter* (Outsiders), which is especially important to me, Hans Mayer makes a remarkable statement that I have not yet gotten to the bottom of: "No attempt to take the monsters seriously and beyond that to accept them as possibilities of the human can succeed without a utopian attitude." It seems to me that the abstract concept of humanity found in the Enlightenment is here turned into a simpler principle of everyday humane action, action that is possible at any time, both in eras of confidence and eras of collapse. But is a "utopian attitude" really necessary for us to behave in a human way in every situation and to every person? The line from Ernst Bloch that Hans Mayer quotes and that can sound especially "utopian" when we read it today may have a future after all, if we think in longer timespans: "Everything is still to come."

Let's remember the words Walter Benjamin dared to put at the beginning of his collected letters, *Deutsche Menschen*, in 1936:

> Of honor without fame
> Of greatness without glory
> Of high office without pay

→ 1991 ←

Conversation about honesty.
If honesty were to consist simply of saying everything
openly, it would be very easy to be honest, but valueless,
unbearable, destructive, virtue maintained at
the expense of others. But where does falsehood begin?
I should say: where we pretend to be honest in
the sense of having no secrets.
To be honest means to be solitary.

MAX FRISCH
Sketchbook, 1949
(From *Sketchbook 1946–1949*, translated by Geoffrey Skelton
[New York: Harcourt Brace Jovanovich, 1977], 257)

Whatever Happened to Your Smile?

Wasteland Berlin 1990

→ ←

Madness can also assail individuals from the outside, which means that
much earlier it came from inside them and went outside.

Ingeborg Bachmann, *Ein Ort für Zufälle*

D ear Dieter Bachmann, is Berlin a "wasteland"? The question
has stuck in my mind ever since you told me—more than a
week ago at the memorial service for Max Frisch—the title of your
next issue and put me under moral pressure to contribute something. It is a truism that the closer you are to a subject, the harder
it is to write about it. But maybe it is time for me to test how much
distance I can put between me and this damned city of Berlin by
writing about it. That's what I thought carelessly next morning; and
it did not seem so difficult as we walked through Zurich in bright
sunshine, through the narrow lanes of the Old City, across the Lim-
mat river, strolled along the Bahnhofstraße, sat on the shore of Lake
Zurich, which really "sparkled" just the way people say it does, and
ate grilled salmon at noon in the Kronenhalle like any run-of-the-
mill tourists. How attractive I found this beautiful, clean, wealthy

Written in May 1991 and first published in the journal *du* (Zurich), July 1991.

city all of a sudden! So much so that alongside of a certain home-sickness I also felt a kind of envy, envy of a world that was intact, at least on the outside; envy too perhaps of those happy beings who are destined by birth and fate to live in it, and who manage to con-tinue living there without conflict, thoroughly enjoying it. But I know that I have been spoiled for such a fate. Because wherever I am, it's never long before the needle of my inner compass begins to twitch more and more insistently toward its magnetic pole, until in the end it points to Berlin. Something in me contracts with pain and joy when, on the evening after our day in Zurich, my Swissair plane heads in for a landing, the western suburbs of Berlin become visible, and then—flat, very flat—the whole city lies open below me, from Tegel to the television tower in the Alexanderplatz. I am addicted to this down-and-out Berlin. I feel it as I write these sen-tences, even though I am writing them in the depths of Mecklen-burg, in the stillness of nature where I come to withdraw from my addiction. For it has become almost impossible to work in Berlin. It tears you to shreds.

I believe I am right in thinking that you value local color and snapshots of the moment. Well, the taxi driver who drove us home was from East Berlin and was very chatty, partly because he was happy to have found some passengers when he did not expect any. We were rare birds, he said. His trade had a pause to recuperate after the total slump brought on by the currency union last year, but that was past. "Have you heard the unemployment figures? Well, then, you know why none of us here are driving taxis. Not even on weekend evenings, which used to be a peak time for busi-ness. I tell you, it's as if it's stopped dead. And the streets are empty. Nobody goes to the bars any more ... Who owns us now? The People's Own Taxi is long gone, a taxi entrepreneur from the West bought us up, drivers and all, but no cars: he gave us new ones, customers wouldn't get into Wartburgs and Ladas any more.[1] But otherwise ... The first thing was, no more fringe benefits. Of course, there was no more canteen food—it used to be dirt cheap—

---

1. The GDR's "publicly owned firms" or VEBs (*Volkseigene Betriebe*) were liqui-dated or sold off at the time of unification, many through Treuhand. Treuhand is the West-German-run organization that privatized East German industry by selling off, liq-uidating, or restructuring firms.

and no more sandwiches at night, or coffee when you come back to the depot dead tired. And they figure everything down to the last penny. If you don't keep on track one month, you are warned that if it doesn't get better next month, you'll have to go. The whole thing is nonstop pressure, and solidarity with other drivers is disappearing slowly but surely—and all that for a thousand marks a month.—My wife? Oh, she's unemployed. The restaurant where she worked as a waitress has closed down. Now she's running her legs off trying to get a job. In the West they just take one look at her and say: 'How old are you? Forty-six? Sorry!' She even answered an ad for a job at a chocolate factory, but there were scads of applicants and they were free to pick out the ten youngest. She didn't have a chance.

"We weren't used to all that.

"Why don't I drive in the West any more? That's what I thought too, at first, when we were going to be united at last. But I'm funny that way: I don't like being treated like a dope. There were passengers who jumped out right away if you didn't know where a street was, but how am I supposed to have memorized the street plan of West Berlin? And the other drivers—to them we just represent the competition. Recently I asked one of them for directions and he said smooth as silk, 'Don't you have a map?' and I answered, 'Thanks a lot, buddy. Maybe I can help you out in the East.'

"No, it's not going well, not at all. They just take us for fools. Or do you see it different?"

"Wasteland Berlin"? The only literal wasteland in this densely-populated "urban landscape" (what a euphemism!) is the broad strip running north to south that was once—"once"? Just a year and a half ago!—occupied by the border installations whose symbolic centerpiece was the Wall. The land around it, off limits to ordinary mortals, developed into a biotype that environmental and artists' groups planned to turn into a park in the middle of a metropolis plagued by daily traffic infarctions: "a belt of luxuriant vivid green winding through the city, a belt against the pursuit of success, status symbols, profit, careerism and consumerism." There you see what unrealistic dreams are still being hatched here and there in this city. "It seems," writes a colleague in one of those recently founded East Berlin publications that has not folded yet, "that Berlin attached such importance to being a cosmopolitan city that it cannot afford to allow a broad, wild green belt, free of commercial fever, to run across it. . . . Anyone here who ignores unexplored possibilities to turn a site into capital is regarded as outlandish."

"WHATEVER HAPPENED TO YOUR SMILE?" was spray-painted on the wall of a centrally located building in Pankow a year or so ago by one of those practitioners of folk poetry who were plentiful at the time. People coming from downtown on the number 46 street-car, whose faces long ago reverted to the taciturn expression they wore before unification, cannot help smiling when they get out at this stop and read the inscription. But it is not an original smile. It is a rather shopworn smile based on memory, if you understand what I mean. All the same, you're quite right to ask if smiling can be considered a normal state anywhere in the world. Is it something one could demand of people?

Well, no. All I am saying is that here, in this city where there has not been too much to laugh about in the period of history that is visible to us, people *did* smile for a few weeks, in the streets and squares, in the shoestores and the streetcars, in the parks and even in hospital wards. The people, mostly young, who stood and sat around Gethsemane Church with their candles in 1989 began to smile in September while chanting "NO VIOLENCE!" That sort of thing annoys every government, which expects those who resist it at least to do so in an earnest frame of mind, and to use violence. That is what the state is geared to. It wants to see the forms of resistance and the forms of suppressing resistance match up, while a state that deploys thousands of security forces in combat gear, armed with police hoses and heavyweight technology, against a few hundred people carrying candles who are calling "NO VIOLENCE!" makes itself a bit ridiculous. To be sure, people stop smiling if you make them stand up all night against the wall of a garage, or beat them up in a police station. But in rare moments of history, highly improbable factors converge so that those who order and carry out such excesses later stop laughing too. I saw this happen in the Great Assembly Chamber of the Red Town Hall, where generals and colo-nels and majors and captains were forced to sit and reply to ques-tions from an investigating commission of which I was a member. They didn't understand much and often didn't tell the truth—but not one of them laughed. Admittedly we could not laugh either, but we did smile encouragingly at each other across the table, or amiably during a break in the canteen, and the magistrate's clerks smiled at us in the corridors of the Town Hall, meaning: Don't be discouraged, carry on. (But I have to report here, at least in passing, because it represents progress, that a few days ago I saw four former Stasi generals sitting close together in front of the TV camera, coming right into our living rooms dressed in well-tailored civilian suits and looking hardly disguised at all. They wore suitable ties, they were conciliatory and roguish in their way, and they made a straightforward offer to cooperate, most especially to keep silent about certain circumstances that perhaps are embarrassing today, involving links among the secret services—but of course they didn't use indelicate terms of that kind. In short, they offered their cooperative silence in return for an amnesty and medical treatment of their former co-workers, with whose growing restlessness they managed to threaten us a little; and they assured us that what lay closest to their hearts was to protect "our state" from harm. When asked which state they meant, they said in unison: Why the Federal Republic of Germany of course!—with which they identified heart and soul.)

Oh yes, they contributed quite a bit to taking the smile off our faces. I'll get to that later. But first, let me come back once more to this smile. Maybe it is a quirk of mine but I think that it deserves to be described, precisely because it was so fragile and short-lived. How could those of us who saw it ever forget it: that shrewd, thoroughly alert, self-assured, disarming smile of the volunteer monitors who patrolled the Alexanderplatz on the morning of November 4, 1989, with their striking orange scarves on which the words NO VIOLENCE were written, while the endless procession of demonstrators started to move—smiling, I swear!—and the good-humored crowds began to gather at the square. The word "sovereign" came readily to mind, one of the most foreign of the foreign words in our German tongue. The people as sovereign. LIBERTY EQUALITY FRATERNITY. Aren't you tempted now to say what many of your journalist colleagues said in the months that followed: How naive they are! How out of touch with reality!

Definitely. The banners and placards of these people, who felt at least for a day that they had won—their smile was also a disbelieving, unpracticed smile of victory—are now gathering dust in a room in the former armory, behind locks and bars. And when, exactly one year after their march, a smaller though still sizable number of demonstrators assembled again at the Alexanderplatz, they understood that they had lost; and on one of their banners that had carried the watchwords of the French Revolution, LIBERTY had been checked off the list with question marks, but EQUALITY and FRATERNITY remained as challenges still to be met.

All that is water over the dam, wrote many of the journalists who descended on Berlin in swarms to observe its nonviolent revolution. Many came to this part of the world from far away, for the first time and amazingly uninformed. They waxed enthusiastic for a couple of weeks, but soon started feeling a bit bored and disappointed. Where was the native population's sense of identity? After a while they couldn't help wondering about that, and began to turn up their noses. A justified question, no doubt; but I will permit myself a grim counterquestion: Do you think you can find out many definite facts about the way of life of—should we call them a species of ants?—if you turn over the stone under which they have eked out a sparse existence for so long? Do you think you can draw sweeping conclusions from the way they scatter in all directions under the slightly disgusted gaze of observers, denying their joint identity without compunction? Is that an indecent comparison? It was the cool gaze of the voyeurs that suggested it.

No stone was left unturned that year. It was a feverish, extremely unreal year in which the body of our society took on strange, new, but very temporary shapes before our eyes, shapes we partly helped to create. We clung to them and tried them out for a time, then quickly abandoned them, or most of them, as in a quick-motion film: commissions, roundtables, associations, all sorts of new structures and resolutions, often whimsical and imaginative, sometimes accompanied by the amused, Homeric laughter of the participants. Scenes, images of the kind you normally see only in dreams. But the remarkable thing for me is that that dream time seems the most clear-cut, exact reality I have ever experienced, an aisle of true reality between two pallid simulations. The flower lady on Ossietzky Street who talked like Carl von Ossietzky, for whom the street was named; the women salesclerks in the after-hours shop on the corner who behaved as if they had just come out of Brecht's play about the Paris Commune and were trying to harmonize the interests of their business with their personal interests: for a few weeks they really were the people they were capable of being.[2] But the flower lady stopped talking long ago, and the saleswomen have all been fired except for one who sits at the cash register and whispers to old customers: "This isn't the way we thought it would be."

How else did you think it would be? you will reply. Today people are hard pressed to give an answer, for they can barely think back to the way things looked before. For a while, the political opposition and the citizens movements talked about how GDR citizens could really take part in publicly owned businesses—for example, through public ownership of shares and by allowing the public a say in policy; because everyone was saying and writing that it would be incredibly unjust if the East Germans, who already had had to pay reparations to the USSR on behalf of all Germans, should now be defeated again for the third time, and once again be stripped of all their possessions . . .

Please, ma'am, that's ancient history. The house on the Alexanderplatz from which a colleague of the legendary Herr Schalck-Golodkowski tried to abscond with a suitcaseful of money in those turbulent times is today the headquarters of Treuhand,[3] "the most important and powerful and at the same time the least supervised economic authority in postwar Germany," which is privatizing eight thousand East German firms that formerly were publicly owned and that tangibly represent the labor of millions of people.[4] Isn't it a little uncanny how the work of two or three generations can just vanish into nothing—not by physical destruction, war, or bombs but in the middle of peacetime, by the stroke of a pen, by the inflexible magic word "privatization"? I'll get back to the subject of magic later on, however.

2. Carl von Ossietzkty: see note 5 to "A German You Can Contradict," above. Brecht's play about the Paris Commune is *Die Tage der Kommune* (The days of the Commune), published in 1956.

3. See note 1 above.

4. Schalck-Golodkowski was a GDR financier who often represented the government in foreign business transactions and reputedly was involved in many shady operations.

One estrangement follows on another. Who is still bothering to ask what happened to our smile? It was squashed between a hopeless past and a future without prospects—for many people.

Hopeless? A book entitled *Geschützte Quelle* (Protected source) has been published by one of our new publishing houses, Basis-Druck. In case this title makes you think of an idyllic nature scene with pure spring water in it, think again. "Protected source" is a metaphor from the poetry of the Stasi and refers to informants who infiltrated opposition groups and distinguished themselves there, posing as reliable allies and often as the initiators of daring actions. Many of the opposition figures who popped up from nowhere in autumn 1989 and were all of a sudden in the political spotlight have vanished since their Stasi files caught up with them; and their close friends, who had trusted them implicitly, had to learn to distrust their trust and to cope with the chill that came when it was all over. The gigantic complex of Stasi headquarters, filled with hundreds of miles of radioactive files, lies like a still gleaming sarcophagus in the middle of this half-city of East Berlin. Is it any wonder that many people—in fact the very ones who did not resist the government in the past and who continued to line the streets and applaud as the parades went by on national holidays—feel unable to walk the hard path from dependency to independent adulthood now that they have seen the revelations about their nation, and awakening from euphoria have fallen prey to disappointment, depression, hate, and self-hate verging on self-destruction? A lot of betrayal has taken place in this city, and it's still going on. Among the things being betrayed are people's convictions, it goes without saying—but I ask you, what good are convictions to someone who is fighting for survival? But people are being sold out, too, and it hasn't stopped yet. Someone sells out a colleague to buy protection and ends up betraying himself. As a precaution, people in responsible positions collect materials—files, book excerpts, letters, documents—which can be put to a variety of uses: to blackmail others; to buy one's way out of trouble; or to be offered for sale to the highest bidder, such as the secret services or news magazines and newspapers. All this is par for the course in times like these, when an era is being dismantled. What I mean is that you can't rely on what you see, at least not in this city. There is a driven, anxious, unscrupulous life and activity going on here under the surface; everyone sells what he can, including himself. How harmless, compared to this, was the close-out sale of devotional articles from the old GDR at the Brandenburg Gate, where a flourishing trade in orders and decorations, pieces of uniforms, flags, and medals was conducted out in the open. Yesterday, however, I read a news item that baffled me: a flag manufacturer's firm reports a steadily growing demand for GDR flags with their hammer and compass and sheaves of wheat. What is that all about? It's easier to see why locally produced food is being sold again all of a sudden, after vanishing almost completely from the shelves of the Kaufhallen—now known as supermarkets—by order of the new owners, having been sneered at for some time by former customers, in their drive to self-destruction. People once again seem open to the notion that cucumbers from the Spreewald, butter from Mecklenburg, and spring water from Lauchstädt are things to enjoy, and occasionally you find shops daring enough to offer nothing but native wares. Even at the Brandenburg Gate the scene has changed again: Last Saturday, 35,000 union members demonstrated there with the message: "We don't want a divided society!"

What has happened? A rather irreverent colleague of mine writes: "I am enthusiastic about unification. Now the world is small, and Berlin is big. Anarchy has perished, liberty has triumphed. The German mark has been liberated. I am the Lord thy God, says the D-mark. Thou shalt have no other god beside me. It isn't advisable."

It isn't profitable either, and profit is the highest commandment in the Decalogue of the new god. In the Berlin Ensemble Theater on the Schiffbauerdamm, this god is even appearing in the form of a trinity and I would like to know what poor Bert Brecht would say if he could see that the search for the Good Person of Szechwan is under way in our city once more. The three blind, self-infatuated gods in his play say, "The world can go on as it is if we find enough good people able to lead a decent human existence." But that's just the point: the good Shen Te cannot be "good" and at the same time be the successful owner of a tobacconist's shop. To live well and to be good are mutually exclusive, so that she has no choice but to change into wicked cousin Shui Ta, at least for a time: "Your original order / To be good while yet surviving / Split me like lightning in two people!"[5] Primitive, you say? Painting the issues black and white? Well, at least the few East Berliners in the audience who can still afford expensive theater tickets respond as if they understand the desperate twists and turns that poor Shen Te goes through as played by actress Antoni, who must give a harsher and more helpless depiction of this Darwinistic struggle for existence than Käthe Reichel did back in the fifties. Reichel could offer a softer, tenderer, more charming portrayal of Shen Te in that earlier time, and her Shui Ta could be a little more comic and ridiculous and less dangerous. What we thought we had overcome has now conquered, and the characters who bring the issue into the theater cannot help showing the effects. And don't forget it was to our country that Brecht addressed the question, "Who would not rather be good than brutal?" even though the story was set somewhere else.

Käthe Reichel, by the way, who has meanwhile become as brassy and sharp and tough as you could wish for, used to accompany a group of protesters opposed to the Gulf War from the Alexanderplatz to the students' vigil outside Humboldt University on Unter den Linden every evening at six. They would walk up Karl Liebknecht Street—we still call it that in Berlin, though all the Karl Liebknecht streets in other cities have already been renamed in the mania that came with unification—and past the defunct Palace of the Republic where Volker Braun once tried to drape the slogan "Peace to the cottages!"[6] Just in time it was revealed that the Palace was contaminated with asbestos. Closed down now, it forms a second radioactive sarcophagus in the middle of what we like to call the heart of Berlin. But that's enough of images laden with symbolism. Sooner or later everybody longs to get back to the present. So let us boldly approach the magical date.

5. English quotations taken from *The Good Person of Szechwan*, vol. 6 of Brecht's *Collected Works*, part 1 (London: Methuen, 1985), pp. 5, 105.

6. Karl Liebknecht, 1871–1919, a socialist politician who helped to overthrow the kaiser and to end World War I, was a leader of the Spartacists' revolt and tried to proclaim a Communist republic from the Palace of the Republic. With Rosa Luxemburg he was murdered by the police as the two were on their way to prison. For Volker Braun, a GDR author (b.1929), see "Reply to a Letter from Volker Braun," below. "Peace to the cottages, war on the palaces!" was the motto of Georg Büchner's revolutionary pamphlet *Der hessische Landbote* (1835), which called for the extensive political and economic reform of Germany.

Fantastic events must be described in fantastic ways. On the night of June 30, 1990, the Great Magician whose coming many people yearned for appeared in our city, raised his staff, and conjured up another world, literally overnight.[7] It's not that the new money rained down from the sky, but it had a beneficial effect from the start by getting the previously somewhat undisciplined masses to line up in well-behaved queues outside savings banks. In fact, it did so not once but repeatedly, because this most important of all transformations, although it happened with precipitate haste, occurred in stages. At last, financial institutions started to sprout up out of the ground in this country. I must admit that the first railcar we saw labeled Dresdner Bank caused quite a stir and really connected us to the rest of the world, but once the magician was on the train, his generosity knew no bounds, and quick as a flash he conjured up the Commerzbank, the Hypobank, and, of course, the Deutsche Bank. (Incidentally, the Weberbank, based in West Berlin, thought it could bring in customers with a big ad inspired by former West German chancellor Ludwig Erhard's censure of the intellectuals, and once again cited Pinscher's critique of "intellectualism": "Literature, ideology, rhetoric, lack of realism, and, on the borderline, the writing trade.")

The magician raised his wand again, and the signboards of new firms appeared above gray shops. Long-cherished desires could finally be fulfilled. And what next? Now everything will be fast and easy, the magician told the people. You need only meet one condition, so small that you will hardly notice it: you must make a little effort to want what all the successful young men with briefcases want—these young men I've brought for your support and example, who are capable of imagining anything in the whole wide world except the possibility that anyone could wish to live a different sort of life than they do.

Of course we agree! many people said. Only there seem to be some small problems. Even the most agile and skillful, who try harder than they have ever tried in their lives and really are quite good at imitating the young men with briefcases—even they give the impression of being phony if you compare them to the originals.

7. The night when the monetary systems of the two Germanies were united.

Keep in mind that the broad palette of diverse human types that a free market economy has to draw on is not needed in a controlled socialist economy and thus simply was not produced. Ours was a nation of bureaucrats and small businesses. Those who wanted to distinguish themselves had to develop imagination and courage tailored to what they were after. So where, in this rather uniform pool of humanity, are we to find the banker (to give one example) who is now so urgently needed? It is a rare exception, a real stroke of luck, if Herr X who works in an East German bank—which now has a different name than it used to—to his inexpressible pride is told by his new boss that co-workers of his caliber are hard to find even in the West and that accordingly they plan to keep him on. Or what about the experienced insurance agent conversant with the logistics, interests, and ethos of his society? Where is he to come from all of a sudden? From "over there" in the West, of course. (Berliners in both halves of the city still say "over there," but at least we are conscious now that we must stop it!) The Western-trained insurance agent comes as a pioneer into this virgin territory. But how can he prevent his new East German co-workers—who may be trained sociologists dismissed from their former jobs—from nervously hunting through stacks of papers and graphs when they are with potential clients and finally admitting that they find the whole insurance business "impenetrable," "complex," and a bit "overblown"? Not to mention the tax system. It's embarrassing to admit it, but my husband used to take just one morning to fill out our two tax returns, back in the underdeveloped days of egalitarianism, whereas today—no, not another word; I'll only say this: people are warned against hiring East German tax advisers because of their inexperience, so we are availing ourselves of the services of West Germans. And who will supply us with managers for the many firms that used to be publicly owned and now are being privatized? Not to mention the small entrepreneurs and businessmen we need, with both know-how and capital to take charge of the many restaurants, bookstores, print works, leather factories, and publishing houses that have not been picked up by the big corporations. And do you think many East Germans managed to save up enough to be able to take part in the bidding when their business or firm is auctioned off? So what all this means is that a whole new upper class is forming in what was the GDR, made up of people coming from outside the country, you say. Yes, that's exactly what it means. And the vast majority of people who are native to this area will once again be the employees and workers? Yes, of course, and they'll be lucky if they can get work at all. Moreover, hordes of our most active young people are continuing to emigrate, while only a relatively small number of well-off people are coming here. You may dimly remember that one reason given for the rapid merger of the two currencies was to stop this sort of thing from happening. So is Berlin a "wasteland"? It sure is.

I am talking about problems of transition. Look, even the saleswomen in one of the former Intershops, which market pressures have converted into a sex shop, are having a pretty tough time putting over their new line of goods. I saw one of them publicly reprimanded by her female manager because she claimed to be unfamiliar with a certain stimulating device requested by a male customer even though the manager had personally instructed her in its use.

Talk about provincialism! We were really living in the backwoods here. Now, at last, there is a brisk trade in the stores, including the McPapers paper suppliers, where on an ordinary morning you are treated to scenes dramatic enough for the stage. A troop of four gentlemen in dark suits and ties invades the brand-new branch, having been sent there from headquarters to check out the business practices of the female branch manager, who is also brand-new. It's worthwhile watching and listening to this woman, who clearly used to work in a simple retail shop, as she struggles to look experienced, competent, cooperative, and capable of living up to her responsibilities in every respect; how the skin on her face starts to twitch, and her head nods compulsively at each gently instructive remark or mild criticism from her supervisor. And once the four have left her shop in formation after noting down their complaints, see how her face changes expression, how she goes over to the woman cashier and sounds off against authority in the good old GDR way.

THE ONLY THING THAT CAN HELP NOW IS MUSIC! is written in large letters on a window shade on the lower Brunnenstrasse.

But the last thing I want to do is give the impression that no one laughs any more in this half of the city. Far from it! A colleague from my publishing firm—who of course was fired some time ago with two-thirds of the staff—tells me that his wife, for many years the editor of a magazine, has just been given notice along with the rest of the staff because the magazine is closing down. Why did that make us laugh? The year before the collapse of the GDR, the Party's Central Committee branch in charge of magazines tried to get rid of this publication, which specialized in reports on the Soviet Union, because it had been too favorable to Gorbachev's perestroika; but the resistance of the editors and solidarity from many other journalists managed to save it. But a harsher wind is blowing now that the "press territory" of the former GDR—that is, of the "five new federal states," or what the federal minister of finance realistically calls the "zone of accession"—has been divided up among the four large West German newspaper corporations. Computations are made, and amputations, where necessary, are performed without emotion. This happened to the poetry division of my publishing firm, on which the firm had greatly prided itself in the past. Poetry did not pay, and had to be eliminated from the publishing program. "Wow," I said, "the government censors couldn't have gotten away with that before unification!" "We wouldn't have let them get away with it," said one of my publisher colleagues.

When she's right, she's right.

That's how it is: within *Homo sapiens*, the most successful mammalian species, the most successful subspecies is without a doubt the representative of the free market economy in all his manifestations. He may join ailing firms—quickly, people hope—as an investor, a figure by now become the stuff of legend. Or he may come as an authorized media agent to take over radio or television networks, or as a media star, appearing Live at Last! Or as a member of one of the numerous evaluation committees charged with winding up the superabundant scientific institutes. Or as a financial adviser to explain to doctors who have not yet set up a practice what it's all about: how as many people as possible can earn something from one patient. Or as a feature writer to tell the intellectuals how they have lived and how they ought to have lived, thereby gaining the applause of fellow feature writers who are now suffering from culture shock, and to soothe their discomfort at having in the past allowed themselves to admire the, ahem, "culture" of the GDR, now so clearly revealed as inferior. And the chief long-term effect of all this is: the ban on utopia! But that is material for a different article, which I would entitle: "Let the World Stay as It Is." Whom have I left out? Oh, yes. The homeowners who are now standing outside on the doormat again, having been all but forgotten by the tenants of the Community Housing Authority. And last but not least, the West Berlin policeman who arrived here recently on the anniversary of the police beatings that took place in East Berlin on October 7 and 8, 1989—he didn't come alone, of course, and was well armed, and supported by the last word in high-tech— to show his East Berlin colleagues the combat-ready and efficient way to evict squatters from the Mainzer Strasse. It's unnecessary to point out that a state that is kept in order can do without commissions to investigate police brutality. But a dozen streets in the Prenzlauer Berg still displayed "Mainzer Strasse" signs for weeks afterward. Typical of the Prenzlauer Berg![8]

People of like mind manage to get together there all the same. Members of the underground, both East and West, still hang out together, or meet again, in the backstairs apartments, in the new presses and publishing houses—also backstairs apartments—that publish the documents that at least describe our past even if they don't succeed in "managing" it. Newspapers and magazines are printed, then fold, and are reborn in a new form. Recently, one of them published the payroll list of two thousand leading Stasi collaborators. They argue and drink too much and squabble in the new cafes, discover that they are close to Kreuzberg, squat in buildings there, and unabashedly start producing artworks; galleries spring up where pottery studios, clothes designers, and basket weavers struggle to survive. Do they take any notice of that magician, whom they certainly didn't summon and whom I too would now like to send on his way? They seem to adjust to him only as much as they absolutely have to, and they have no need to resist or to keep away from the sorceror's apprentices and the flood of little keepsakes they have brought with them.

8. Prenzlauer Berg is a bohemian district of Berlin where artists and other inhabitants have traditionally been activists and members of the counterculture.

Yes, you say, but what about all the others? Doesn't every child know the laws of the free market? Not in this country, kind sir. In our city, what children want first of all is to drink their fill of Coca-Cola and to read their fill of Donald Duck comic books. And, don't forget, even the adults here didn't imbibe with their mother's milk the belief that private property is the most sacred of goods, and so they don't take it for granted as you do; and perhaps they still have a troubled relationship with money. But the most disturbing thing is that while their brothers and sisters in the West have been able to develop antibodies to certain aspects of the free-market economy in the course of a forty-year intensive learning process, people here are not yet immune to anything. *Horrible dictu*, they are—or were—gullible. They actually believed the politicians' promises, the advertisers' gushing; they believed the lottery owner who claimed they would make their fortune with the number they got in the mail; they believed the media were independent, and that the petty scoundrel on the street would not cheat them.

Here I will draw to a close, first admitting that I have given neither a complete nor an impartial picture. I have remained partisan—as perhaps one is bound to be in this united city with its two societies where we can't help seeing that we don't know each other, that our foreignness to each other goes deeper than it did when the Wall was still keeping us apart so that each side could pity and envy the other, and when—bitter as it may be for East Berliners to realize it—West Berliners really had no reason to wish for unification. But now the two are supposed to live together, and they clearly feel threatened by each other. The people of the East are supposed to give up everything, not just what they found disturbing or unacceptable; they are being asked to deny, in retrospect, that their lives had value. Germans in the West are being asked to give away part of what they have only recently come to view as good and precious. Each project their fears onto the other. In the West they think: Those people in the East are lazy and backward, and all they want is money. And in the East they think: Those people in the West are arrogant know-it-alls and want to make a big profit at our expense.

The only thing that will help is to practice talking with each other, in small groups and large groups—a laborious, painful, and often wounding process but one from which we all may come out changed. Practice sessions of this kind are happening, though too rarely, I believe. A year from now, things could look different. As one of those tireless graffiti artists has written on the wall, EVERY-THING'S GETTING BETTER, NOTHING'S GETTING GOOD.

Yours sincerely,
Christa Wolf

Rummelplatz, the Eleventh Plenum of the Central Committee of the Socialist Unity Party, 1965

A Report from Memory

➤➤ ◄◄

I will try to tell you how we—a group of writers, artists, filmmakers, and painters—saw, experienced, and evaluated the period in which the Eleventh Plenum was held. Admittedly I did not expect the Eleventh Plenum to have the impact it did, but the fact that it "deteriorated" into a meeting about the arts came as no surprise to me or to many others of us. There were warning signs.

I will tell the story in chronological order, because that sometimes makes the structures more concrete and easier to examine. At the end of November 1965, a meeting was held in the Council of

First published in *Kahlschlag. Das 11. Plenum des ZK der SED* (Clear-cut: The Eleventh Plenum of the Central Committee of the Socialist Unity Party) (Berlin: Aufbau Taschenbuchverlag, 1991). This is Christa Wolf's contribution to a discussion held at a colloquium at the East Berlin Academy of Arts in June 1990 which looked back twenty-five years at one of the periodic campaigns of censorship waged against artists and dissenters in the GDR. The Central Committee was the most powerful body in the GDR's ruling Communist party, the Socialist Unity Party, and included bureaucrats in charge

State. Walter Ulbricht liked to have meetings with artists, which often turned grotesque. In this instance I was still going up the stairs when Hans Koch, then chief secretary of the Writers' Union, came out to greet me. He was looking very pale and said, "We're going to be slaughtered here today!" I was confused because I didn't know who or what was on the chopping block. A paper by Max Walter Schulz was read—he was not present—and after that no one spoke, which was embarrassing. During this break, a number of people scurried around trying to drum up contributions to the discussion and whispering about the real topic of the meeting, namely a manuscript by the novelist Werner Bräunig and an issue of *Neue Deutsche Literatur* in which part of the manuscript had been printed. That was the starting point of the government's censorship campaign.

Werner Bräunig had written about the early Wismut period, when the Soviets were beginning to mine uranium in the GDR. This was also the theme of Konrad Wolf's film *Sonnensucher* (Sun seeker), which was banned for years. After the break, Walter Ulbricht used a reprint of selections from Bräunig's novel published under the title *Rummelplatz* (Amusement park) as an example of all the damaging tendencies in many other artworks, films, and the like that the government was to attack during the plenum.

It was clear to us that something critically important was being

---

of various branches of the arts and media, among them German Radio and DEFA (*Deutsche Film Aktiengesellscaft*), the German Film Company. In the mid-fifties, and again in the early sixties after the Berlin Wall was built in 1961, a relative relaxation of censorship occurred when artists were allowed to participate more in the so-called "international style," but fears of Western influence, along with internal economic problems, resulted in a new attack launched at the 1965 Eleventh Plenum on perceived dissenters. This general assembly became a landmark event, notable not only for the resistance of Christa Wolf and others to the censorship campaign as described in the essay, but also because it banned the poet-singer Wolf Biermann from publishing or giving public performances of his work in the GDR and led eventually to Biermann's expatriation in 1976, destroying the hopes of many GDR intellectuals that the repressive social system could be reformed internally.

1. Wismut AG, a uranium-mining firm with plants in various parts of Soviet-occupied eastern Germany, was a political bone of contention in the GDR as many Germans, including Communists, sought a political identity independent of the Soviet Union, which initially owned most GDR industries and centrally managed the GDR economy. Founded in 1945, Wismut AG originally was Soviet owned, but in 1954 it became a joint GDR-Soviet holding as a result of the de-Stalinization instituted especially by Khrushchev in the mid-fifties. De-Stalinization was resisted by

set in motion and that we had to prevent it. Several people spoke to that effect, including me. Originally I had planned to give a different speech. I intended to warn that our art was in danger of being killed off by the demand to turn it into banalities and to bar it from dealing with conflicts, and I also wanted to speak about a trip I had made to the Federal Republic, where people were working to form a democratic art. I wanted to say that we would be giving up enormous possibilities if we did not establish contact at last with West German authors like Peter Weiss and Heinrich Böll, and a number of others too of course, and open a discussion with them from which both sides had a lot to learn. Today it is hard for people to understand how essential it was, back in the autumn of 1965, to make this kind of appeal.

At that meeting, and then at the Eleventh Plenum too, I deliberately said the opposite of what people might have expected. In my talk at the Council of State meeting, I took some of my original idea and blended it with remarks about the main theme that came up in the assembly. So on that occasion I was already expressing resistance to the attacks on Bräunig, and I did so again later in the talk I gave at the Eleventh Plenum because I saw that the attacks were setting a pattern and that Bräunig's text was being used for a buildup to a far broader attack on the arts.

After I had spoken—this is just another small detail—Walter Ulbricht was given the issue of *Neue Deutsche Literatur* that had Bräunig's text in it, with notations in the margins listing the criticisms that Ulbricht had already put forward with passion in his speech. This was the first time he actually had the text in his possession and had read through it. I know this because I was sitting very close to him and was able to observe him.

Anna Seghers spoke too.[2] She defended Bräunig and calmed

GDR leader Walter Ulbricht, who at the time of the Eleventh Plenum was the most powerful figure in the government, being chairman of the Staatsrat, the Council of State, which had become the ruling body in 1960 when Ulbricht abolished the office of president. Erich Honecker, later first party secretary and then Ulbricht's successor, was a leading member of the Politburo at the time of the Eleventh Plenum, and his wife Margot, later minister of education, was also present and active at the assembly.

2. See "The Faces of Anna Seghers," below.

things down; then others spoke, but not about Bräunig. In any case, our protest had some effect. The aggressiveness of the attack was toned down in the government's concluding remarks, when we were told that Bräunig could of course write about the Wismut period provided that he took into account what things were like then: all he had to do was to write stories accurately, because, "after all, we do not forbid anyone to do anything." Anyhow, it seemed he was no longer being accused of malicious intent.

After the conference, Hager's personal adviser said to me, "You people have no idea what you stopped from happening here today!" Then I realized they would probably not put up with this defeat. But at first it seemed as if an attack on the arts had actually been prevented. For the time being there simply was no one around who spoke against Bräunig.

I believe this conflict destroyed Werner Bräunig, though how that happened is another story. He died in 1974 at the age of forty. His novel was never finished. In 1981, 170 pages of it were published as a fragment.

The main attack on the arts came at the Eleventh Plenum, but in a form I did not expect and which infuriated me—a report from Erich Honecker. I believe the report had really been drawn up by the Politburo; it was not written to exclude Walter Ulbricht or to step up opposition to him, as many thought.

A grim atmosphere reigned at the plenum. Right at the start we were told that we might look at Erich Apel's diary if we wished, that it showed that depression was what had driven him to suicide, and that health care for Party workers had to be improved. I still reproach myself for not having had the courage to say I would like to read it. No one did; but I ought to have done so.

It was clear to us all that the assembly stood under the shadow of Apel's suicide, and we all believed it was related to the Soviet trade agreements. It was rumored that these treaties were being used to put the GDR in a position that would deprive it of its independence, that the country was letting itself be sold out, and that Apel did not want to share the responsibility for this.

And then of course there were great difficulties with implementing NÖSPL, the New Economic System for Planning and

Management of the Economy,[3] and problems with young people. We had the very clear feeling that the "discussion" of the arts was being used as a substitute for confronting the economic problems that had piled up in the GDR, that we were being made into scapegoats. That was a powerful motive for starting a debate aimed against the arts at this particular time. The hope was to divert attention from other things, for they could count on the agreement of the masses who had conventional tastes in art. If they attacked these "beatniks" or criticized films with erotic scenes in them, they could of course be sure of support from inhibited and dependent people who always strongly resisted liberal ways of thinking, and still do so today.

Of course I knew that no one in the Central Committee had yet spoken against the statements in the report of the Politburo. So when I spoke, I felt as if I were standing alone in front of a steamroller. It's unlikely I could have managed to do it if I had been left to my own devices. But a group of us who were artists used to meet each evening during the assembly. Most of us were members of a generation who lived a politically committed life in this country, who saw the conflicts, and who had a very strong sense of the danger that would threaten our commonwealth if the contradictions

3. The "New Economic System" (NÖSPL, Neues Ökonomisches System der Planung und Leitung der Volkswirtschaft) was instituted by Walter Ulbricht in 1963 when it became clear that the Seven-Year Plan of 1959–65 was not producing the desired results. NÖSPL introduced some decentralization and market-economy reforms as advocated by the Soviet economist Evsei Liberman. The West German "economic miracle" had been financed by U.S. aid through the Marshall Plan, but the Soviet Union prohibited the GDR from accepting Marshall aid; imposed long-term, severe reparations; required export of a large part of GDR production to the USSR and other Soviet bloc nations on terms favorable to the Soviet Union; and continued to own and control GDR industries for a long period—all measures that prevented the resource-poor GDR from successfully recovering from the destruction of World War II and establishing its economic viability as a separate nation. The Soviet measures resulted in heavy production quotas for GDR workers and a shortage of essential consumer goods, which in turn caused continual emigration of GDR citizens to the West and a serious drain on the work force. It was to stop this drain that the Berlin Wall was built in 1961. Cf. Henry Ashby Turner, *The Two Germanies Since 1945* (New Haven and London: Yale University Press, 1987), and the U.S. Government's *East Germany: A Country Study*, compiled by the Federal Research Division, Library of Congress (Washington, DC: Government Printing Office, 1988).

were not resolved in a productive way. We thought if it didn't happen now, it would be too late. We had the feeling this was one of the last moments when development in the GDR could be steered in a direction that might make this nation an alternative to the capitalist Federal Republic We wanted to strengthen the socialist initiatives to the point that the GDR could become "competitive" intellectually as well as in other ways. We saw ourselves as allies of those in economics and science who were thinking and working along the same lines. We had personal contacts with them, we had talked with them. There were even a few people in the Central Committee with whom I could speak openly about these matters.

That evening after the assembly, I joined Konrad Wolf and discussed with him and others what was going on. You might say we were "forming a faction," but of course our aim was not to form an opposition group with a political program. I spent the night in the home of Jeanne and Kurt Stern. We talked very excitedly far into the night, asking what we could do, what we could still salvage. For we knew that a major housecleaning was under way.

One of the films under attack was shown to the Central Committee. They had a briefcase with materials in it. It was like psychological warfare. The Central Committee members were systematically gotten into the right mood, and it was an incredible feeling sitting there among them. I didn't go to the film showings; I couldn't have stood it. And then on the second day, when Paul Fröhlich, the First Secretary of the District Council of Leipzig, compared the political situation among artists in the GDR with the Petöfi Club in Hungary—that is, with counterrevolutionaries, as he understood it—naturally I was extremely alarmed.[4] That evening Konrad Wolf said, "Now you must speak. What is happening now will turn into a disaster if we do nothing to stop it." That night I didn't sleep. Next morning I signed up right away to talk to the assembly.

4 Paul Fröhlich: "But counterrevolution and reactionary activities also help to generate ideas that are hostile [to ours]. We still remember and are familiar with the role that the Petöfi Club played in Hungary, although we cannot compare the situation in Hungary at that time with the situation in the GDR in our own time. I would like to make that very clear. But we must be reminded of it." Minutes of the Eleventh Plenum, as quoted in Institut für Geschichte der Arbeiterbewegung Berlin, Zentrales Parteiarchiv, IV 2/1/189, p. 122.

I only had a few notes jotted down on a scrap of paper, and, interestingly, my turn came almost at once. I was the second or third person to speak. They gave me no time to prepare, and I spoke excitedly and in a less formulated way than I would have wished. Moreover, I was interrupted by constant heckling, from Margot Honecker among others.

Right at the start I rejected the comparison that had been made between the Writers' Union and the Petöfi Club. That was the first point at which I was interrupted; but this comparison was the main thing that had moved me to speak. I was all stirred up; I spoke in an unfocused way and throughout the first part of my speech I was concerned with convincing the Committee that it should not view artists as the enemies of our state. If you should read my speech today, you would find it hard to understand unless you knew the atmosphere in the chamber and the historical background. A quarter of a century has gone by since then. Many things I said then sound absurd today, and the value of my speech can be determined only by comparing it with the tone and content of the other speeches. We—that is, others as well as I—only gradually came to realize that we were doomed to disappointment in our hope that, despite everything, we could contribute to changing this nation through art, through critical art. Differences of opinion arose along this difficult road to realization, splits that had already begun at the time of the assembly. Many stories could be told about that. It was right afterward that I began to work on *The Quest for Christa T.* The second part of my talk, in which I begged the assembly to call off the attack on individual works of art and on art in general and thus to prevent the consequences that were sure to follow, was regarded as provocative.

After my speech I went out into the foyer to calm down, while inside the assembly people began to argue about what I had said. Anna Seghers, who was there as president of the Writers' Union, invited me to accompany her to the East Asian Museum. I resisted the idea: "Not now of all times!" "Yes," she said. "Now is exactly the time." Then we walked across the broad road outside the Central Committee building. She was looking very unconcerned; I took her elbow and said, "Don't get run over!" "Oh," she said, "I was run over once before, and I could write very well afterward." She was referring to the accident she had in Mexico, after which she wrote "The Dead Girls' Outing." [5]

So we walked together to the East Asian Museum, and when we came to the Processional Road and the Gate of Ishtar, she said, "Look, back then it was forbidden to make any representation of human beings, and they made such beautiful things. But in this country there is no ban on depicting human beings. And believe me, all the rest will pass." And she made a bet with me that in one year "all this" would pass. Then I said, "No, no way." We bet a cup of coffee. We never talked about it again.

We went to look at the sculptures in the East Asian Museum, and she ran her hand over the backs of a number of the female figures. "They're enough to turn you gay," she said. That was just her way of telling me to put things in their proper place. "Now is a difficult time. I have experienced very different times. Now perhaps one can't depict people who are *sad*, but the time will come . . ."

Later on, when as nominees to the Central Committee we were given the internal minutes of the proceedings, I found it instructive that Fröhlich's reference to the Petöfi Club and to counterrevolution had been removed from the record of his speech, and so had the reply to it that I had given in my speech. When my talk was printed in *Neues Deutschland*, it was cut down even further and lost its punch and its point.

So the Eleventh Plenum as a forum on the arts did not happen out of a clear blue sky. Of course people did not seriously believe that the films that no one had even seen yet had been driving young people out into the streets in Leipzig. But they wanted to smash any link between various movements in the society—those pressing for change in the economy and those pressing for realistic portrayal in art—merely as a precautionary measure before things got out of hand, and to find a scapegoat so that they could avoid having to discuss the real problems and could remove these problems from public view. In my opinion that was the main purpose for staging the assembly.

5. "Ausflug der toten Mädchen," a 1946 short story about exiles, concentration-camp internees, and other victims of the Nazi regime, from which Seghers had fled to Mexico, having been denied asylum in the USA owing to her Communist affiliations.

I should also say that before the assembly there had been a connection between the economy, the general life of the society, and art, and that this connection was severed by the Eleventh Plenum. The Bitterfeld Conference of 1964 is now treated only as a joke, and in large part it was comical and ridiculous.[6] You could write a comic play about it. But a number of artists took it seriously; they went into the factories as they had been challenged to do and took a look at what was going on there. *Spur der Steine* came out of meetings of this kind.[7] And I would not have written *Der geteilte Himmel* (Divided Heaven) if I had not been in a factory. When it became clear that the links between artists and factories were allowing artists to gain a realistic view of what went on in the factories and to form friendships with workers, managers, and people in other professions, and that they were beginning to be informed about economic realities in this country, that was the point when the possibilities opened up to us by the Bitterfeld Conference were closed down. There were continual hints about this at the Eleventh Plenum: "Of course we don't want to prevent you from doing anything, but you have to look at things the right way."

This meant that the opportunity for us to intervene through art—an opportunity we had seized with enthusiasm, and we were not at all dissatisfied with the results—had been crushed. I know that several reports written afterward on topics of this kind were not published. Also, there were clear signals that the targeted films were to be banned. After this, we could not carry on friendships and connections with certain firms, with workers' brigades and econo-

6. In 1959, a conference was held in Bitterfeld, near Halle, to set up a program to develop socialist art in the GDR. It encouraged artists to become "artist-workers" by associating with workers and performing manual labor before writing about contemporary life, and to bring workers into the arts. A follow-up conference was held in 1964 to reexamine the program, which had failed to produce the expected results. Christa Wolf's novel *Der geteilte Himmel*, written in 1963 (translated by Joan Blum as *Divided Heaven: A Novel of Germany Today* [Berlin: Seven Seas Books, 1968]) was the most important work to come out of the Bitterfeld program. It won Wolf a major literary prize and a reputation, both in Germany and internationally, as an artist of criticism and dissent, because it described the division of Germany realistically and revealed some of the reasons for the economic blight in the GDR and for the flight of GDR citizens to the West.

7. *Spur der Steine* (Sign of the stones) was a popular 1964 novel by Erik Neutsch, which was also made into a film.

mists, except on isolated occasions. The ties between artists and industrial workers were broken as far as possible. Artists were repeatedly criticized for having "detached" themselves from the working class, from the people, but, in actual practice, contacts between people from different levels of society were made as difficult as possible. This is a time-honored technique of domination.

I would also like to explain why the film *Fräulein Schmetterling* (Miss Butterfly) was never finished. During the Eleventh Plenum it wasn't yet in as advanced a stage as most of the other films, with the exception of *Spur der Steine*. It could not yet be shown and was not yet at the center of the controversy. Permission was given to continue work on it. A rough cut was made of it, and this rough cut was shown in early summer 1966 to the Film Advisory Council of the government film agency.

At the time we felt this film was unsuccessful, that it did not clearly express our intention. It was the first film made by Kurt Barthel, who was a student of Konrad Wolf.[8] The principal role was flagrantly miscast, being given to a young and inexperienced Czech amateur actress. The dramatic elements were not fully worked out either, and the film did not have a light enough touch, it was too direct, too didactic. When we took part in discussions or were asked to make a comment, we were in the unhappy position of having to keep saying, "First read the script, then let's look at the film." There were also some differences of opinion between Kurt Barthel and the rest of us.

In the discussion at the Film Advisory Council, the opinions of the viewers—who were not very numerous, by the way—were divided. All the working artists who were present based their views on the intentions of the film team; they emphasized the passages in which these intentions were realized and tried to understand why other parts had not succeeded, and so on. All the officials present started from the premise that the film had gone wrong from the start, even in its intention.

For example, Hans Koch told us that Bieler's *Zaza* and *Fräulein Schmetterling* were the films that had depressed him the most. They

8. Kurt Barthel, 1914–67, known as "Kuba," was a lyric poet, dramatist, and film scriptwriter who became a member of the Central Committee of the Socialist Unity Party.

were like Bergman's *The Silence*, he said. Later he retracted the remark. (*The Silence* was the official personification of decadence and nihilism.) The philosophical concept behind Bergman's film, he said, was to show the eternal inability of adults to communicate with each other. We were insisting on an unresolved conflict in relationships between individuals. The film showed a lack of ideas, Koch said, and an intellectual passivity. He demanded that the conflict be resolved. Nowhere in the film was any pledge given that change was even possible, he said. He criticized the camera technique: the new buildings were never shown within a city landscape, there was a certain lack of "warmth" and "homeyness" even in the visual language of the film.

Horst Brasch, a senior official, gave a very harsh speech. He said that now was not the time to talk about intentions but to judge the result, which in turn would reflect the intention; in general he found it depressing. In our works of art, we had to contribute to the advancement of society by recognizing its positive elements. He failed to see any positive effect on society in this film. Ideologically it was incorrect. How ought and how will our society one day become? That is what the film had to show, he said. People in the future should be cleverer and better than we. The creators could overcome their crisis only if they would address their subject in this way.

Günter Schröder was there, too.[9] He wondered if I really was the author of this screenplay; he said he could hardly believe it. The material contained all the erroneous and harmful ideological views criticized by the Eleventh Plenum; it did not give a true picture of our reality and did not embody the socialist image of man. It was a crude counterfeit of life in the GDR. It showed the exact opposite of the conditions that were normal at the present time. Above all, he said, film had to do with ideology, and in this area our film was a total failure.

Then filmmaker and author Wolfgang Kohlhaase tried to cool things down, but without success. Heinz Kimmel from the Central

9. At the start of 1966, after the Eleventh Plenum, Horst Brasch was made undersecretary in the Ministry of Culture, and Günter Schröder, who previously had worked with Kurt Hager in the Central Committee administration, was made chief screenplay editor at DEFA, the government-run German film company.

Council of the "Free German Youth" organization was very concerned too, of course, and said that the screenplay, like the film itself, showed a concept that clearly was to be deplored, and that a whole series of ideological views were expressed in it that could not help but lead to this sorry result.

I will skip over the rest of the discussion. Dr. Maass, head of the Film Department, summed up by saying that the film would be dropped and that a million marks had been wasted. He said he was disturbed by the fact that they were forced into not showing films that had already been produced. It brought harm to our republic that must be of concern to us all. The film tried to exert an influence hostile to our republic and represented an enemy within our republic. The film distorted the reality of our republic and expressed a philosophy that had nothing whatever to do with our philosophy. But what was seen in the underlying concept and on the screen, Maass contended, must previously have been inside the heads of the people who made the film. It represented an intellectual attitude, an ideology, that had objectively hostile effects, and that the Eleventh Plenum had abolished. We now had to deal with its causes, he urged.

Work on the film was halted after that. The director has reviewed it and the material does not seem to warrant our completing it now.

What we wanted to do with this film was summed up by me in a statement I made at the time: People should not give up prematurely the things that they long for and settle for dull common sense.

Two Letters

→→ ←←

I. TO AN ACADEMY

I. TO AN ACADEMY

September 1991

Dear Colleagues,

Although I had not expected it, the fate of this Academy has been very much on my mind in recent weeks, the way one thinks about people, things, or institutions when one is about to lose them. The question I think we have to answer today is this: Is it a loss to dissolve this Academy, and, if so, for whom? Each of our members will answer the question differently, and it would probably be a good thing if as many as possible would answer it here today, in public. When I was elected to the Academy in 1974, my reaction was not emphatic but rather skeptical. Later, after November 1976, the Academy became the only place for years where I could still meet colleagues, discuss, make suggestions, offer semipublic criticism, and even give public readings.[1] I had Konrad Wolf to thank for that

Letter I, "To an Academy," was a speech read at a plenary session of the East Berlin Academy of Arts in September 1991. Letter II, "To Wolfgang Thierse," was first published in the German edition of this book.

1. After Wolf Biermann was given permission to perform in the West and then denied reentry into East Berlin and stripped of his GDR citizenship, GDR intellectuals experienced a crisis that led a number of them to emigrate to the West, while others looked for alternative means of protest or were driven deeper underground.

but not only him; there were other colleagues too, including many who worked with the Academy.

This Academy is being dissolved because those in charge of arts policy in Berlin, and apparently some in the new, formerly East German states of the Federal Republic as well, think it represents "leftover baggage" inappropriate to the new political landscape, and also because they don't recognize it as the legitimate successor of the Prussian Academy of Arts, which is what it was intended to be when it was founded. Instead, the Arts Academy on West Berlin's Hanseatenweg claims and has been granted this right of succession; and it is not intended for there to be two arts academies in Berlin.

We, the members of this Academy, were not quick enough to recognize how things stood, and then we didn't react as fast and as resolutely as we should have. We didn't know exactly what we wanted, whereas the other side did know exactly and took action. We let time slip by, in the illusion that the European Society that Heiner Müller wanted to found could be related in some way to this Academy, or that a regional academy representing some of the new federal German states could take over the tasks, membership, and assets of our Academy of Arts, at least on a limited scale.[2] These two institutions may perhaps come into being—especially if we promote them—but they will not be related to our present Academy or dependent on it.

All that was accomplished in forty years, all that was collected, published, taught, stimulated, and made accessible to a deeply interested public through this establishment—or, more accurately, through our various establishments, in various branches of the arts—this treasury of German culture will disappear as a living, growing organism when our institution is dissolved. To the list of our omissions we must add the bitter reproach that we failed to make our newly expanded public aware of what sort of cultural life has gone on here, and, more especially, we failed to convey that life to the persons in charge of evaluating the assets and further financing of the Academy, who know nothing whatever about it. We began too late to call on qualified colleagues to help us draw up a history of the Academy, the kind of assessment of the past that I believe

2. Heiner Müller, 1929–1995, was a GDR poet and dramatist.

people have a right to expect from us even though, on the other hand, we all rejected the sort of exercise in "self-purgation" in which a few individuals who are regarded as being "in the right" would be given the awkward task of passing judgment on the others. The realization that it is impossible for us to draw up a history leaves me, I admit, with a residue of dissatisfaction. Like others, I consider it essential to remodel and change this Academy. The collapse of the GDR, whose Council of Ministers called on our founding members to establish the Academy and ratified its later members, has eliminated the framework within which we had been measuring our achievements and omissions. The first public events we organized in autumn 1989 showed that the Academy was buzzing with change, showed that its members were stirred by the democratic movements in the country. This atmosphere should have led us to begin an open, ongoing dialogue about our activities. We needed to express at last the differences of opinion about politics and arts policy that divided and still divide members into groups within each branch. The Academy has not been a homogeneous structure, and of course it has gone through various phases. Since I have been familiar with it, it has always been—among other things—a forum for art and artists who would not otherwise have had much public exposure in the GDR. Generally speaking, the Academy has used the privileges it was granted to foster a spirit of open, critical debate within its own relatively "sheltered" environs.

We have lived with contradictions that we have often been unable to resolve. Many of us were aware of it and confronted the contradictions. Our experience both in the past and at present is that conflicts are denied or glossed over as insignificant. On the other hand, the trend to liquidate and dissolve everything in the former GDR—a trend that is affecting more than just this Academy—is causing people to adopt an attitude of defensiveness and self-justification instead of engaging in self-examination and self-knowledge. This Academy is the embodiment of conflicts and contradictions in a stage of German history which, after all, was not simply an "accident," a "mistake," or a mere deviation from the paths of righteousness. If the Academy vanishes, taking with it a great part of these past conflicts, then those of us who are alive today will lose another opportunity to learn about them, and so will those who come after us. The real history of the people who lived in the GDR is being demonized and made to disappear into a dark hole of forgetfulness. The more this plan succeeds, the less hope we have of confronting the real history of Germany—including the varying lines of tradition in its art—instead of a phantom. My concern about this issue perhaps entitles me to quote a couple of passages from the correspondence I carried on in July–August 1979 with the then director of the Academy, Konrad Wolf. It grew out of my intense reaction to certain things that happened in our branch and out of his question to me, Did I want to end my work with the Academy? He asked me, for example, whether in my books I intentionally played off "people of sensibility" against the "pragmatic manipulators," and he went on to ask: Is there "an unbridgeable gap between us, too? Or is it a field of tension that brings the risk of being torn apart but also the possibility of achieving something productive in the long run? That may sound very simplistic, and it is not exactly new [we had spoken about my 'situation' from time to time] . . . Ought I, for example, to 'condemn' you because you have withdrawn to a great distance, no doubt for well-considered reasons? Nonsense. It's like this: the most important thing is that you write, and if this is the only way . . . But can it work in the long run?"

In my letter of reply, I wrote him that indeed I was well aware of the tension between those who think and those who act, and that I could "derive a great deal of stimulus, anger, amusement, and productive zest from contradictions . . . even if they are very harsh and call me myself into question." Then I went on:

But I can no longer derive anything productive from this thinking in false alternatives and the behavior that stems from it or that it justifies. An insidious revaluation of all values is under way and continually gaining speed, which is destroying or has destroyed those intellectuals who are searching for alternatives to consumerism and to the alienation practiced in capitalism. This has gone beyond tactical behavior by this side or that. In whatever direction we turned, we always stood with our backs against the wall, unable to maneuver, confronted by slogans—Growth,

Prosperity, Stability—and by the risk of war and the risk of counterrevolution; and, recently, blamed for the slow-down in disarmament on top of all the rest.

We see that all this is not working and can tell it is not going to work. And in this case, it seems to me, to hold onto any official position one has, now that no one is actually capable of "taking action" any more, becomes increasingly an act of self-deception. The field of tension you write of has long since collapsed, because one of the two poles between which it was possible for tension to be generated has simply been eliminated. This can be done rather elegantly or quite crudely; it happened crudely. It can be done with or without pangs of conscience. Those affected can submit silently or supply pretexts by hitting out and by using sometimes dubious methods of combat. None of this changes anything in the predetermined result. Anyone who justifies holding a responsible office by saying that if he carries out its duties he can "prevent something worse from happening" is simply deceiving himself and others. Because everything bad is carried out and will be carried out, whoever the official who does it may be.

I have been referring not to you in the above but to someone else. For now comes the contradiction (because of course my thinking and action are not free from contradiction either): I honestly wish that you would continue to be director for a long time yet, and endure the tension without ceasing to feel it.

Perhaps, absurd as it may sound, your situation is even more difficult than mine, given your life history—precisely because you are a person of sensibility and not a "pragmatic manipulator" . . .

Those among us who were closely acquainted with Konrad Wolf know how greatly he was strained in this field of conflict. In the life and death of Konrad Wolf I see tragic elements. It would be unforgivable of us to let lives like his be sucked into the dark hole along with the rest. What I would have hoped from a remodeled East Berlin Academy of Arts is the study, description, and publica-

tion of its achievements and failures, of the conflicts and the courage to face contradiction that it provoked, and of the reasons for
adaptation and compromise, not all of which stemmed from cowardice or convenience. To accomplish this, however, the members
of the Academy needed first the will and then the opportunity to
renovate this institution. One way to fight for it is through the law.
Another way is for our plenum to resolve that all the members place
their mandates at its disposal, and that a founders' committee
elected by the plenum should call on a number of members still to
be determined—including both old-time and younger members—
to represent our Berlin Academy of Arts in the future.

For the question remains: Once this Academy is dissolved, who
will engage in a vital way with its history and carry on the lines of
tradition to which it was particularly committed—that of German
antifascist literature, for example? In the meantime, the public,
who continued to attend our Academy events in large numbers until very recently, are losing a place where they can confront their
own past, and possibly reorient themselves to the new conditions in
a way that is not linked to memoryless conformity and self-denial.
(For example, for two years we have been meeting in a discussion
group here in the Academy's halls to which I have invited artists,
scientists, and other interested parties so that we may inform ourselves about contemporary issues. I know of no other body that has
advanced the process of self-understanding over so long a period
and in such an open atmosphere.)

Where will such events happen in the future? Who is to carry
on the responsibility that is the product of our past? Surely not the
West Berlin Academy of Arts, with which I am familiar, having
been a member for some years. Admittedly it has taken over the
heritage of the East Berlin Academy of Arts, since by means of a
"special power" it is taking control of the archives and collections
of this Academy, which are in excellent condition and, incidentally,
have enormous material value. But it can take over none of the specific tasks that I have outlined, for which it lacks the staff, the information, and, of course, the will. Oddly enough, relations between
the two academies, which were headed toward a good working relationship before the collapse of the Wall, have subsequently cooled
rather than strengthened. The West Berlin Academy sees no possi-

bility of accepting additional members of our Academy—by changing its bylaws, for instance. Instead, it is accepting only a few artists
from the former GDR, and in many branches a clear resistance to
us is detectible, not only for political but also for artistic reasons.
Many members of the West Berlin Academy judge and condemn us
without knowing us and the work of our Academy. Just as it has
been suggested to the public at large, they see that the most important thing has been salvaged, namely the archives and collections. People don't realize that one of the special features of this
Academy lies in its ensemble of members, contributors, and re-
searchers, along with the fund of archives and collections.

Whatever the future fate of the Academy may be, I propose that
one weekend in December we should once again hold an "Academy
Day" in our traditional style. On this day, perhaps as a farewell but
in any case as a commemoration, each branch should present artistic achievements of its deceased members, our eminent predeces-
sors who in the past founded this Academy and were active in it—
works by Becher, Brecht, Bredel, by Fühmann and Heinrich Mann,
by Anna Seghers and Arnold Zweig, to name only a few from the
area of literature.[3] We would have to come up with the money for
this meeting ourselves, if necessary with the help of art lovers who,
like us, don't want to see erased from public consciousness the tradition embodied by this Academy, and by this Academy alone in such
concentrated form.

II. TO WOLFGANG THIERSE

September 21, 1991

Dear Wolfgang Thierse,

Your suggestion of a "tribunal" is flitting through people's
heads and raising clouds of dust. I feel rather skeptical about it.

3. Johannes Becher, 1891–1958, was an expressionist poet and social activist; Willi
Bredel, 1901–1964, was a socialist novelist imprisoned by the Nazis who fled to the USSR
and later was active in the GDR; for Franz Fühmann, see notes to "Reply to a Letter
from Volker Braun," below; Heinrich Mann, 1871–1950, was a novelist, brother of
Thomas; for Anna Seghers, see "The Faces of Anna Seghers," below; Arnold Zweig,

When an injustice has occurred in the eyes of the law, humanely interpreted—and no doubt that is something many people could agree about—it is up to the courts to act (although, admittedly, in many cases this won't lead to "justice" either, because the legal standards set by the victors promote other interests than merely to restore humane behavior. The needs for revenge and for self-congratulation far outweigh the will to draw distinctions, to take historical developments into account, and to consider one's own role during the time when the world was divided into two camps.) So the "tribunal" would be for everyone other than the victors and would function as a moral authority in a thoroughly amoral and frequently immoral world. Any standards we could set there would have to be quickly forgotten, next day or next week, if we are to adjust to the political conduct of the world's new masters. What choice do the masses of "ordinary people" have except to adjust? Things are different for us, for intellectuals. So we hold a tribunal, okay. Historical associations inevitably arise: the Nuremberg Tribunal, the Russell Tribunal,[4] and so on. But in our case, who are the judges supposed to be? Who are the "just men"? And who is to help us, the accused, overcome the psychological barrier that the word "tribunal" erects in our minds?

I think, and, in fact, now is the second time I have been through this experience, that the people who are really guilty—the ambitious, the cowards, and the toadies who deliberately worked their way up on the shoulders of their colleagues, not hesitating to betray them when it was necessary—don't develop a sense of guilt. I don't think they can be reached by any moral or judicial verdict. They are well armed against it. But people of the other type, those who knew they could not live here in the GDR and remain "just" and "guiltless" but who nevertheless stayed because they wanted to sustain an opposition and to help people and were then worn out by the insoluble contradictions and the permanent conflict—these

1887–1968, the German-Jewish novelist known for his World War I fiction portraying Prussian militarism, was stripped of his German citizenship by the Nazis.

4. The Russell Tribunal was established to judge crimes of Western nations and Japan in the Vietnam war. See *Prevent the Crime of Silence: Reports from the Sessions of the International War Crimes Tribunal founded by Bertrand Russell, London, Stockholm, Roskilde* (London: Allen Lane, 1971).

people are now tormenting themselves once again. Of course they are the target of the Western media and see themselves (again) being excluded and neutralized. It may be that a tribunal of the kind you suggest would intensify the guilt feelings of these people even further and make their paralysis permanent. At least, that would be a result. Or it could be that only West Germans should be judges, because traditionally they have been in the position of being the just ones. That is worth thinking about and and perhaps would clarify matters at least.

I am among those who warned, long before October 3, 1990, that unification would make self-critical examination of our past very much more difficult, insofar as unification amounted to the larger, wealthier part of Germany annexing the smaller, poorer part. At the time I had not yet realized the full extent of the West's attitude of defensiveness toward us, which borders on actual loathing. The tendencies to demonize the GDR, to turn it into a phantom and its inhabitants into monsters while disregarding history as much as possible, were only beginning to show themselves. True, you can point to a dozen articles in intellectual periodicals in which this is no longer happening. But the desired effect has already been achieved among "ordinary" West Germans. Fear has allowed them to be injected with an image of the GDR that is totally removed from reality, and this in turn is causing or at least encouraging former GDR citizens to revert to a defensive attitude that verges on obstinacy and self-righteousness, an attitude unfavorable to self-criticism. I fear that their mood might become downright explosive if a tribunal were to be instituted against them now, on top of the rest. You would have a hard time explaining to them what you "really" have in mind.

So what is to be done? Like you, I believe there is nothing more important than the "self-critical analysis" you write of. It is made inexpressibly more difficult by attacks from ignorant or malevolent victors. Our despair about this, if we dare to formulate it, is dismissed as "nostalgia" and stuffed back down our throats. Perhaps we ought to try to create more opportunities for people to talk with their counterparts in the way I have experienced for the past two years in the discussion circle at the East Berlin Academy of Arts, where intellectuals from East and West can express their views. At this moment in history, I know of no other method that would include a substantial number of people. The East Berlin Academy will no doubt be dissolved. A West German in a position to know is said to have stated at the recent media conference that the intention is to "smash" the intellectual potential of the East. Once again, this makes life easy for those here who want to resist reform, including those in the Academy.

October 3, 1991. I have just heard your speech on German Radio. I agree with much of what you said. I too have often described a certain type of intellectuals here in the East as "*Tuis.*" [5] But in your talk I found once again that the "other side" was not given enough of a hearing, nor was the history; but of course that can't all be done in half an hour. I would say too that there were serious differences between the attitudes of the intelligentsia in the sciences and in the arts, which had to do with their social position and the resultant differences in their degree of dependency on the system.

Another thing: When I look at the West German artists and scientists and their academies and highly paid institutes, I wonder: Where among these men and women is the courage to stand up to the thrones of kings? Oh, I could go on and on.

5. Brecht left a fragmentary novel in which he used the word *Tuis*—an abbreviation of *Tellectuelinns*—to describe false intellectuals who let themselves be bought to produce ideology useful to the rich and powerful.

"The Truth of Our Tongues"

The Stories of Grace Paley

→→ ←←

" I don't know. I used to know," Grace Paley says, when asked what
is the "central concern" of her stories. Was she being coy? It
would be hard to find a less appropriate word for her, if I am really
going to talk about her and her stories and not just send her greetings from Mecklenburg to Vermont, where she now lives during the
summer. Hi, Grace! So now I am supposed to introduce your stories
to readers, male and female, who don't know you yet. I can see she
doesn't believe in "introductions," she shrugs her shoulders and is
silent. They are inimitable stories that cannot be retold in other
words, I say; but if Grace knows anything about them, she knows
that. Her father already rubbed her nose in the fact when he said:
"I see you can't tell a plain story. So don't waste time."[1] The father
is canny and resigned at the same time, while his daughter, pa-
tiently and a little sneakily, seems to concede everything yet keeps

First published as Wolf's Introduction to the German edition of Grace Paley's collected
short stories and poems, "*Die schwebende Wahrheit.*" *Erzählungen und Gedichte* (Leipzig: Reclam Verlag, 1991).

1. Quoted from "A Conversation with My Father," in Paley, *Enormous Changes at
the Last Minute* (London: Virago Press, 1979), p. 166.

trying to persuade him that the unhappy wife and mother in her story, whose blatantly unjust fate upsets him so, could *change* in the end and her life could take a different direction ("She's my knowledge and my invention").[2] But elsewhere Grace, untroubled by the apparent contradictions, confesses, "It was possible that I did owe something to my own family and the families of my friends. That is, to tell their stories *as simply as possible,* in order, you might say, to save a few lives."[3] I believe she means this not just metaphorically but quite literally too. She takes a dim view of the future of our earth. "Of course, because of this planet, which is dropping away from us in poisonous disgust, I'm hardly ever home."[4] Which she thinks is part of the reason why she has written only short stories, and, she believes, too few of them, and no novels. Instead of novels we have this peculiar web of narrative, voices, reports, observations, which at bottom are all connected.

It's clear to me that there is no way to get the better of her, so I keep reaching for her book, leafing through it, getting absorbed in it, being caught in the same wake. Her words and sentences elicit a different sort of admiration and enthusiasm from me than any other prose, and at the same time I feel this sharp pang: How *does* she do that! Form is a matter of grace, she claims tersely somewhere or other. Sure, sure. But all the same, one must be able to find out something about it. I no longer shrink from marking up her stories with a pencil. The catch is meager, as I expected. What have I finally managed to jot down? In the first story, "Goodbye and Good Luck," I wrote a single word in the margin: "Dialogues!" An almost irritated note of appreciation. What I meant was how the actor Vlashkin says to Rosie, his lover of a lifetime more or less, "You are losing your time. Do you understand it? A woman should not lose her time." To which Rosie replies: "Oi, Vlashkin, if you are my friend, what is time?"[5]

How true, and what do I mean by this bit of Germanic literary

2. Ibid.

3. Quoted from "Debts," in ibid., p. 10 (Wolf's italics).

4. Quoted from "Listening," in *Later the Same Day* (London: Virago, 1985), p. 209.

5. Quoted from "Goodbye and Good Luck," in *The Little Disturbances of Man* (London: Virago, 1980), p. 17.

accountancy: "dialogues"? "You are all right? Really, Rose? Your health is good? You are working?"—"My health, considering the weight it must carry, is first-class."[6] But that's how people really talk, Grace Paley says. You should just hear the way people talk here, she says: it amazes her.

She's speaking about New York, the culture of the Lower East Side, the unique blend of diverse immigrant tongues in the melting pot of American. Grace Paley's parents, immigrant Jews, spoke Russian at home; later she lived with her small children in a neighborhood of Jewish families of various backgrounds, along with Puerto Ricans and Poles. Born "all ears," she has worlds of opportunity to hear people talk—in the park with the other mothers, in the supermarket, at home with the neighbor women, at demonstrations and sit-ins, distributing leaflets, in cafes and the cheaper restaurants.[7] And she listens, listens, listens. The language of place. The "truth of our tongues." How sizzlingly they tell each other their opinions, how imaginatively, aggressively, irrationally, illogically, and aptly. Grace Paley creates whole surrealistic portraits out of speech alone. She knows whereof she speaks. Once we took a walk together along streets that bordered her own neighborhood—streets full of abandoned buildings and unemployed young people given over to drugs and crime, many of whom walked up to Grace to say hello and tell her about themselves. She knew them; she and her husband cared about them.

Back to the stories. Very often they are compositions for voice which, it seems to me, need no commentary beyond a delighted sigh: So that's how people are. And maybe all that this benevolent storyteller achieves at the end of 487 pages is that we turn our sigh into a question: Is that how we people are? Well, isn't that a lot? More than most storytellers achieve, who set out to do so much more? She wants nothing more, she says, than to know how people are living at this moment in time and history. This is hardly a modest program for a writer, but in any case it is one that frees her from trying to do things that don't belong on paper, one that allows her to wait, sometimes for years, until a subject is ripe to be

6. Ibid., p. 19.
7. Quoted from "Faith in the Afternoon," in *Enormous Changes*, p. 32.

written about. "There is a long time in me between knowing and telling."[8]

As far as I can see, she is not concerned about any definition of art, either "high" or "low." She knows that the real experiments happen in what you write about. That has been true ever since there was art, but people keep forgetting it—and actually that's something to do with class, she adds reflectively. And so it is, though this too becomes debatable if people try to deny the existence of class. Along with experimenting on content, however, Grace Paley gives a markedly female shape to her material, a shape that really is part and parcel of the experiment. She describes how she suddenly notices that she has woven or created a sort of container into which the story comes and settles, a container resembling a cup or a plate or a cistern or a washtub. Who could read this and not picture women going about their traditional activities, weaving baskets, making pottery, producing fibers? Paley *asks* her stories to come, asks carefully, cautiously, to avoid wounding them. The form is a gift. A gift, to be sure, that does not come from outside, and that she has to work hard for.

As I write this, I keep hearing a sentence from Virginia Woolf that I read recently and reluctantly, much as I am otherwise inclined to trust her sentences. It is all the better if a buyer can forget the writer's sex when he comes to buy a book, she says—because a writer has no sex. Admittedly she did not write the sentence in the first person but in the third, and used the pronoun "he" to refer to this ideal book-buyer; but I cannot help recognizing that to a large extent she shares the views of the dream customer that we—myself included—would like to recreate today. But not so Grace Paley. Beyond doubt she is a writer—almost by accident, she thinks; she could easily have remained an unpublished author—but she has a sex and does not deny it. You could even say this is the source of her inspiration—meaning not just the sum of all her positive impulses but the sum too of all the sorrows, fears, hurts, all the intentionally inflicted insults, misunderstandings, disrespect, and misinterpretation stemming from myriad sources that a woman is subject to today, not to mention the sum of all her own omissions, errors, and

8. Quoted from "Debts," p. 9.

faults of the sort to which women are especially prone in societies where they must raise children in hostile milieus, where they cannot give their children many things that they need, and where these same societies, or various institutions, make them feel guilty about it. No wonder a considerable number of women writers have renounced having children, or have even constructed a theory about it like Simone de Beauvoir, who said that only a woman without children could preserve her intellectual independence. Grace Paley, on the other hand, says that although she could not write without living, she could not live without her children.[9]

A woman with small children is bound to write differently than a man does, or than a woman without children does. Her time gets broken into small segments; her ability to concentrate, which may never have let her down before, wears thin, and she may never regain it. She must get used to feeling that the intensity and time she devotes to writing is intensity and time taken away from her children; and she must endure the ongoing feeling of guilt and resist the ongoing temptation to give up. She discovers how hard it is for a woman to do justice to herself—for writing is one way of doing that. Who could be interested in this rubbish, she wonders. She was very interested in it, Grace says, but she didn't have enough social ego to write it down until she had developed it to the point where she could tell herself that it didn't matter what other people might say, what the media might say, because they always tend to show contempt for women's "self-pity." They get nowhere with Grace Paley, because it is her nature, she says, to be tough and cheerful; and that is exactly the mixture that makes her prose explosive. No tearfulness, no appeasement, not a trace of self-pity, but something akin to ruthlessness toward others and herself. Vitality and especially humor join with it to form a unique alloy of joie de vivre and hopelessness. Life is tragic and the world may be nearing its end, she says—but that doesn't release her from trying to understand it.

By her example you see what children can mean to a woman writer: an intimate connection to life's most living core. A wealth of unfathomable details comes from her shared life with children, which can never deteriorate into mere observation. It is a source of

9. See dedication to *Later*.

immediacy, verbal wit, originality, finesse, and tenderness, which can very well count as aesthetic categories if you decide that you absolutely have to have categories. It gives empathy too. I know of nothing that can sensitize a person more deeply and lastingly than association with children—sensitize in the broadest sense, because children, especially her own children, force a woman to take the state of the world seriously. "I *had* promised my children to end the war before they grew up." [10] Grace Paley has been protesting in the streets ever since the Vietnam War.

Women, women friends, and family are her favorite themes; she's never done with them. The dark life of women, she says, is what started her writing in the first place. Women seem remarkable to her: how strong they are. But having a tough time does not mean being a victim. She doesn't overdo it. She doesn't allow her characters to kill themselves. Writers who do, she says—referring expressly to Tolstoy and the death of Anna Karenina—have no idea how terrible a life people can endure. In the families of women, mostly women without husbands who have been friends since childhood and are playground mothers like her, she finds the same hopeless confusion, the same chaos, that is seen in any normal family and that everyone is therefore bound to recognize—provided they have no illusions about their own family life—even if their outward circumstances are very different; even if the family in the story centers on a woman named Faith who runs the household, cooks, struggles, quarrels with the children, types "with one hand ... behind my back," [11] holds long discussions about life with her women friends, makes short work of her ex-husbands and potential lovers, despairs of her parents in the old people's home, and grabs her piece from life's great cake with insatiable appetite; even if a family like this has its own kind of craziness, a domestic climate that cannot help but seem overheated, unwholesome, and exhausting to a member of some other clan.

Faith is a marvelous character. The sound of her name reminds you of "Grace"; it implies loyalty and trust. Faith is Grace's projection of herself onto the horizon of literature, which both intensifies

---

10. Quoted from "Wants," in *Enormous Changes*, p. 5.
11. Quoted from "A Subject of Childhood," in *Little Disturbances*, p. 139.

and magnifies the original. Faith as a character amplifies every impression that passes through her: the blows of fate, injustices, everyday injuries, love and its disappointments, close friendships with women; the commonplace rudeness, meanness, and thoughtlessness to which a woman is subjected; the frequent poverty; all the happenings she could hardly endure without irony and self-mockery.

Grace "is" not Faith. Sometimes she is more like Faith and sometimes less. She is closest to her in the texts from the Peace Calendar for 1989, "Midrash on Happiness," "Conversation II," where Faith's mouth speaks Grace's words.[12] Grace plays with her character, who has very distinct features of her own and at the same time is a kind of medium for herself. "Faith really is an American," she says, "and she was raised up like everyone else to the true assumption of happiness."[13] Faith, Grace says, permits her to speak for her people, that is, for her friends: her life and theirs are interchangeable. That may sound like extreme modesty or even self-denial in the art business, where almost everyone tries to achieve a distinctive style, an individual profile, and to set herself apart from all the rest; but it may simply be a sense of reality. Grace Paley isn't shocked or insulted by the idea that her individual life is just part of a society's biography, especially a social biography of women. She is interested in the way real memories blend into invented characters, the way precise individual characters are formed out of the diverse, inexhaustible pool of a group. Grace Paley obviously needs this group—"my people"—not as a storehouse of material but to live and survive. Ellen, one of her friends, telephones her "two weeks before Christmas" to say, "Faith, I'm dying." Faith feels she is dying herself. "What's so great, Ellen? What's the big loss? Live a couple more years. See the kids and the whole cruddy thing, every cheese hole in the world go up in heat blast firewaves . . ." To which Ellen replies, "I want to see it all."[14] Intimate friendship with women is part of the essence of happiness for Grace Paley.

12. War Resisters League Peace Calendar 1989, *365 Reasons Not to Have Another War*, by Grace Paley and Vera Williams (New York: War Resister's League, and Philadelphia: New Society Publishers); reprinted in Paley, *Long Walks and Intimate Talks* (New York: Feminist Press, City University of New York, 1991).

13. Quoted from "Faith in the Afternoon," p. 33.

14. Quoted from "Living," in *Enormous Changes*, pp. 59–60.

A central motto. If she were drowning, she says, she would still "see": she would look up at the sky.[15] Her poems, which are being published here in German for the first time in a sympathetic translation by her friend Marianne Frisch, are shorthand notes made with her eyes wide open. In the 1989 Peace Calendar she turns reports on political actions into fragments of the human tragicomedy in which she is taking part.

She is incorruptible. She breaches convention without apparent effort, she ignores the judgment of the "world." The relations between her characters are measured by their humanity, and the characters can be as amoral as they wish to be and must be, without ever departing from this standard. The underlying values without which any group would be simply a band of marauders seem incredibly enduring in some ways and changeable in others. These values are reinforced and changed, or at least renewed, by what the group does or fails to do together, by their talk, by the stories that Grace Paley writes about them. "What's going on? I'll tell you what: life is going on. You have an opinion. I have an opinion. Life don't have no opinion."[16]

15. "Drowning (I)," in Paley, *New and Collected Poems* (Gardiner, ME: Tilbury House, 1985, 1992), p. 7.
16. Quoted from "Zagrowsky Tells," in *Later,* pp. 158–59.

Woserin, Friday, September 27, 1991

->>- -<+-

I wake up at 5:00 A.M. and am determined to go back to sleep, but I already know I will fail as I have failed so often in recent weeks, with sleep running away all the farther the more determined I am to catch it. So I try another tactic: I am quite indifferent as to whether I wake or sleep. On the contrary, lying awake and losing myself in my thoughts is far preferable to wasting time sleeping, and if I can get my thoughts to free-float, I secretly hope they will be caught in the whirlpool of weariness and churn down into the dark abyss of sleep. But my thoughts are wide awake and don't fall into my trap; one by one they troop open-eyed and mocking past my inner eye. Well, all right then, I'll watch it getting light outside. There's a whole literature of observations of that kind made by poor sleepers; it's really a shame that I don't know when the first signs of dawn will replace the darkness that's still outside the windows now and that doesn't exist outside our windows in Berlin.

A short time later I reach after all for the book that's lying on the old chair next to my bed. I didn't actually plan to reread the whole of Solzhenitsyn's novel *Cancer Ward;* I really only wanted to find out if it contributes anything to the basic hypothesis of the speech I'm working on, about "Cancer and Society"—working too

First published in the German edition of this book.

late, too slowly, with insufficient concentration—and am I supposed to be comforted when my husband Gerhard tells me on the telephone that I always feel this way? I've forgotten. Leafing through the book, I realize how much of it I've forgotten. How could I not remember—seeing how I pay so much attention to beginnings—that the book starts with the line: "On top of it all, the cancer wing was 'number thirteen'"?[1] And that the failure of the official Pavel Nikolayevich Rusanov to acknowledge his superstitiousness about the number thirteen reflects his inability to tolerate the truth about his illness—the illness that starts him on the bitter path of insight by robbing him of all his privileges at a single stroke, and annihilates him socially before he reaches biological death? How is it that it didn't strike me the first time I read the book that Kostoglotov, one of the main characters and a counterpoint to Rusanov, is first seen through Rusanov's eyes—as a sort of cutthroat—and that we first learn the nickname that Rusanov gives him and only later discover his real name? And why do I have to overcome an inner resistance each time I'm about to pick up the book? I read the first few chapters, making a mental note when I recognize something. Yes, Kostoglotov compels his young fellow patient to read a book, and at the same time he impresses on him: "But remember, education doesn't make you smarter" ... "So what does make you smarter?" "Life, that's what."[2]

Suddenly a child is trotting around my feet wearing Anton's striped T-shirt, his favorite garment, but it isn't Anton, although in my dream I "know" I am responsible for him now while his parents are "far away." It's another child with whom I am wandering through the many pillared corridors of a large house, it's a pretty little girl called Svetlana who implores me to adopt her. (A couple of days ago Anton told us, "As long as Mommy and Daddy aren't here, I'm your son.") I wake up hearing the sentence, "Isn't it the wickedest thing to make a person angry?"

It's 7:30. But I admit it's light outside now, the rectangle of the window stands out clearly behind the curtain. What does that sen-

1. The English translations of Solzhenitsyn passages are quoted from Alexander Solzhenitsyn, *Cancer Ward*, translated by Nicholas Bethell and David Bury (London: Bodley Head, 1968), p. 1.
2. Ibid., p. 25.

tence mean? Did it come from a different dream? And "Svetlana"? Why Svetlana? A Russian name—not surprising considering what I am reading. But doesn't it mean "the bright, the radiant one"?

I pull back the curtain, the sky is a gray cloth, a couple of birds start up out of the elder bush under the window. They'll be back in no time and go on making free with the elderberries. In my bathrobe I cross the hall to Anton, who is sitting on the ground by his bed in his pajamas and studying a Donald Duck comic book. I know you can't talk to him when he's reading but I keep trying; I ask how he slept, express my concerns about the cold floor, don't even shrink from wishing aloud that he should get dressed, and in return reap a series of variable grunts and a long plaintive look to which I respond unfeelingly ("Man, but I'm in the most exciting place!"). I use the old and contemptible technique of blackmail—"Well all right," I say, "I'll just eat ham and eggs by myself"—"Oh, you really kill me," he says, and becomes absorbed in his reading.

While I am in the bath, the little radio announces that in the Bundestag yesterday opinions clashed over the new regulations on abortion. Members were presented with six different drafts of the law, ranging from the proposal of Alliance 90 and the Greens that women should have the legal right to terminate an unwanted pregnancy and that Paragraph 218 should be eliminated without replacement, to the draft by a "pro-life" group from the Union that would permit abortion only if the health and life of the mother were threatened.[3] Male hypocrisy is complicated because the hypocrite is often unaware of it and of how the concern for "unborn life" masks the ancient power struggle for control of wife and child. What sickens me is that those who hold this fossilized attitude need it to preserve their own self-esteem, and so it cannot be dissolved by any argument or by sympathy with the life that is already born. I miss other parts of the news while pictures go through my mind of how I drove through the villages with Rosemarie E. in our bright

3. Bündnis 90, or Alliance 90, was a coalition made up of Social Democrats and members of New Forum and other citizen groups that had helped to bring down the old GDR government; they generally wanted a socialist alternative state rather than immediate unification. They put up candidates for the March 1990 elections, and in the aftermath of unification they continued to act as a pressure group on issues like abortion, which had to be newly regulated so as to apply a single law in both parts of Germany.

red Trabant—when was that? the end of the fifties, the beginning of the sixties?—to a village in Brandenburg whose name I have long since forgotten, where she disappeared into a house with a doctor's nameplate on the door; how I drove around the corner to wait for what seemed to me an endless time until at last she came out, pale as a sheet, walking with small, cautious steps, sat down silently beside me, and groaned softly. I drove off without a word and we said hardly anything throughout the long journey. Then I took her home and put her to bed, and for the next few days I felt a terrible dread as fever set in and her temperature soared. But there was a woman doctor who, although she would not have performed an abortion herself, was willing to prescribe the right medications without asking too many questions.

So the UN Security Council has finally concluded a universal and comprehensive arms embargo on the former Yugoslavia. The European peace conference that has convened in the Hague and will present its findings in the first week of October expressly welcomes the embargo. I try to picture the scenes that must lie behind the incredible report: Heavy fighting south of Dubrovnik. The words that involuntarily spring to mind—"There must be something we can do!"—give way to the pervasive sense of helplessness that overcomes me more and more often.

I find Anton in the same position I left him in almost half an hour ago, crouching on the floor in the only open space left, surrounded by hundreds of Lego blocks in every color of the rainbow that I know he intends using to complete an extensive zoo. The zoo's foundations are already on view under the table along with a horde of native and exotic plastic animals, all of whose names and habits he knows and for which he wants to build the appropriate habitats. I involve him in a conversation about the biotopes of tropical rainforests, at the same time handing him his clothes, which he actually puts on, absorbed in thought. He thinks about what material he could use to reconstruct a bit of tropical rainforest and, as he does so, supervises the production of his fried egg, of which he has an ideal image that no actual earthly egg can live up to—well, hardly ever: it must be a perfect circle, the white no longer "squishy" but the yellow liquid enough so that he can draw it out into a network of rivers and streams.

Cautiously I bring the conversation around to the subject of school and ask whether he thinks he can make friends in his class. Of course, he says: Tobias is as good as being his friend already. "But it's funny, you know, usually the girls want to be friends with me." "Why is that?" "Because I protect them, that's why." There followed a long, detailed description of a chivalrous battle waged for a girl named Sophie against her attacker Steffen, who used the meanest tricks but simply could not prevail against Anton's left hooks and surprise kicks and in the end was sent off with a warning that he would not forget so easily. "Okay," I say, "but look, didn't you ever have the feeling that the others were envious because you already knew how to read and they didn't?" "No, why should they? I was the one who was bored, not them." "And if your teacher had you read stories aloud—didn't anyone say you were a show-off?" "No, why should they? They've seen for themselves that I really know how to read." "Oh, so show-offs are people who boast about something that they can't really do." "Sure, what else?"

While I wash the dishes, Anton insists we retrace the travel route of his parents again in the atlas and on the little globe, and again he wants to hear the verse: "In Europe everything is so big, so big / And everything in Japan is so small." Neither of us knows much about Nepal except that the people are said to be very poor. "I don't think there would be any point in my sending them any of my clothes," Anton says after a while. "The children wear very different clothes there, I saw it once in a photo." "Otherwise you would send them your striped T-shirt?" "Sure," says Anton.

He negotiates with me about whether we could wash out the remaining mustard in the glass jar so that we would have one more in the series of mustard jars that he thinks are "awesome." He is concerned about whether the mustard manufacturer can afford to give us a glass jar along with the mustard; he says it must be awfully expensive.

Carola comes down the stairs and takes charge of Anton, I finish dressing, it's started to rain softly, I cross the damp field to the car, exchange a few words with Carola about the horde of elderberries that grew this year, every year we have more, we still have juice from last year in the cellar, but should we leave all the berries to die? She plans to get a pail and pick berries with Anton. With the car key already in the lock, I straighten up again and look around. The old, rather run-down house with its red brick, its green door, its white window frames, which need painting, incidentally. The linden trees of different heights to the right and left of the entrance, their leaves just beginning to turn. Overhead the sky has turned dark gray. I have been storing up images like these for some time, a sort of packed lunch to carry with me in the more difficult days ahead. Now Carola is clapping her hands. A gigantic flock of crows starts up out of the taller linden tree.

First I drive across the short stretch of cobblestones. The old road is to be covered with a layer of asphalt as soon as possible, because that is what the mayor and most of the townspeople want. We are not enchanted by the prospect of our quiet village street being turned into a racetrack for speeding cars, but other residents hope that this customer-friendly road may attract investors and buyers—for example a purchaser for the manor house by the lake that used to belong to a publicly owned firm in Berlin and now stands empty—so that vacationers will come back again and a few jobs will be created for the unemployed women in the village.

I turn off onto the narrow tarred road that was laid by the cooperative and crosses their fields—but are they still "their" fields? I don't know—and I try, as I always do at this spot, to take a look at the nest of the osprey that for several years has been raising its young up on an electrical pylon. Has it already left, headed south? I see no trace of the ospreys, but the geese are moving across the sky in wedges. Each year you can predict from the time of the geese migrations when the winter will start and how severe it will be.

On the road to Sternberg, which I know in every detail, it occurs to me why I have developed a resistance to reading Solzhenitsyn's *Cancer Ward*. Suddenly I see myself sitting in a lounge chair on the terrace of our house in Kleinmachnow with that book in my lap. It's a warm sunny afternoon in autumn, the poplars have shed their first yellow leaves onto the concrete of the terrace, it's a perfect idyll, and I am afraid. September 1968. Gerhard has gone to Potsdam with our daughter Annette; she has been summoned to be questioned by the Stasi. Her boyfriend was stopped on the road because he was driving too fast on his motorbike, he had with him a German translation of *Two Thousand Words* by the Czech writer Vaculik, and when he was questioned he said that he had heard the same views expressed in our home. His place was searched. We didn't want my diaries to be found at our place and so for the first time we hid them; and for the first time, two men showed up at our door. I wondered what they could prove against Annette and what we ought to do if they held her in custody. I was trying to distract myself with the Solzhenitsyn book, it wasn't working very well, and a faint sense of fear or at least discomfort still attaches to the sight of the book. Now that I know where it comes from, I'll be able to ignore it.

Arriving at what used to be the polyclinic, I find the atmosphere in the physiotherapy section down in the basement is the same as ever, even though the individual divisions of the clinic have been forced to privatize. Frau N. tells me about it while she treats me with a stimulating electrical current. It's so nonsensical, she says, to break up a medical unit that functioned so well, whose different sections were so well coordinated with each other. It just couldn't be true that everything in the East had to disappear, even things that had been successful. Even in economic terms it was madness for expensive equipment not to be used in common by all the doctors—not to mention the great disadvantages for the patients, who had had specialists available for almost all their ailments within a single establishment. I ask her whether at least they are gaining some financial advantage. "Oh, you know," she says, "we only get 50 to 60 percent of what West German physiotherapists are paid. They told us recently that if our training was really that good, we could have found good jobs over in the West. So we're being punished for not leaving our patients here in the lurch.— That's twenty minutes, right?"

I lie there listening through the partitions to the conversations going on in the other cubicles. The big event is being discussed from every angle: last week there was a break-in here during the night. So now they are going after the hospitals and clinics; what can the burglar have been looking for, there really aren't any treasures lying around here, but since then the night portress has been afraid; that's understandable, your life just isn't safe any more, just think how the traffic has increased, you daren't cross the street. I lie there and enjoy the Mecklenburg dialect and Mecklenburg's ruminative pace. In the end I have to remind Frau N. that I must mark down on my card what I owe her for the treatment: "Oh, that's not so important," she says and waves it aside.

I roam through the furniture and housewares store to see what changes the past year has brought to the products. Housewares too are approaching what is available in the West. The furniture is as ugly as ever, East and West alike. I buy a package of wooden clothespins guaranteed to be of old GDR manufacture, and an equally dusty garbage bin made of rubber that is hidden behind all the snazzy new garbage bin models. And in the supermarket next door, formerly a consumer coop and now part of the Kaisers chain, I feel no urge to buy. I leave with little more than a chicken—no longer called a "broiler" as in the days of the GDR—and basmati rice.

In town I miraculously find a parking place at the market and walk along a couple of streets inspecting the new shops and the ones that have been refurbished with new advertising signs. A new, modern textile shop stands on one corner: a pullover for Tinka's birthday. I spend a long time hunting for Conrad Bächtle Strasse before finally realizing that it must have been renamed Kütinerstrasse. Before, I never gave a thought to Conrad Bächtle; now I would like to know who he was. The Bureau of Church-Owned Farmland is located in a splendid old Tudor house that has been renovated. I need to speak with the woman in charge about a few square meters of land that we neglected to have surveyed years ago when we bought our property. This was no problem back in "GDR days," as people call them now, since land was not worth much then and, moreover, people didn't speculate in land. The verbal assurance that we would eventually have the survey done was enough to satisfy both parties, and our neighbor uses the patch of land next to us while respecting our customary rights. I am amazed to hear myself bargaining with the Church land administrator about the sale of this tiny plot of land; she seems unresponsive. Basically, the Church is not selling any more land, she says, and behind her words I hear the message that, given the new circumstances since unification, she is sorry that it ever did so. I suppress my chagrin, drop off my letter to the Church board, and warn myself as I leave not to lose my good humor. Why should I be immune to the effects of the "new circumstances," which in part involve a new relationship to property?

I get a treacherous urge to go to the discount store by the market and make purchases that I suddenly feel cannot be postponed—heavy bottles, heavy bags. As I pack up my wares at the counter, I hear a man behind me ask the cashier, "Isn't that——Christa Wolf?" The woman says yes, and the man replies, "Honecker gave her a fancy house too." Business as usual, I think, and I turn around and grin at him, meeting a glassy expression with which I am quite familiar. He isn't from around here. Is that supposed to make me feel better? When someone tries to push past me as I go out the door, I push back as impolitely as I can, and force my way out first. "So, there it is again," I say half-aloud on my way to the car.

The day has brightened up, the sky now is a thick pane of milk glass with a bright light just behind it. The sun breaks through for a few seconds at several points in my journey home. I enjoy the driving; I sing "Across the lake, across the lake we go" and "On a tree a cuckoo sat." Depending on which song I sing first, it starts off a whole series of songs of a particular type. This is the forest-and-field series that includes "A hunter blew his horn," which with its multitude of verses nearly fills up the time between Dabel and Borkow. This time I notice how many of the linden trees, newly planted two years ago, have grown bigger. Most have already developed a tiny crown. They are instantly transformed in my imagination into full-grown lindens cutting a dark-green swath through the rolling landscape; an adornment. I won't live to walk in their shade—or how fast do linden trees grow? "And their branches rustled as if calling to me," I sing at the top of my voice as I drive into the yard. Anton is there, they have picked three bucketfuls of elderberries, Carola is sitting by the rock stripping the berries from the stalks; Anton has built a bizarre landscape of branches and stones on the ancient granite that we brought to the front of the house from the lake in a daring enterprise involving several men and some high technology. Both are hungry for the potato fritters I promised them, which I finally make, using prepared potatoes rather than freshly grated ones and feeling a little guilty about it. They taste good with sugar and cranberries. We try to picture what Anton's parents may be eating in Nepal. I notice that Anton, who avoided talking about his parents right after they left, now talks about them more and more often. On the other hand, he avoids any conversation about school; the most he says is, "Yes, yes, I'm going back." But he can't say what it was that made him so afraid on his first days of school that he couldn't sleep or eat and had to throw up in front of the school building. "Isn't your teacher nice to you?" "Oh yes, she is."— "Do the other kids pester you?" "No, they don't." "Shall we practice writing a bit more today?" "Yes, let's."

I lie down. The relief of a nap each noon, a little holiday in the middle of the day. Solzhenitsyn. Reading, I become absorbed again in this familiar grief that has been with me for a long time and will not leave me again. I find the exact passage I need for my lecture "Cancer and Society": Kostoglotov tells his adversary Rusanov about a book he is reading that says that very little research has been done so far into how the development of a tumor is related to the central nervous system. Yet there is a remarkable relationship! There can even be a spontaneous recovery, though it occurs only rarely. "Do you all see what that means? Not a cure, but recovery! Well?" Then the incredulous silence is broken by one of the terminally ill men who says, "For that you no doubt need . . . a clear conscience," and Rusanov retorts in outrage: "That's idealistic drivel! What does conscience have to do with it?"[4] Solzhenitsyn himself experienced a spontaneous cure of this kind.

Anton wakes me; he needs to get physically close to someone, lies down next to me, cuddles up to me, lies perfectly still for a while, then wants to read his beloved Jandl poems. He knows where the book is, fetches it, insists on my reading aloud to him even though he knows the poems by heart and recites them one after another so that he can laugh himself silly beforehand. " 'I / wanna / wash / the dishes / Wash yourself / my child.'—'Merry Christmas!' " he demands and I read,

> open up the door-y
> open up the door-y
> dear master can come in-y
> dear master can come in-y

4. *Cancer Ward*, pp. 158–59.

christmas merry
christmas merry
and I'm only a dog-gie
christmas merry
christmas merry
and I'm only a dog-gie

I make an effort to read the texts with exactly the same diction as Gerhard always does, but I notice that my reading leaves something to be desired. Anton is generous and shows his satisfaction. We are both in a good mood.

The sun really breaks through in the afternoon; I grant myself permission to sit with my coffee and newspaper on the bench behind the house, my favorite haunt for reading, planning, and making notes. The headline of the Schwerin newspaper says PRIVATE INVESTORS BEGIN TO BITE. "We recognize that there are motivated and well-trained workers in eastern Germany," announced Birgit Breuel, the director of Treuhand, at a press conference yesterday.— The planned firing of thousands of East German shipyard workers will take place only if there is a simultaneous offer to enrol them in a job creation scheme. Twenty-four thousand men and women are to lose their jobs in three waves of dismissals by 1993.—The crisis in East German agriculture is nearing a climax. The Minister of Agriculture reckons that four out of five agricultural workers will lose their jobs by 1994.—The debate about the right of asylum continues.—A miners' rebellion in the Romanian capital has brought down the government.—The sub-post office in Jesendorf reports heavy consumer demand.—There are no more Soviet nuclear weapons left in eastern Germany.—8,100 military draftees have been called up from the new federal states.—Frau Honecker has been granted a German passport.—By the end of June, 2,073 road deaths had taken place on East German highways.

I fold up the newspaper and interrupt the interior newsreel I have been watching. I look for the newspaper's masthead. Publisher: Dr. Hubert Burda. Just two years ago this paper, with the same layout, was the party newspaper of the Socialist Unity Party. I wonder how many of the editors are still staunchly carrying on with their work.

It's after four. Finally I get to my desk. I am aware that my lecture on Cancer and Society is only a pretext to confront the question that has interested me the most for some time, and that along with other questions has been washed away by the absolute primacy of the political in the past two years: What is "mind"? What is the relationship between the mental principle and the brain? How are we to picture the mutual penetration of matter and mind, including in the human body? And so how do "mind" and "psyche" affect the body cell that suddenly "degenerates" into cancer? Too many quotation marks, I know, but how can I express in language this unity of Mindbodysoul? In fact there is quite a simple way to express it: I just have to say "human being." Only we're trained to always think of "human being" as divided into three parts.

I review my notes on my conversation with Hans Peter Dürr.[5] He distinguishes between "material, concrete" and "real."[6] He sees no signs of a change in the one-sided thinking of scientists: They consider "real" to be what is measurable, he says, and they screen out all the rest of the vast domain of reality. Thus the question of "waves versus particles" is fundamentally mistaken, in his view. The notion that an atom is a particle and that it remains identical over time is completely wrong. Let's take an atom of iodine, Dürr said. The statistical average of all iodine atoms decays at exactly the rate determined by physics. But the individual atom is free to decay in the next second, or quite a bit later than the statistical average. Chaos reigns on the level of the microcosm; and mind, as the source of all creativity, proposes a multitude of creative ideas. Some of these alternatives petrify into matter, the "waste product of the mind," which is governed by more or less mechanical laws like the matter of the macrocosm and of the mesocosm, in which we live. Of course we love to establish such laws, which give us the certainty that we shall rediscover objects we need in the same place and condition as that in which we left them. But this is not how things are in the microcosm, where everything is still open.

Dürr does not picture the birth of the cosmos from mind as a kind of "big bang." Instead, this primal birth could have taken the form of a primal question with an alternative yes-or-no, this-way-

5. See the bibliography to "Cancer and Society," below.
6. German: *zwischen "real" und "wirklich."*

or-another-way element in it. Each possible reply to the question was linked in turn to other questions with their own variables, and so on and on, so that the number of possibilities would multiply at a dizzying rate. This immense reservoir of possibilities could have created such structures as "time" and "space"—which in this context no doubt warrant being put into quotation marks—thus forming a canvas onto which reality could be projected. Why ever not?

The same excitement grips me now as on that afternoon six weeks ago when we were sitting on our veranda in Berlin and Dürr introduced the phrase "horizon of expectation." A horizon of expectation formed, which brought about an event. There was some probability that an event would occur at the point of maximum expectation; but it was by no means certain.

A poetic principle, I said, and he said: "Why not? At some point, science and poetry may coincide again."

Automatically I transfer his examples from science to history, to events I have experienced. Didn't we all feel, in the fall of '89, that our common horizon of expectation had grown dense—that it had a suffocatingly dense consistency? And wasn't this dense concentration bound to produce "the event," to burst out with it? We had the physical sensation of being dragged into an immense concentration of energy that had not been present a few weeks or even a few days earlier.

Quickly I jot down a few lines to use in my lecture: the meaning of expectation.

The fact is, you are not necessarily lying if you tell a patient that the outcome of his or her illness is uncertain. Statistical probability loses its absolute validity when you look at the individual case. It is always conceivable that the process that is disrupting the precarious balance of the cell and that has driven it to multiply at breakneck speed may be reversed. And perhaps we may learn to feel awe again at the miracle of that balance.

For an hour or two, or even longer, I shed the feeling that it's "too late," the feeling that is now such a permanent part of my life that I am no longer even conscious of it. The clamp opens up, a life of something like freedom becomes possible, I am out from under the yoke of false, destructive needs. By the same token it must also be possible to live a life in community, with others, and not just blindly and furiously against them. So maybe the aged Faust's grandiose self-deception isn't the last word, I think. And do we really need a word at all, isn't a perceptive glance, an unselfish action, more effective now than worn-out language? Shouldn't we . . .

My thoughts are racing. Anton appears in the doorway, by the door where I put up the big poster of Virginia Woolf's face. He has just seen a film about animals on TV. He asks if I know how the survival of turtles off the South Sea islands is tied to the price of bananas. I don't know, so he tells me. Well, sea turtles feed on jellyfish, right? And toxic pesticides and herbicides are sprayed on banana plantations, right?—"Oh, and then the poison gets into the sea, and the jellyfish die . . ."—"No. Well, yes, but that's not the main thing. It's that when the price of bananas is very high, the bananas are packed into plastic bags so they won't be damaged in transport because they are so valuable, get it?"—"Got it."—"And a lot of those plastic bags, which are made of transparent plastic film, go into the sea, and the turtles think they are jellyfish and eat them, and then the turtles die from starvation or suffocation."—"But that's terrible."—"Yes, it's terrible."—"But when the prices are low and they don't use plastic bags, the workers on the plantations get lower pay."—"Of course. They can hardly live on what they get as it is."—"So: the turtles or the people?"—Anton is silent, thinking. Then: "I have an idea. I could paint a giant poster and hang it up in our grange hall. I could paint a sea turtle on it, very realistically, and I'd have someone write underneath it: 'Do you want me to die?'"—"Why have someone else write it?"—"There are lots of letters I don't know. And then I'd put pieces of paper by the cashier's for people to sign saying they would pay a higher price for the bananas even if they are transported without plastic bags."—"Good idea," I say, "and now we'll practice a couple of letters, shall we?"

We sit side by side at the desk in the big room. Anton haggles with me: "What? Two rows of 'Mama' and two rows of 'Mimi'? And then numbers too?"—"Come on, let's get on with it!"—He writes without concentrating, doesn't want to make the effort, and occasionally breaks off to play with his sand kaleidoscope, enjoying the landscapes that he can form with the sand between two panes of glass. I water the geraniums in the window, observe the changes in the sky. How early it gets dark now. "Do you know what would be even better?" Anton says. "If the people sign saying that they won't buy any more bananas that are wrapped in plastic bags."—"That would be better. But would they do that?"

Carola has made mangel-wurzel rolls and wheatballs in her kitchen. The kitchen is filled with the sweet scent of elderberry juice being squeezed from the juicer. A battery of bottles is already standing on the the window ledge. We talk about the qualities of elder, about the early departure of the cormorants, about the fact that the village shop is due to be closed soon—it isn't economical and the supply of cigarettes and alcohol gets stolen every couple of weeks—and later the post office will close too. Where will the old women in the village go to buy groceries then? Where will they meet each other? Anton says: "Hey, I have a better idea. The people who own the plantations are rich, they said that on TV. They should get less money and the workers more, even if the bananas are cheaper and are not packed in plastic bags. Otherwise, the workers simply ought not to pick the bananas."

Carola takes Anton to bed, reads him his evening fairy tale; I am summoned for the Good Night Song, which Anton insists must on no account be "The Moon Has Risen." Finally he tells me why: because of the "sick neighbor" in the last stanza, whom Anton can't stop thinking about once he hears the song. So we agree on "A Little Star Stood in the Sky," using an improvised tune, and we agree that he may continue reading. For half an hour? Okay. We assure each other that Anton's parents will be home in three days, that we will pick them up at the airport, that they will probably be very tanned.

A murder mystery on television. A rich man lays a trap for his wife's lover but then shoots the wrong man. I get annoyed, as I do almost every evening, that I can't tear myself away from a thriller no matter how silly or boring it is. I ask myself again if the entire TV debris of decades is still stored inside me; and what might I have done if I had not been sitting in front of the tube, which is my concession to the Zeitgeist? Right after the final scene the telephone rings; Gerhard knows I must not be interrupted until the film is over. No, there was no sun in Berlin, no rain either, the weather was overcast. Too much mail, you really must learn to throw some out.—Rituals.—"Listen," I say: "'On Being feed with joy unspent'—does that ring a bell?"—"Goethe."

"Where in Goethe? I need to know the opening lines."—"It's a late poem. Summarizes his worldview. Just a minute: 'Eternal is being, for laws serve / The living treasuries to preserve ...' It goes on something like that."—"That's no use. I need the beginning."

The electricity fails twice during the political news of all things, reminding us that we are not living in the heart of civilization. Then the late-night talk show goes off without a hitch. Incredible, I say a number of times, hearing and seeing how a sequel to *Gone with the Wind* is being planned and paid for. So the woman who is to write this sequel is an employee of the author's heirs. "Lots of luck," I say, once again comforted that I was not born in a later time, if all the writers are to be the employees of various interest groups ... "For laws serve / The living treasuries to preserve / That the All wears for ornament." Who says those lines? I think that's how the poem ends; my memory can still cough up something when it comes to Goethe. In the kitchen I prepare the chicken with mushrooms for tomorrow.—Goethe no doubt came to mind in connection with my thoughts about Dürr, so the first line must be related to the same subject. Now I remember that it's a long poem. It's remarkable how scientists today are showing an interest in Goethe's premonitions again—even in those theories of his that are actually "false" about the nature of light, on which he took issue with Newton. "Itself to find in boundlessness / The self with joy becomes selfless ..." No, that's not it. Though there are some lines in it ... "The eternal in all things moves on / To nothing must each thing be gone / If it chooses still to be." Those lines could be from the poem I am looking for. Or maybe not.

The chicken pieces are sizzling away, a pleasant aroma is spreading through the kitchen, I slice the mushrooms, I feel I'm now very close to the line I'm looking for, the rhythm is working inside me, trying out different words, new lines, and then it's there, quite clear; there is no other way my poem could begin. How late it is, but it's not midnight yet, I telephone Berlin, I hope you're still awake, so listen, this is how the poem begins:

To nothing can no thing be gone
The eternal in all things moves on
On Being feed with joy unspent
Eternal is Being: for laws serve
The living treasuries to preserve
That the All wears for ornament

"Just a moment and we'll have it. The poem is called "Legacy,"
it has seven stanzas and it belongs to the very late group written
between 1828 and 1932."

"That's what I thought. But there must be an earlier poem in
which he claims the opposite, namely that everything has to decay
into nothing, and quite economically he used the same line: 'The
eternal in all things moves on.'"—"Very good. We should look into
it some time. But not any more this evening, okay?"

To my great annoyance the mushrooms are spoiled; I won't be
able to save the dish by cooking a raw potato with it. I take my
edition of Goethe's poems to bed with me, not only because I still
have to find that poem but also because I want to experience the
beneficial effect that Goethe's poems always exert on me. I leaf
through the book, feel the effect I'm after, and find what I am looking for, too. It's called "One and All" and could be compared line
by line with "Legacy," which was written just ten years later and
to my amusement ends with lines that could not be more anachronistic:

To presage what noble souls will feel
Is of all work the most desirable.

Cancer and Society

→→ ←←

What entitles me to talk to you here on this subject? Hardly anything more than would entitle anyone else to. I know or have known
people who suffered from cancer, many of whom died. They include
close relatives and women friends with whom I waited to hear the
results of their tests, whom I visited in the hospital, who shared
with me, sometimes over a period of months, the ups and downs of
their illness, and whom I saw shortly before their deaths. Their
faces were the first thing that came into my mind when I received
the invitation to give this talk. I thought about my relations with
these very different people; whether and how our relations changed
as a result of their illness, and whether I had been able to deal with

Lecture given at the annual conference of the German Cancer Society, October 24, 1991,
in Bremen, and first published in *Scheidewege*, no. 22 (1992/93). The balance of this
note, notes 1 and 2, and the bibliography (except for bracketed substitutions and addi-
tions) were prepared by Rainer-M. E. Jacobi and published with the German text.
  This text, we hope, will introduce the "other side" of Christa Wolf's varied oeuvre
to the many readers who may not yet be familiar with it. This and other nonfiction
texts of a similar stamp, which Wolf describes as a "sideline," reveal more clearly than
many of her literary works certain interests that are all the more authentic for being
pursued quietly. They reflect motives and purposes in her work that have not been addressed in the recent press debate, or earlier in the public response to her writings in
the GDR. The lack of public notice suggests that this side of Wolf's work involves concerns that have always gone beyond the superficial divisions of East and West, and for

the change. What came into my head next were the titles of books. I saw that several books in which "cancer" played a role had been especially important to me. I realized that Christa T., the central character in one of my early novels, *The Quest for Christa T.*, falls ill and dies of cancer of the blood, leukemia—and that at that time certain West German critics assigned a symbolic political meaning to her death. Then I thought of my long-term critical examination of science and occasionally of "scientific" medicine, and of my intense—though scientifically untrained—interest in the "new thinking," not just in politics but in the sciences as well. A style of thought is emerging from various disciplines that appears to be moving toward a changed picture of the forces at work in this world, and of the motivations of our own lives: a picture that is surprising and exciting. I wish I could talk about all that here—fully aware of my incompetence and in a questioning spirit.[1]

For instance, why did I accept the lecture title that was proposed to me in the first place—"Cancer and Society"? Did I yield to the suggestion that there is a special connection between this par-

---

that very reason are considered suspect, if not downright dangerous, by both the old ideologues and the new. In short, her writings pose critical questions about the structures of our modern industrial civilization. By this we mean not only the obviously crisis-ridden economic and political structures but, more importantly, the mental structures of our modern culture and way of life that feed into them. The question of the relationship between illness and society thus goes far beyond some aspects of contemporary medicine that may merit criticism, and becomes significant in terms of anthropology and cultural philosophy.

This text may aid in the recognition of that other and more basic dimension of Christa Wolf's work which, like its manifestly political dimension, addresses the question of human beings, their failings, their jeopardies, and their opportunities.

1. Without claiming completeness, I shall list a number of essays that document the "other side" of Christa Wolf's work and show its continuity over many years: *Lesen und Schreiben* (1968); ["The Shadow of a Dream: A Sketch of Karoline von Günderrode" (1978); "Speaking of Büchner" (1980); "Illness and Love Deprivation: Questions for Psychosomatic Medicine" (1984).] These essays are included in the collection *Die Dimension des Autors* (1986) [translated as *The Author's Dimension* (see footnote, p. 3 above)]. In the same context we should mention the lectures *Voraussetzungen einer Erzählung*, which accompany Wolf's 1981 novel *Kassandra* [translated by Jan van Heurck as *Cassandra* and *Conditions of a Narrative: Cassandra* (New York: Farrar Straus & Giroux, 1984)], and *Störfall. Nachrichten eines Tages* (1987), a discussion of the nuclear accident at Chernobyl [translated by Heike Schwarzbauer and Rick Takvorian as *Accident: A Day's News* (New York: Farrar Straus & Giroux, 1989)], with the documentation of the debate that followed, *Verblendung. Disput über einen Störfall* (1991).

ticular disease and "society"—that is, all of us? If so, I would then have to ask myself what I regard as the prominent feature of our society. One striking feature, it seems to me, is a certain addictive behavior on the part of many people, a compulsion to activities that we can't give up—or, conversely, an inability to do things we ought to do—even if we know and read and hear and admit every day that our behavior is suicidal, and even if many experts and scientists compare us to lemmings. What stands in the way between our insights and our actions? What blocks us, for example, from sharply reducing our exposure to harmful substances, at least those that directly produce cancer? What stops us from developing alternatives to nuclear energy more quickly? More than once I have seen the enormous capacity of cancer patients for self-deception, even if they earlier had said they wanted to know the whole truth no matter what. Since I myself was once close to death—though not from cancer—I know that there are conditions in which one is so weak that one cannot physically endure "the truth." But what is "the truth," in a case like that? And in our everyday language, should we be allowed to apply the same words to any phenomenon we consider outrageous even if the situations have nothing in common—for example, to say that criminal behavior in society is "malignant" just as there can be a "malignant" growth of cells, or to equate human behavior with the behavior of the body by applying to both a word like "derail"? Wouldn't it be a good idea to investigate such verbal analogies to see what they imply?

I

Let me tell you about a letter that reached me only today. Someone with whom I am not otherwise acquainted wrote to me about a seven-year-old boy with cancer who does not have long to live and whose dearest wish is to receive a record number of get-well cards so that his name can be listed in the Guinness Book of Records. His wish can easily be fulfilled, the letter says, if I will write him a card and then ask ten more people to send him cards too, each of whom in turn must ask ten others so that our efforts will "snowball."

It may help to illuminate our topic if I try to describe the contradictory feelings this letter gave me. My basic feeling was sympathy for the terminally ill boy and an anticipatory sorrow mixed with anger. But this feeling was cut off by a deep sense of embarrassment that is familiar to me from situations in which completely inappropriate behavior is displayed, whether by me or another. I also felt uneasy because it seemed to me that nothing could be more "inappropriate" than to criticize what might be the child's last wish. And yet, how *could* it be his heart's desire to hold the record in a field he had not chosen but that had been invented for him by cancer, his sickness unto death—and how could it be that the most important thing to him was not the affection, the sympathy of the people who wrote to him, but their number? In a macabre way—so I thought, or rather felt—this British boy is a child of our time and of its upside-down values. And I am a child of our time too. I tried to satisfy my mixed feelings by splitting up my behavior. I wrote the boy a card as I was asked, but being a strict opponent of chain letters I did not write the other ten. Should I have done so? Ignored my discomfort, unconditionally accepted and supported the sick boy's desire for a record? I still don't know.

I shall avoid suggesting that there is any direct connection between the inability of people in the industrialized nations to give anything up—to renounce the uncontrolled multiplication of our needs—and the inability of cancer cells to halt their uncontrolled growth. The challenge of my theme, I believe, does not lie at this level of images, analogies, and metaphors to which the phenomenon of "cancer" seems to lend itself, partly because its very name is so loaded with associations that it often tends to be applied metaphorically. I shall keep in mind Susan Sontag's argument against the use of "illness as metaphor," but I shall also question it. Certainly language exists in a social context. So how do we actually talk about cancer? *Do* we talk about it, in fact?

Oh yes. When you first begin to pay attention, you get the impression that cancer is a favorite topic of the media, along with AIDS. It is a disease that serves the whole spectrum of our needs as consumers, needs that, in part, the media create in order to abuse them but in part find ready and waiting and set out to satisfy, and that range from serious scientific interest—or an interest that is disguised as scientific—to a deep-seated urge to sentimentality and

to simple, unvarnished sensationalism. On television, scientists—
a physician, for example—talks about the "three pillars of cancer
treatment," to which he says there are no alternatives; and I picture
the roof of a temple held up by marble columns, beneath which the
modern clinic conceals itself with its temple attendants, its priests,
and its gods dressed in white coats. I once visited a sacred grove of
Aesculapius in Greece, and thought that in the natural setting and
the stillness there I could detect a hint of the spirit of the place,
even after so many centuries. With its fasting, purification rituals,
curative sleep, and stimulation of dreams it clearly reflected a
different understanding of illness and its cure than do our hospitals.
Surgery, radiation, and chemotherapy are the three "pillars" of cancer treatment that the specialist spoke of. Don't be afraid that I
might try to debunk this therapeutic strategy, as it is often termed.
Undeniably, the large number of alternative treatments for cancer
that have developed recently—treatments actually in use even
though academic medicine disputes their effectiveness—indicates
dissatisfaction with the standard treatment. One point of criticism,
it seems to me, is that standard practitioners, while acknowledging
the truism that a doctor's job is to treat not an appendix, a gall blad-
der, or a cancer but the "whole person," are hardly equipped to do
so. To treat the person, the "personality"—that's what we call "ho-
listic medicine," but what is it really? What does it involve? And
doesn't it, too, begin with the dialogue between doctor and patient,
with language?

II

Often the doctor does not use the word "cancer" in the initial conversations. A favorable biopsy result is described as "not malignant"; an unfavorable result is frequently paraphrased—I'm not
sure if this is still the case—by the mysterious term "borderline."
After this, the entire arsenal of treatment methods may be brought
to bear, communicating to the patient, without words, the doctor's
opinion of the patient's condition: the surgeon's scalpel "speaks" instead of the word. The word "cancer" has remained taboo among
those afflicted, despite the growth of information and despite the

daring way we have grabbed it by the hair and dragged it into popular magazines. Magical thinking and feeling, of which we still have an abundant store, shrinks from the everyday use of the word, as if pronouncing it might bring it down upon our heads. People nowadays use word processors, and recently I too have started to do so, but when the time came for me to give a code name to the file in which I stored this text, I avoided using the obvious and unmistakable word "Cancer" and instead chose the neutral term "Lecture," which characterizes the material much less precisely.

But isn't the word "cancer" in fact dangerous? Doesn't every doctor know from experience that it can actually kill someone? Don't many people still regard it as a synonym for "no hope"? And can't hopelessness kill? Maxie Wander, whose book *Leben wär eine prima Alternative* (A great alternative would be to live) attracted great attention after her death, wrote before she knew her diagnosis: "Thinking about cancer is like being shut in a dark room with a murderer. You don't know where and how and if he will attack." It probably can't be expressed more clearly than that. Then, after her operation, she found she had to suppress her true feelings in order to find out the truth, which was so important to her: "If you make a fuss, they never tell you the truth. So you have to simulate courage, serenity, cheerfulness. And I managed to keep that up." Her woman doctor spoke to her about "sites of instability," which were "widespread" and "inclining to multiply." "Of course she is lying," wrote Maxie Wander. "I am alarmed by the prospect of being transferred to Ward Five, the cancer ward (which is never called that!)." And then she ends up where she "belongs, on the cancer ward." Alexander Solzhenitsyn's book of the same name was published in German translation nine years before Wander fell ill, and she must have read it. I have only now realized that some sentences in these two very different books are interchangeable—not only because there apparently are laws governing the way in which cancer sufferers deal with the different phases of their illness, but also because the two authors have in common the fact that they crave truth and reality. In Solzhenitsyn's novel, Kostoglotov, the man who comes from a concentration camp and the experience of exile, gets hold of a textbook on disease anatomy because he wants to *know* instead of having to believe the doctors "like a rabbit." It is depressing to see how the patients have to use up some of the strength they need to fight their illness in order to escape from the twilight where other people confine them in the belief that they are "sparing" them—the question is, who is really being spared?—and to emerge into the glaring light of reality. They spend their time pondering the meaning of veiled hints. Maxie Wander: "What the doctors said in the next few days not only pointed to cancer—that was more or less obvious already—but suggested that they had apparently not removed it all. I deduce this from the few words I gradually drag out of them. Why do they avoid looking at people when they talk to them? Why can't they explain the situation to the patient more clearly?" Later, when she kept pursuing the search for her real diagnosis, they resorted to deceiving her with falsified medical records and insurance certificates, and she became as uncertain about her true wishes as anyone else: "Probably it's right after all for the doctors to keep their fears to themselves and not speak of their true findings. If I knew there were cancer cells in my lymph, I would lose all courage to live."

III

Is there a connection between the widespread inability to handle the truth of a serious illness and our deeply ingrained habit of deceiving ourselves, and letting ourselves be deceived, about the role we are playing and the society we live in? And is it also connected with our view of illness as merely a limitation rather than as a spur to deeper reflection? Competitive individuals that we are, we are never taught to respond in a *human* way to weakness, breakdown, loss of meaning, failure or defeat, except in Sunday sermons. The models that function automatically are not understanding, sympathy, and the attempt to accompany others into their crisis even while risking challenge to ourselves, but rather defensiveness, denial, abandonment, the shifting of responsibility to institutions, and the attempt to shield ourselves as long as we can. I say this because I want to make clear that many doctors who avoid the truth when dealing with patients are behaving normally, complying with norms, conforming to their society.

⤙ 95 ⤚

As I wrote this, the title of a book kept running through my head: *Der Wahnsinn der Normalität* (The Insanity of Normality) by the Swiss psychoanalyst Arno Gruen. A radical title, and a book of radical theories based on the idea that nearly all members of our culture are turned in the wrong direction in early childhood because parental love is shown to be dependent on the good behavior of the child. The result is a pathological adaptation, a relinquishing of self that to a large extent counts as "normal behavior" and is rewarded, whereas rebellion, even the insistence on developing autonomic needs, is viewed as abnormal and punished with guilt feelings. Thus we must look into ourselves to find the early source of all our guilt feelings. But more dramatic, more tragic are the lives in which conflict, rebellion, and the struggle with guilt feelings are not even allowed to arise; in which the pressure to conform cuts people off from their true needs, entangles them in the net of a false reality, and prevents them from truly living their lives. Will we ever discover how much the individual cells of our body "know" about the self-denial and self-destruction we experience in the social and psychological realms, and how they may try to deal with it? How can we know if our body isn't the place where we act out the contradictions we experience from the unreasonable demands of society in the broadest sense and from the threat of losing our integrity if we are unable to manage the contradictions in a way that is consistent with our system of values? How can we hope to experience "health" in the physical sphere if we have ceased to fight for our integrity as persons?

Fritz Zorn, the author of the book *Mars*, states categorically that "the harm that is caused by faulty upbringing can be so great that in its most extreme forms it can manifest itself as a neurotically determined illness, such as cancer, as now seems to be the case with me." He regards his tumor as "swallowed tears": "I could no longer squeeze inside me all the suffering I had dammed up and swallowed for years. It exploded from the pressure, and in the explosion it destroyed my body. This explanation of cancer seems to make sense because there really is no other explanation. Admittedly, doctors know a lot about cancer, but they don't know what it actually is. I believe cancer is an emotional illness in which people who are consuming a great deal of pain are in turn consumed by this pain after a certain period of time. And because people of this kind are destroying themselves, techniques of medical treatment do no good at all in most cases."

IV

Among the "little books of cancer"—to use the term coined by Peter Noll, another Swiss, to describe the vast literature that cancer sufferers have produced about their experiences with this fateful and uncanny disease and that consists in autobiographical histories like Noll's own book, *Diktate über Sterben und Tod* (*In the Face of Death*)—two works embody the opposite social extremes, Fritz Zorn's *Mars* and Alexander Solzhenitsyn's *Cancer Ward.* Could there be life histories more different than theirs—the scion of a very wealthy Swiss middle-class family, and a penniless convict from the Gulag, a man without rights, an exile? Where can we find a common denominator—something apparently independent of outward circumstances if we are to take seriously Fritz Zorn's theory about the origin of cancer—that prepared the way inside them for a cell, or a small group of cells, to pursue their crazy growth without being recognized by the immune system? (And what does "inside them" mean, anyway? Where? In the immune system? In the brain? In the psyche?) What makes the cells adopt a growth that is not progress, where our measure for progress breaks down? Is it perhaps—I ask this with all due caution—the false norms of their society and the overwhelming pressure to conform to them the point where the extremes meet, and where identical or similar patterns of experience are laid down in men as different as Zorn and Solzhenitsyn?

Cancer, Adolf Muschg says in his literally hard-hitting introduction to Fritz Zorn's book, is a "disease in quotation marks," which, confusingly, is not really a disease at all but "an asocial process of the biological norm." And of course what is asocial is criminal in our society, so we deploy an arsenal of combat methods to fight it, answering force with force in techniques that we can only describe in the language of the police and the military: "Miracle Anti-Cancer Weapon on the Horizon?"—"Computer Images Unmask Tumor."—"After Three Months, M. L. Lost His Toughest Battle."—"Full-scale Attack on Tumors with Laser Beams?"— "Area Bombardment of Cancer."—"Tumor Base Launches Battle against Cancer."—"Fighting with Finesse: New Front Is Opened in Cancer Therapy as Molecular Biologists Aim for 'Guided Missiles' with Pinpoint Accuracy against Tumors."

Here, as in other areas of life, militaristic and impersonal thinking and language are indissolubly tied to the language of sentimentality and cliché that is really the other side of the same coin: "Gino, 4, Has Cancer: State Denies Mother Money for His Care."— "What More Must Parents Endure? Struggle with Authorities over Child Sick with Cancer."—"Little Joe's Last Wish: A Grave next to Papa Cartwright."—It is a form of psychological warfare that plays on the emotions of the enemy as it does in any other kind of war. But in this war the front lines are peculiarly blurred, and a reporter for the popular press who is out to produce headlines must keep in mind that his catchy titles strike not only at the hated disease but at many of his readers too, if they are cancer sufferers.

V

Despite the heavy competition from AIDS and numerous other themes for horror tales, cancer continues to be a tried and true instrument to generate fear. Why is this? Why—Susan Sontag's protests notwithstanding—does cancer still lend itself so aptly to use as a metaphor, and why is it used this way even by writers of the calibre of Heinrich Böll, who, in his introduction to Solzhenitsyn's *Cancer Ward*, describes Rusanov, a narrow-minded and thoroughly corrupt bureaucrat who of all the characters is the least able to bear the truth about his illness, as "a social cancer"? And in the early diaries of Maxie Wander, we read, "These petty bureaucrat types are the cancer of society, every society produces them, why not ours?" "Cancerous," "malignant," "metastasized" are terms we hear, read, say, or write almost daily. To cite just two examples from newspapers and magazines that I selected more or less at random: one author demands that "the domination of money as the medium of taxation should be rationally reduced" so that money will not continue to "penetrate all spheres of life like a cancer." And the head of the Berlin Physicians Association states in an interview, "Today, optimal techniques of coded accounting have already become more important than the optimal care of patients. At this point, the system of paying a nationalized-insurance doctor for each individual service performed is threatening to degenerate into a sort of mafia. The majority of doctors are suffering under this malignant mandatory system." How do doctors really experience their own "insanity of normality"?

To summarize my impressions, I would say that our strategies for controlling fear are not putting us in closer touch with ourselves and with the reality that we live in and are trying to suppress but, rather, are leading us farther away from ourselves and into dead zones of alienation. If our suspicions are correct and there is a link between our way of life and the diseases we manifest, then our strategies are taking us in a vicious circle, back to our suffering and also back to our cancer. Having made the disease into an obsession, we then have to domesticate it again by sensational reports of success ("Growth Factor Discovered in Cancer," "Cancer's Weak Point Revealed at Last"), or we have to mystify it ("The Great Mystery of Cancer," "Mistletoe Therapy, the Sacred Plant against Cancer"). To my surprise, there also seems to be a strong inclination to make cancer patients themselves responsible for their illness. Guilt is the stony heart of nine-tenths of all the clinically diagnosed cases of cancer in America today, writes American author Grace Paley. And as proof we have blaring headlines: "Responsible for Their Cancer"—75% of cancers are caused by the wrong life style, the article says; and poverty comes from having no money; but it's better not to ask the root cause of either. This brings us to the much-described and much-quoted notion of the "cancer personality." Even if we avoid classing all women in this stigmatized group for simplicity's sake—"Cancer, a Women's Disease"—nevertheless, psycho-oncologists have assisted in drawing up an impressive list of traits that supposedly characterize the cancer personality. This personality "makes a effort to conform," shows a tendency to "take things hard, to resignation and discouragement, to compulsive behavior and pseudo-selflessness"; it is characterized by "not standing up for oneself, rigidity, repression of emotions," by the "failure to own up to one's desires, so as to look good on the outside," by a "discrepancy between inside and outside with a positive facade concealing a negative interior." This discrepancy in turn makes it increasingly necessary to "cover up egoistic motives and goals," so that the author of the article I am quoting cannot help being reminded of the inwardly divided character of Dr. Jekyll and Mr. Hyde, "in whom the respectable citizen is turned outward while the brutal persecutor of his fellow men, the dark side of the personality, is experienced only in thoughts, or goes unnoticed."

This claim, which borders on religious zeal, is helpful I think, because it makes clear that the so-called "cancer personality" is simply a normal citizen suffering from the usual divided personality—and, in fact, the dual personality of Dr. Jekyll and Mr. Hyde has always been interpreted as that of a normal man, ever since Robert Louis Stevenson invented him in 1886. It is interesting that this largely accurate psychogram is taken to represent only a certain group, as if this group is being asked to take upon itself the symptoms from which the whole society is suffering so that the remaining, "healthy" part can be spared some of the ills that an efficiency-oriented society imposes on us all. We should be on our guard, I believe, lest the "cancer personality" be made into one of the victims of the large elements in our society who in times of crisis feel an overwhelming need to target anyone weaker, making others into scapegoats who carry the unloved parts of their own personality—"There but for the grace of God go I"—and whom we perhaps feel unable to love, just as we cannot love things in ourselves that cause us guilt.

VI

Isn't it true that cancer brings us all face to face with basic questions—not just the cancer sufferers but also those with whom they are in contact, including relatives, physicians, all the rest of us—and doesn't it challenge the whole context of normality we are used to? Do we let ourselves respond inappropriately and ineffectively to the signal "cancer" in order to preserve the normal behavior that we feel we cannot live without? Ever since Galileo studied the universe by observing its parts through a telescope; ever since scientists including physicians obeyed this commandment in the belief that the tinier the "components" they could isolate under the microscope, the closer to reality they were; ever since "unscientific" became the most painful thing they felt anyone could say about them—ever since then, a language evolved that is suited to this kind of thinking and action, is as "normal" as the practice it derives from, and fortifies and reinforces this practice. Here is an example: "Practical psycho-oncology could be described globally as a strategy whose characteristic feature is the amplification of experience and action on the part of all those involved in interaction . . . while expressly preserving ethical principles."

I had to give up my attempt to restructure this sentence, because I do not understand it. Is simplicity automatically suspect? Must we use technical jargon to drown out the silence that we would need if we listened to the language of our body—the language that psychoanalyst Georg Groddeck called "the speech of the Id"? "It is self-evident that the Id, if it does not achieve its goals by simple means or if the goals are too many and too difficult, does not draw the line at inducing simple constipation or simple hoarseness but resorts to septic appendicitis, peritonitis, intestinal obstructions, tumors of the larynx, cancer." Even simpler, even less scientific, are these words of Paracelsus that I would also like to quote: "The highest grade of medicine is love."

Is it possible that the most up-to-date medicine, traveling in a giant time warp, is once again coming close to this statement and bringing all its useful, indispensable tools and methods along with it? I took the liberty of looking into some books by doctors who are *not* oncologists—for example *Awakenings*, by Oliver Sacks, who observed the spectacular changes undergone by patients suffering from post-encephalitic syndrome after treatment with the medication L-DOPA and, as a result, came to profoundly distrust the mechanical approach to treatment that ignores a patient's life history, what he calls "assembly-line medicine." He says, "The dialogue about how one is can only be couched in human terms, familiar terms . . . and it can only be held if there is a direct and human confrontation, an 'I-Thou' relation, between the discoursing worlds of physicians and patients" (p. 225). Moreover, "There is nothing alive which is not individual . . . Yet modern medicine, increasingly, dismisses our existence, either reducing us to identical replicas reacting to fixed 'stimuli' in equally fixed ways, or seeing our diseases as purely *alien* and bad, without organic relation to the person who is ill" (p. 228). Sacks would like to see a case history narrated as "an integral combination of science and art" (p. 229). Thus he is not embarrassed to use words we would normally find in works of literature, like "empathy," "reflection," "understanding," even "reverence," "affliction," and "emotionally shattering." He invokes morality and feeling, speaks of the "creative impulse." This physician, like an artist, seems unable to get along without the unquantifiable thing, the un-thing that we call "inspiration."

VII

Are the two branches of the tree of knowledge that are farthest apart—science and art—destined to come closer again? Can they rediscover a common language? But how can they reach an understanding unless they begin with "the human being," that largely unknown creature who has succeeded in withdrawing from scientific methods, from isolating, dissecting, measuring, and counting, from his abolition and his status as an abstraction, and taken refuge in art?

Everything depends on what in a culture is said and believed to be "real" and in agreement with social convention, and is imprinted on each new member of the culture with his or her very first breath so that members, as far as possible, will spend their lives sliding along the track of this reality without deviation and without experiencing the slightest doubt—and, indeed, as we are now seeing in the newly merged Germany, they will for the most part react aggressively when this worldview is shattered. But how are we to live with the dissolution of all certainties about what "reality" is, and how is a physician to live with it? What are we to make of the message of modern physicists that there is literally no solid ground under our feet? That the famous "basic particles of matter" sometimes take the form of a wave and at other times the form of corpuscles, and that as physicist Hans Peter Dürr expresses it, "In its form and structure, reality or what we call reality essentially depends on the methods and instruments we use to perceive it." So if the highest goal is precision, clarity, and exactness of expression, which includes medical diagnosis—and in order to achieve diagnosis a process, an organ, a disorder must be removed from its context and investigated without valuation and emotion—the result may be that some of its essential properties are misunderstood, for example its ability to surprise, its indeterminateness. Dürr says one cannot predict the specific behavior of each and every particle; one can only glean a statistical average based on the behavior of large numbers of particles within a limited timespan. The future, he says, is not determined, it is not simply a linear development of the present. It is a "future present," a genuine new creation, and a new act of creation is in any case not dependent on the previous act: each present moment, depending on its structure, builds up a "field of expectation" concerning possibilities that are potentially realizable in the course of successive presents.

Field of expectation—I pause at this term. A poetic phrase that calls up in me a whole web of living associations, that starts vibrating strings that would not have been stirred by a verdict of finality. What was unthinkable before suddenly appears an exciting possibility, one that in fact has always been there and was merely concealed. Can it be "true" that what we call "reality" is only the currently "completed phase" in an immense store of potential reality? Is "matter," so to speak, the "petrified waste product of a living spirit" (Dürr)? Ought we to end our fixation on cancer as the "granite of material events" (Viktor von Weizsäcker) and start trying to reinterpret this syndrome which bears the accursed name "cancer" and has "engraved itself into the consciousness of most people as our body's Public Enemy Number One"?[2]

2. The material presented here, though it may appear very modern, nevertheless was "known" in medicine at the beginning of the century, if in a concealed and perhaps even a suppressed form. Viktor von Weizsäcker (1886–1957), whose work for the most part fell prey to this "suppression," believed it was not enough to question only the "what" of illness: we also have to ask "Why?" "Why at this time?" "Why in this way?" and "Why not in a different way?" Von Weizsäcker felt that the sick person's life history, social integration, and conflicts were integral to understanding his or her unique illness, and it seemed obvious to him that an understanding of this kind could be gained only by that "peculiar form of knowledge," the interpersonal encounter. The loss of an objec-

Do we perhaps only "have" cancer if we know it? And, in that case, can we perhaps learn how not to have cancer? Otherwise, what can explain the rare but inexplicable cases of spontaneous cure? Solzhenitsyn, when asked how he was able to overcome and survive his incurable illness, countered with a question of his own: Who else would have written the books he still had to write if he did not do it?

To put the question differently: What effect do our thoughts, does our "mind," have on our body? Or is that stating it too dualistically? Is "nature"—including the nature of us humans—and what "holds it together at the core" (as Goethe put it) something quite different from the substratum that we view under the microscope? If "I" am hopeful or despairing, does each one of my cells "feel" hope or despair?

Human cells—I read in Deepak Chopra—have somehow "evolved to a state of formidable intelligence," and "the first thing that is killed in the laboratory is the delicate web of intelligence that binds the body together" (*Quantum Healing*, pp. 39–40, 41). Taking advantage of the naïveté that goes with my lack of scientific training, I mentally relate Dürr's "field of expectation" to this "web of intelligence." I cannot resist putting into the same context the methodological approach of Rupert Sheldrake, who speaks of "fields of morphic resonance" in his search for the memory of nature, and I also include the views of James Lovelock, whom Sheldrake regards as a kindred spirit and who, in his Gaia model of our earth, regards our whole planet as a living, animate organism. It gives me a certain pleasure to list the names of scientists who, I would say, take a quasi-poetic view of their disciplines. Physicists, physicians, psychologists, physiologists, biologists, biochemists, ecologists are coming together, discarding the mechanistic world view, and as they do so are encountering familiar objects in unex-

---

tive way of thinking that came with illness also meant a "loss of reality." People's illnesses, he felt, offered them the possibility of learning the truth about themselves and their way of life.

Interested readers are referred to the edition of Viktor von Weizsäcker's collected works, the *Gesammelte Schriften*, which Suhrkamp began to publish in 1986. Among the remarkable "parallels" between von Weizsäcker's epistemological reflections and insights and the natural-philosophical implications of quantum theory, see C. F. von Weizsäcker, "Gestaltkreis und Komplementarität," in *Zum Weltbild der Physik* (Stuttgart: Hirzel, 1976), pp. 332–66.

pected contexts, or are seeing these objects reveal properties and capabilities that were previously hidden. This is the "new thinking" in the sciences that I mentioned at the start. I must content myself with just hinting at all that is happening.

VIII

But how does this new thinking and research, how do these new horizons of possibility, relate to our topic? Perhaps they encourage openness to new questions. For example, what would happen if both patient and doctor were deeply imbued with the conviction that the calculation of statistical probability has no place at the bed of a cancer sufferer? That the future is never absolutely determined—and, above all, that it is not certain that the patient will have no future? And that it is a person who is diseased rather than an organ, and therefore the person may be helped by remedies that were not taken very seriously in the past and that apply only to this individual?

All I can do is ask questions. All I can do is testify that when I was gravely ill and near death, I was helped not only by antibiotics that were specifically attuned to fight a certain species of bacteria, but also by the poems of Goethe—by their sound as well as their content, which called up in me a living web of associations; by their beauty, which had never moved me so deeply before, and by the happiness I felt when I suddenly "understood" lines like this

Everything passing
Is only an image.[3]

I no longer understand these lines as profoundly as I did then, but I believe that they touch on the riddle of our existence, on the question of whether and to what degree the structures of all material and mental existences are connected and can change into each other, support each other, promote or hinder and destroy each other. But *if* our thoughts and ideas are as real as any visible, tangible, measurable particle of matter—that is, if they are as capable of pro-

3. These lines are from the "Chorus Mysticus" that ends Goethe's *Faust*, Part II.

ducing effects—then what prevents us from calling up and developing the thoughts and ideas that are creative, beneficial, constructive, and curative?

The hierarchical and bureaucratic power structures we live in—the same structures by which we organize our so-called "health system"—surely block us from moving about freely in these new zones of creative thought and action, because they persuade us that freedom means being allowed to abuse our inclinations and abilities, and that the march of the lemmings into the abyss is "free" in its own way. This is the freedom to choose death, even the death of our species; it is the freedom to be irresponsible.

A woman I know who had an operation for suspected breast cancer and whose histological report happily showed "no indications of pathology," wrote to me, "The surge of joy I felt also allowed me to discover something else that shocked me at first: I had in me a tendency to let myself die. I 'needed' the threat of death in order to risk exposure to situations in which I was fragile, wounded, and vulnerable, and which I would not have allowed otherwise. I was forced to assume total responsibility for the course I took. I discovered in myself the belief that it is possible to be deeply close to others only in the face of death. I hope that such drastic measures are no longer needed now, especially since I have had so many good experiences."

I don't know if large numbers of individual experiences of this kind can create a pattern of experience—or "field of resonance" as I imagine Sheldrake would put it—where the predominantly destructive impulses of our time could be removed and neutralized. I doubt it. But in conclusion I want to pass on to you the optimistic prognosis of an American doctor, Jeanne Achterberg, whose program is made clear by the title of her book, *Imagery in Healing:* "There is drama, here, as the elusive mysteries of the human mind begin to unfold—drama unparalleled ... in any other arena. The scientific paradigm shifts, the metaphors blend. It is a good time to be alive" (Introduction, p. 10).

Bibliography

Achterberg, Jeanne. *Imagery in Healing: Shamanism and Modern Medicine.* Boston and London: New Science Library, 1985.

Chopra, Deepak. *Quantum Healing: Exploring the Frontiers of Mind/Body Medicine.* New York: Bantam Books, 1989.

Dürr, Hans Peter. *Das Netz des Physikers. Naturwissenschaftliche Erkenntnis in der Verantwortung.* Munich and Vienna: Carl Hanser Verlag, 1988.

————. "Naturwissenschaft und poetischer Raum—Begreifen und Spiegeln der Wirklichkeit." Manuscript. PEN Club, Presseclub Concordia Wien, 1991.

Eccles, John C., and Hans Zeier. *Gehirn und Geist. Biologische Erkenntnisse über Vorgeschichte, Wesen und Zukunft des Menschen.* Frankfurt/Main, Fischer Taschenbuch Verlag, 1984.

Gruen, Arno. *Der Wahnsinn der Normalität. Realismus als Krankheit: eine grundlegende Theorie zur menschlichen Destruktivitä.* Munich: Deutscher Taschenbuch Verlag, 1989. Translated as *The Insanity of Normality: Realism as Sickness: Toward Understanding Human Destructiveness* (New York: Grove Weidenfeld, 1992).

Jonas, Hans. *Materie, Geist und Schöpfung. Kosmologischer Befund und kosmogonische Vermutung.* Frankfurt/Main: Suhrkamp Verlag, 1988.

Lovelock, James. *Gaia: A New Look at Life on Earth.* Oxford: Oxford University Press, 1987.

Noll, Peter. *Diktate über Sterben und Tod mit Totenrede von Max Frisch.* Zurich: Pendo Verlag, 1984. [Translated by Hans Noll as *In the Face of Death* (New York: Viking, 1989).]

Sacks, Oliver. *Awakenings.* New York: HarperCollins, 1990.

Sheldrake, Rupert. *The Presence of the Past: Morphic Resonance and the Habits of Nature.* New York: Times Books, 1988.

————. *The Rebirth of Nature: The Greening of Science and God,* New York: Bantam, 1991.

Solzhenitsyn, Alexander. *Cancer Ward,* translated by Nicholas Bethell and David Bury. London: The Bodley Head, 1968.

Sontag, Susan. *Illness as Metaphor.* New York: Farrar, Straus & Giroux, 1978.

Wander, Maxie. *Leben wär' eine prima Alternative. Tagebuchaufzeichnungen und Briefe,* ed. Fred Wander. Darmstadt and Neuwied: Luchterhand Verlag, 1980.

————. *Tagebücher und Briefe,* ed. Fred Wander. Berlin and Weimar: Aufbau Verlag, 1990.

Will, Herbert. *Georg Groddeck. Die Geburt der Psychosomatik.* Munich: Deutsche Taschenbuch Verlag, 1987.

Zorn, Fritz. *Mars.* Munich: Kindler Verlag, 1977. [Translated by Robert and Rita Kirner as *Mars* (New York: Knopf, 1982).]

The Leftover Baggage of German History

Correspondence with Jürgen Habermas

→→ ←←

November 26, 1991

Dear Christa Wolf,

I am grateful to you for inviting me to the Academy function last Thursday. The thoughtful contribution from Jens Reich and the wide range of the contributions from a prominent circle were instructive as to the moods and conflicts of the people who were most active in effecting the changeover in the GDR. As a visitor from the West, I admit I felt a bit like the member of a theater audience watching a lively drama from his box. I was moved by the ongoing discussion about a "Zero Hour." People were strangely inspired by this slogan,

This correspondence was published for the first time in the German edition of this book. Jürgen Habermas (born 1929), professor of philosophy at the University of Frankfurt and a leading representative of the Frankfurt School tradition of social thought founded by Adorno and Horkheimer, is the author of many books, particularly analysis of the Frankfurt School and of major Marxist thinkers. The Academy referred to in the first sentence of the letter is the East Berlin Arts Academy.

which the audience fed to the speaker and did not entirely fit the tenor of his speech.

I can readily understand the feeling of having thrown your old baggage overboard and of standing now at a new beginning. Intellectuals in eastern Germany are right to feel that they have been involved in an exceptional event and have gone through experiences that are out of the ordinary. Their lives have accelerated in the whirlpool that sucked them in, and it will be exciting to see how they process the confrontation and what they produce from it — especially the younger people, whose membranes are still quite open. In a similar way, dear Frau Wolf, our generation has worked on the years before and after 1945, which supplied enough raw material for a lifetime. On the other hand, the talk about a "Zero Hour" was not entirely convincing. Once the decision was made that the West German monetary and civil law system would prevail throughout Germany, the people of the GDR "acceded" to the Federal Republic in more than merely the constitutional sense. The mode in which unification took place could not be better symbolized than by the far from identical twins Schäuble and Krause, and what the two of them hatched out set the direction in which we had to go, so that those who consented to the accession had little choice but to adapt and submit, and certainly no more scope for political action. The resulting image of a hasty surrender is thus not entirely inaccurate.[1]

But if it isn't so easy to make a new beginning, then it is all the more urgent for us to have understanding and cooperation between those in both East and West who do not follow the mainstream. My main reason for desiring this cooperation is not that I think we need a coalition — and soon you in the East will be as used to seeing intel-

1. Günter Krause (born 1953) was a GDR politician, head of the CDU/DA (Christian Democratic Union / Democratic Awakening) party in the GDR's assembly, the Volkskammer, in 1990. He led the GDR in its negotiations with the FRG to draw up national agreements for unification, and was rewarded with the post of minister of transport in the new government. Representing the FRG in the negotiations was Wolfgang Schäuble (born 1942), West German minister of the interior who in November 1991 became chair of the CDU/CSU, the largest party bloc in the Bundestag. The two are "twins" because they were heads of the respective CDU parties in the two Germanies (the CDU being the only party that had branches in both countries), but nonidentical because of the disparity in the actual negotiating power they held and in the extent to which they represented their national populations.

lectuals on the left denounced by right-wingers as we are in the West. No, the reason we must get together is the regressive tendencies described by Friedrich Schorlemmer in his clear-cut and determined verdict.[2] Even though the Socialist Unity Party regime with its worn-out slogans has been inveighing against right-wing radicalism for forty years and has treated it as a threat from outside, it was the party itself that hatched out the threat from under its own wings. Something of the mentality of the thirties and forties seems to have been preserved. In any case, following unification a critical mass of resentment has built up, which has also changed mentalities in the West. As in the thirties, of course, the regressive attitudes in Germany also reflect shifts on the international scene. I'm referring to the "national fronts" that are growing stronger every day in almost all Western countries, as well as the ghosts that are rising up from nineteenth-century tombs in the nations of central and eastern Europe. But in postfascist Germany, the same phenomenon means something more.

The new feature in the old Federal Republic is above all the fact that the elements of the extreme right, which previously were separated, are now uniting in an explosive combination. Nationalist democrats and republicans are joining forces for the first time with violence-prone youth, skinheads and hooligans, and both groups are now entwined in a wide-branching network of right-wing media intellectuals with whom increasing numbers of conservatives are mixing more and more openly. The borders between the groups had already frayed in the last decade: the liberal conservatives seem to have lost their inhibition about contact with right-wing radicals and proponents of Germanomania. The intellectual climate in general seems to have made a definite shift. The liberals are becoming nationalist liberals, while the Young Conservatives are becoming militant German nationalists. The question of the "two dictatorships,"[3]

2. Friedrich Schorlemmer (born 1944), a German Protestant theologian and SPD politician, worked in the peace and civil rights movements in the GDR and in 1989 cofounded the citizens group Demokratischer Aufbruch (Democratic Awakening), the only citizens group brought into Kohl's Alliance for Germany party in the March 1990 elections that decided the fate of the GDR.

3. I.e., Nazism and Stalinism.

which until recently was hotly debated among historians, has been settled for some time: from now on, one no longer needs to differentiate between them. We can almost feel happy if the regime that justified industrialized mass murder on racist grounds is at least mentioned in the same breath with Stalinism. Subtle minds have long been occupied with drawing other sorts of distinctions, aimed at making clear to us the comparatively humane and civilized features of National Socialism. Words that once were punctiliously avoided are now being used in an inflationary way—as in the phrase "Auschwitz in our souls"—as part of this cleaning up.

East German intellectuals, in their specific experiences and impulses to reform, may be more advanced than we are in the West. But if chances for a *new* start in the Federal Republic lie in going in the opposite direction, we should keep in mind how important it still is to prevent attitudes in Germany from shifting too far backward and to the right. We West Germans depend on the liberal and left-wing intellectuals in the former GDR if we are to keep the web of a halfway civilized political culture from tearing under the new strains. By "strains" I certainly do not mean the notorious financial "costs of unification" but, rather, the problems that are coming from outside and are further warping the fabric of society inside the country. If we react to these problems in the wrong way, the result could be grave damage to the internal constitution of the Federal Republic, which was achieved with great effort during the postwar decades.

One of the problems coming from the outside is the economic immigration from the South, and now from the East as well, which was caused in part by the First World and seems more or less inevitable. Today it is serving as a litmus test to how we will react tomorrow. Are we putting an end to the compromise of the welfare state? Have we already accepted living with an underclass that includes 20 to 30 percent of the population? Will a majority made up of "prosperity chauvinists" take a hard line toward the outside world and become repressive internally? At least since Reagan, if not before, you can observe in the large cities of the USA how the "insiders" can survive only through a neurotic defense system to block their awareness of the "outsiders." Will we too close our eyes to a structural minority of helpless people whose only remaining means of protest is self-destruction and who have no chance of changing their situation by their own efforts? Are we accepting a pattern of segregation that shows sheer contempt for all the notions of social justice that were taken for granted in past traditions, from the Enlightenment and the workers' movement? These questions will find no intelligent answer in the ever more trying conditions that obtain now if right-wing populism starts to spread in the Federal Republic too, with the SPD and the CDU both adapting to it while the FDP throws its principles to the wind and members of our "green FDP" merely cultivate the mentality of left-wing renegades.[4] The old images of a Communist enemy, which time after time allowed us to consolidate our collective identity during times of crisis, have been shattered — but our new enemy-images are drawn from the old repertoire. The grandsons of neoconservative grandfathers are tinkering around in West German newspapers, writing subtly tailored articles that already bear a first distant echo of the thuggish slogans of the Reich, now displayed on the war banners of football hooligans.

This pessimistic diagnosis led me to comment on one consequence of German unification which to my astonishment met with complete incomprehension from East German intellectuals. In the little volume of interviews that I sent you (*Vergangenheit als Zukunft,* Pendo Verlag, Zurich, pages 50–51), I said I felt that one of the worst aspects of the heritage the GDR was bringing into an expanded Germany was its devaluation of our intellectual traditions, both the best traditions and the weakest ones.[5] The meaning of my remark was clear within the context: "This 'nation of workers and peasants' abused progressive ideas, quoting them in its political rhetoric in order to legitimize itself. It contemptuously turned them into lies by practicing them inhumanely, and thus brought them into discredit. I fear that this dialectic of devaluation will prove more ruinous to intellectual health in Germany than the concentrated resentment of five or six generations of anti-intellectual, anti-Semitic,

4. SPD = Social Democrats; FDP = Free Democrats; Green FDP = Green Party environmentalists allied with Free Democrats.

5. Translated by Max Persky as *The Past as Future* (Lincoln: University of Nebraska Press, 1994).

false-romantic, Germanophile obscurantists." Richard Schröder and Friedrich Dieckmann reacted with absolute fury to this comment. But why?

There must be a misunderstanding here, and I wonder if it could be related to a view that was barely mentioned in your Academy discussions last Thursday but was spelled out in the "Theses for a United Berlin-Brandenburg Academy of Arts," the paper you gave me when we said goodbye. It states:

> Not only in the East but *also in the West* of Germany, which was divided by a rigorous security system and was torn apart internally, adaptations were made to the mentality and culture of the superpowers that dominated in *each of the two fragmentary states*. These adaptations have left their marks, and have led East and West Germans to develop different identities. Decades of living with a border that splits up one's country and causes intense opposition between the two halves is limiting to thought *on both sides*. The dual nationhood of Germany has affected both populations inwardly. It has created an intellectual and emotional bias in the East and *in the West*, which among other things has led *both* countries, in their different ways, to distance themselves from the potential of their tradition in the unified German culture that existed before.

The italics, which are mine, mark the places where I feel doubt. I believe this remarkable theory of convergence sets up a false symmetry. The theory has its supporters in the West too, of course. But the fact that prominent friends like Martin Walser and Dieter Henrich share your view does not make it any truer.[6] I cannot form a judgment about the life histories of intellectuals in East Germany, and I must leave it to you to decide whether you believe that your literary production has been "biased." But I consider false your view that our life histories here in the West were limited and deformed in the way you state — and false in a *dangerous* way, because of its

6. Martin Walser (born 1927), is a contemporary FRG novelist.

devastating implication that we should return to the old intellectual continuities, which we resisted successfully for the first time in modern German history at the cost of considerable effort and going against the dominant climate. It would surprise me very much if there were any difference of opinion between us about which traditions we wish to continue, and which not. Please understand the following remarks as an attempt to make sure of this consensus. I have always regarded the intellectual openness about Western traditions that became possible after 1945 as something liberating. Some people may have experienced the division of our nation as more disturbing than others did. But what West German intellectuals produced in the postwar period does not seem to me to show any damage—at least not the symptoms you diagnosed—which would indicate that any of us felt cut off from impulses in our mental life that were worth preserving.

Please do not misunderstand me. If I insist on drawing distinctions about this matter, it is by no means because I want to claim any *merit* for one side while denying it to the other. We are both from the same generation, and we share the same "Patterns of Childhood."[7] For this reason we also share the same basic attitudes, which if I am not mistaken motivated us in a similar way to break not merely with the political heritage of the Nazi regime but also with the deeper-lying intellectual roots of the German elite who applauded it and with their washed-out version of the German mind. I can well imagine, and I have been thinking this since November 1989, that if by chance I had not grown up in the Rhineland but had found myself in 1945 living east of the Elbe instead, I would have identified with the antifascism of the returning Communists and would have become a Party member and begun a career; and because this is a hypothetical case, no one can say today when and where that career would have ended. It was for much the same reasons that I became a socialist even in Adenauer's Germany, which was not the usual thing; and I discovered Western Marxism at the same time as the early Lukács, and by my own choice became

7. An allusion to Wolf's 1977 novel about her Nazi upbringing, *Kindheitsmuster*, translated by Hedwig Rappolt and Ursule Molinaro as *Patterns of Childhood* (New York: Farrar, Straus & Giroux, 1980).

Adorno's assistant. Nor did I hesitate to write my qualifying thesis as a university lecturer under the direction of Wolfgang Abendroth.[8] I can document all this in a perfectly clear-cut way, and yet—without the slightest implication of arrogance—I can say that we in the West lived in circumstances which, in the intellectual sphere as well as in others, were not forced upon us or even limiting but made it possible for us to experience our Western orientation as something liberating.

This westward orientation did not imply a warping of the German psyche but rather the practice of independence. Our unreserved assimilation of the whole range of liberal traditions did not merely include—if I may take myself as an example—American pragmatism from Peirce to Dewey, rational law of the seventeenth and eighteenth century down to Rawls and Dworkin, analytical philosophy, French positivism, and French and American social science from Durkheim to Parsons; but it also extended to elements of the German tradition which up to then had been suppressed or marginalized: to Kant as an exponent of the Enlightenment and not as its so-called conqueror, to Hegel as a radical interpreter of the French Revolution and not as its opponent, to Marx and Western Marxism, to Freud and the Freudian left, to the Vienna Circle, Wittgenstein, and so on. The German émigrés returning from the West were more important to us in this process than the wasted remnants of our own tradition that had survived National Socialism.

In this connection, I remember some comments of my friend Albrecht Wellmer several years ago during a conference about the Frankfurt School of Critical Theory. They make clear that our spontaneous attention to the traditions of the West during the fifties was actually what made the uncorrupted elements in our tradition accessible to us. Figures like Heidegger, Jünger, or Carl Schmitt could not have done this for us.[9] In order to see the universalist, liberal, and

8. Theodor Adorno, 1903–69, German sociologist and philosopher, was a cofounder of the Frankfurt School of Critical Theory; Wolfgang Abendroth (1906–85), was a professor specializing in public law and the social sciences, and a committed socialist.

9. Ernst Jünger (born 1895), was a novelist who celebrated a militarist and nationalist cult of the dead but who after the Nazi period advocated humanist ideals. He was a friend of Carl Schmitt (1888–1985), a specialist in government and constitutional law who became a Nazi party member, rejected pluralism, and studied ways to establish the legitimacy of absolute state power.

subversive features of the German tradition, you must first have recognized its anticultural elements. Wellmer explained how the Germans of Frankfurt, returning from their exile in America, played the role of catalysts because they

> made it possible to think of a radical break with fascism that did not involve an equally radical break with German cultural tradition, that is, with their own cultural identity. I believe the enormous influence exerted by Adorno and Horkheimer — an influence that was not just critical in a destructive way but above all was liberating — is due primarily to this unique combination. It was Adorno, especially, with his extraordinary productivity after the war, who cleared away the rubble under which German culture lay buried and made it visible again. He did this as a man of urban civilization who did not succumb to the allure of the archaic yet who kept his romantic impulse intact; a man who took for granted the universalism of the modern age, yet did not ignore the traces of distortion in the existing forms of humanism. He was the rare case of a philosopher who belonged at the same time to the modern era and to the German tradition.

Lukács certainly philosophized with a wooden hammer when in 1955 he traced the "path of irrationalism from Schelling to Hitler." But even this heavy-handed method could not cover up the element of truth that shone out of the very title of his book, *Die Zerstörung der Vernunft* (The destruction of reason). Wouldn't we be throwing away the good effects of this act of clarifying self-reflection if today we were to resurrect that old mixture of vague and profound thoughts that we had to struggle with for so long? The view that all we did was to conform to the mentality of the winning side, and that we have been "intellectually and emotionally biased" down to the present day, is one that is now being circulated among us in West Germany by people like Syberberg and Bergfleth, who want us to sink back into the German swamp.[10]

10. Georg (György) Lukács, *The Destruction of Reason*, translated by Peter Palmer (Atlantic Highlands, N.J.: Humanities Press, 1981). Hans Jürgen Syberberg (b. 1935), is a contemporary film director.

Clearly, nothing can be more alien to you and your friends than that kind of attitude. The current upheaval of your lives creates special kinds of vulnerability. This makes it more complicated to understand each other, and demands more than the usual amount of sensitivity in the way we deal with each other. I also see that it can bring a feeling of relief if people can believe they have shared a common fate. But agreeing prematurely that symmetries exist between us would be a false courtesy that can only lead to new illusions. For this reason I plead that each side should work on its own postwar intellectual history, and beware of overgeneralizing on the basis of its one-sided experience. If we try to turn Germany into a one-pot stew, the result could be something that neither of us wants: the history of the GDR may get swept under the rug as West Germany writes its own victor's history. In our newspapers, I am reading articles whose gist is that the history of the GDR might be interpreted as one part of a common German fate. But that is not true even in our own generation—and how much less true it is for the younger generations who make up the great majority of our population today! We in the West in fact have not lived under Stalinism, nor do we know anything about the complex circumstances of life in a post-Stalinist society. To pretend that we do, or even to act as if our separate postwar histories represent two shoes that are part of the same pair, helps no one. The only things that can help in this tricky situation—in any situation—are observation, thought, and the drawing of distinctions.

For this reason, I admire your initiative in creating at least a small-scale substitute for *your own* East German public within the East Berlin Academy of Arts. The former GDR has been deprived of the opportunity to hold its own debate about its fate in forums organized by its own public—and not just since Super Illu and Mühl-fenzl.[11] Western editors are pulling the strings now, and Western voices are drowning out those in the East. At least the intellectuals should get to understand each other, realizing and going beyond the distances that separate them. But appealing to features that we supposedly have in common, an approach that is well meant

11. I.e., not just since unification.

but based on false conclusions, merely forces us into following a path set by others so that we end up ratifying the mistaken scenario of annexation and subservience designed by Schäuble and Krause.

In the sincere hope that we will soon find the opportunity— that you will grant me the opportunity—to continue our conversation face to face, I am

With gratitude and warm regards,
Jürgen Habermas

December 7, 1991

Dear Jürgen Habermas,

I am happy to have received your letter. Today I can write you nothing more than a fairly extensive "confirmation of receipt." I believe we would benefit from a thorough dialogue about the problems you see.

For example, I and many people I know do not at all have the feeling that we have "thrown the old baggage overboard and are standing at a new beginning." Quite to the contrary, our baggage is getting heavier and we are prevented from making a new start— and in fact, it would look a bit absurd anyhow for sixty-year-olds to be starting over. And I share your opinion about the "accession" of the GDR and its results. A "Zero Hour," which many people may have wished for, is not available—nor was it available in 1945— and the sooner people who consented to the accession shed this illusion, the sooner we can get back to talking about history.

For us, intellectuals of the left on both sides of the former border—that border that used to be dense and material and still exists, not just "in people's heads" as the phrase goes but in the sharply differing conditions in which the majority of people live—for us intellectuals, I think that talking about history means talking of our own life histories, our personal biographies. I fully share your concern about the various elements that are joining together to form an explosive combination. This is happening before our very eyes, while we are still being warned against trying to draw any parallels between this and any earlier period of German history. There is a faith-healing approach to the disastrous developments in eastern Germany. Soon the proportion of "insiders" to "outsiders" here may no longer be two-thirds to one-third but the other way around. And given such social burdens, how can people develop democratic structures capable of carrying the load? Where will young people without jobs and prospects find an outlet for their fear, their aggressions, and their rage?

Rhetorical questions—just to show that I understand your concern for preserving the web of "a halfway civilized political culture" in the former Federal Republic.

But now to the core of your letter, whose central message I can only begin to address today.

I am not familiar with Friedrich Dieckmann's and Richard Schröder's reaction to the statement of yours that you quote. So I am reduced to reading it again in the context of your interview, to see how I react to it myself. I feel annoyed by it too; but during our discussion at your home in Frankfurt I had already noticed your fear that through the legacy of Stalinism we East German intellectuals might drive you, the West German intellectuals, back to stages of intellectual argument that you had already put behind you. I was dismayed by this fear, which Margarete Mitscherlich appeared to share and which I had not expected. In part I explained it by what you admitted was your unfamiliarity with conditions here, with how they had evolved, and also with the conditions under which intellectuals lived here and with their attempt to assert themselves and to articulate their views in opposition to the dominant ideology, which they had recognized as a false attitude. I am speaking here only of the intellectuals. Probably the sharp reactions that you experienced to your remark stemmed from the impression that you, like others, failed to see and acknowledge the work being achieved here by opposition writers. But especially, I too doubt your prediction that the misuse of progressive ideas through "inhumane practice" will prove "more ruinous to intellectual health in Germany than"—okay, than the "intellectual" heritage of National Socialism. I doubt it, for one thing, because there are intellectuals in the West and the East who consciously resisted this practice and maintained a critical attitude. But I also doubt it because National Socialism, with its resentment-laden "ideas," penetrated deeper into the national consciousness and is maintaining itself there longer than pseudo-Marxist and genuine Marxist ideas could and can.

This represents a discussion topic all on its own. Be that as it may, your remark, which is provocatively sharp, seems to me to warrant detailed discussion—as does your sketch of your own paradigmatic development, which I regard as the core of your letter and is the most interesting to me as a writer. From your letter and interviews I gather that you view your development—as I view my own—as having been in opposition to a restorationist system or against restorationist tendencies. You say your opposition was based on *intellectual* impulses that you derived from the West, from the spirit of the Enlightenment. Intellectually too the East has played no role in your life. Couldn't this be viewed as a limitation? The breadth of your intellectual horizons even in your early years is something that one must acknowledge, not without envy. We, or at least I, had to catch up on much of that material later, and I was able to do so because we/I had access to Western literature. Without that opportunity I certainly could not have gone on living here. Lukács, to be sure, did play a large role for me early on, and later I had to learn to distance myself from certain dogmatic judgments of his about particular German writers and literary currents. As a university student I became acquainted with Marxist literary criticism in a thoroughly stimulating form that encouraged me to go on thinking over the years. Moreover, my first encounters with Marxism as a social theory and a philosophy were with the real thing, not its counterfeit and parodied form. Above all, I began early to study psychology, and Freud, Mitscherlich, and Reich became central to me. No, it's true that after a certain phase I did not feel cut off from Western thought; nor could I have written the books I did if I had been. Admittedly I was also very open to the literature of the East, to the work of Russian authors, especially authors of the last century, and then to Soviet literature, and after a certain point to dissident Soviet writers in particular. I formed friendships with them, I felt a direct empathy with their fate, and when we meet today, a word or a look is enough for us to understand each other. I would not want to have missed that part of my life. Many people I knew from that time are dead. What remains of that experience will disappear with the collapse of the Soviet Union, because it is no longer needed and in demand. I don't mean it will vanish for me, but with me and with those of my contemporaries who still know something about it.

To my amazement I am saying this soberly, without any feelings of self-pity or regret. While saying it I have strayed from the subject: that paragraph in my statement to the Academy which apparently troubled you, perhaps even hurt your feelings. For myself I must say that I only gradually worked my way out of bias, dogmatic prejudice, credulity, inhibition—gradually and with great difficulty, pain, and existential conflicts. I can remember clearly each stage in this process, including the relapses, halfway measures, anxieties. Literature helped me. When you write, you can't lie, or you get blocked. Perhaps you have been spared such conflicts. All the same, when I think of many of my West German writer colleagues—and they are the people we are talking about, aren't they, along with other artists, not the philosophers and social scientists on both sides?—I'm aware that we have based ourselves on different lines of tradition within the one German literature—and at times on different literatures of other peoples and regions of the world—depending on whether we lived in the GDR or in the Federal Republic. And also I must confirm that people's exposure to certain specific intellectual movements and resentments and avoidances depended on which side of the Wall they lived on. (Once again I am referring to literary people.) In general, we in the East knew more about the West and about living conditions there than our Western colleagues knew and know about us and the conditions of our lives, simply because we were more interested.

But I notice that I am circling around the theme, not pinpointing it. I am sure of this much: we have different histories, we should insist on that, and we should begin to tell each other these histories. Would you be prepared to make your letter, or the problems it addresses, the starting point for another discussion—assuming that another of these discussions takes place at the Academy next year? It could happen at the end of January. (Until the 26th I will be in treatment at a health spa.)

By the way, the co-report on Herr Henrich will be given by

Lothar Baier. I have sent him your letter, with the notation that it is only for internal use. I will still try to invite Albrecht Wellmer and Claus Offe for December 19; thank you for the suggestions.

Greetings and best wishes to you and your wife for the New Year, which very likely will not be a peaceful year for any of us.

Yours,
Christa Wolf

Trial by Nail

→→ ←←

I was sitting in a room—I think, or I tell someone I haven't met yet—when nails started growing toward me from both sides, or, to be exact, from in front and behind too, that is from all four sides; believe it or not, there were people there, maybe a hundred, I mean an audience to whom I was to give a lecture, while privately I wondered how much farther these nails would dare to poke out because they had already perforated the canvas walls, had been hammered through them. It seemed to me that these fields of nails had already grown out by millimeters since I had cautiously approached them, concerned to keep my distance, and had given myself up to their churn and swirl, to their tugging current, and to the splitting and cracking of the fabric that tried to resist them. The barrel studded with nails on the inside in which the wicked woman is rolled down the slope into the river was one of my first images of terror, wasn't it, yes I remember though I no longer know which fairy tale it is.

This essay was first published in the catalogue for Günther Uecker's show *Aufbruch* (Erker Galerie, Sankt Gallen, Switzerland, 1992). Günther Uecker, born 1930, is a sculptor and exponent of "concrete art" who specializes in reliefs and objects studded with nails which study the effects of light. The German title of this piece, *Nagelprobe*, literally "nail test," is equivalent to the English "acid test," but Christa Wolf plays on both the literal and figurative meanings in her title and in the body of the essay.

And then there was that iron mold shaped like a human figure into which they forced the victim, the person being interrogated, so that by a clever device they could gradually move the nail-sharp spikes in the lid closer to his soft, quivering flesh—that's how I imagine it—until he was willing to confess and admit his guilt; or the woman was finally ready to confess that as a witch she had fornicated with the Evil One—that's what I'm thinking. She could have done it earlier, couldn't she, or does she need the trial by nail in order for the truth and nothing but the truth to be driven out of her at last, drop by drop along with her supply of blood, of which the queen has to shed only three drops into the snow when she pricks herself with the needle—or the nail, whichever it was—and was it from her finger? I think, feeling uncertain for the first time—in order to see her child white as snow, red as blood, and black as the ebony from the colonies, that very durable, heavy, fine-grained ornamental wood with which the German fairy tale is already familiar—the same tale that later has the wicked stepmother dance in red-hot slippers.[1] Oh Karoline, about whom I have just been reading: how privileged you are to have been able to choose your own method of death,[2] the sharp-pointed polished dagger. That's what I think, and now I am telling you.

With

little nails

b

e

s

t

u

d

ded

1. The nail-studded barrel is from the Grimms' fairy tale *The Goose-Girl*, while the queen who pricks her finger to envision her daughter is from the Grimms' *Snow White*, which ends with the wicked stepmother being forced to dance herself to death in iron slippers that have been heated in the fire.

2. "Karoline" is the romantic poet Karoline von Günderrode, who committed suicide in 1806 by stabbing herself with a dagger that she had chosen as the instrument of her death and had long been carrying around with her.

I remember the threat that was uttered every night; my mother could not know how she sang me awake with her lullaby.[3] The diminutive forms "little nail" and "nail-let" (*Nägelein* and *Nägelchen*), were used in early modern High German, and even in Middle High German when the songs and fairy tales were born, to designate the clove pink, the carnation, weren't they?—that fragrant wild and garden flower whose name derives from the spice known as cloves, the dried bud of the clove tree native to the Moluccas and the Philippines whose shape resembles little nails.

We can't go on this way, or can we? But now let's get down to brass tacks, or make nails with heads on them as we say in German, I mean those sharp-pointed instruments you hammer into an object, consisting of shaft and head and made of metal (iron, brass, zinc, copper, and so on), or occasionally pegs made of wood that are used to fasten or connect and most often are forged from hard-drawn steel wire or squared wrought iron, or cast from strips of sheet metal or steel, with a tapering rounded or polygonal shaft, and with a swaged or cold-pressed head that is shaped like a blunt cone, or is flat or rounded.

But many nails have no heads.

And many people have a big nail in their heads, that is, they have a swelled head, and no doubt I'm one of them, I admit that. I mean, one never learns all there is to know about the forms of vanity and self-conceit—that's what I say. I never finish learning.

And there are some people who hit the nail on the head. Some invariably hit every nail on the head. Or they hit every head without fail. They hit everyone else's head without fail, that's what I think. Some people are infallible, I say. Envious? I ask myself. Anyhow I have to ask if I am envious.

But the "envy nail"—*Neidnagel* or *Niednagel*, a word mean-

3. This is a line from Brahms's Lullaby—"Lullaby and good night, / With roses bedight, / With clove pinks bestudded." The German word for "pinks" is the same as "little nails" and thus can frighten a child, as Wolf describes. The standard English translation of Brahms's Lullaby bypasses the potentially frightening phrases in the German original. Instead of "little nails," the English has "With lilies bespread," and for the closing line it uses "Lay thee down now and rest, / May thy slumber be blessed" instead of the more disturbing thought in German, "If God wills, in the morn / You'll be waked up again," which Wolf addresses later. For the complete German and English texts side by side, see *The Fireside Book of Children's Songs* (New York: Simon & Schuster, 1966), pp. 18–19.

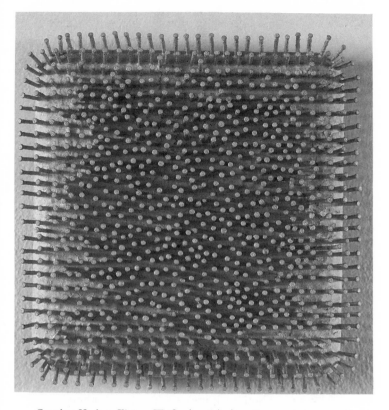

Günther Uecker, *Kleines Weißes* (1958/59), nails mounted on wood, actual size. Courtesy Erker-Galerie, Sankt Gallen, Switzerland.

ing "hangnail" which derives from Low German and has been adopted into High German or has "wandered" into it in a way that has always been a mystery to me—has nothing to do with envy, of course, nothing to do with jealousy, resentment, zealotry, malice, those things you can always count on, I think—those passions you can always count on among us humans, I think, enviously—which I suspect may be why the artist has resorted to nails, to these "*mediators of optical tensions.*"

And the envious chambermaid comes back into my mind, the one from the fairy tale called *The Goose-Girl* who actually is allowed to decide her own punishment, namely, that barrel studded with nails on the inside, which—so I find out when I reread it—

wasn't rolled down the hill but was dragged up and down the streets by white horses. And once the sentence was carried out, the young king married his rightful wife and the two of them ruled their kingdom in peace and happiness.—But to get back to the hangnail, the *Niednagel*, or in its older form *nijpnaghel*, is a word whose first syllable derives from verbs meaning to nip, pinch, squeeze, tweak; because as everybody knows, the broken skin at the edge of a fingernail turns into a pinching, squeezing, painful nail that we nevertheless feel compelled to touch over and over, to tear it further, to repeat and increase the pleasurable pain that is the mediator of emotional tensions, of signals from an underworld that a child is allowed no other way to express. "Lullabye and good night / With roses bedight / With little nails bestudd-ed" my mother sings, I remember. A child lies in bed pierced—larded, so to speak—with a multitude of very small nails, and "If God wills, in the morn You'll be waked up again," the singing mother threatens. She also promises that God *will* will the child to wake up; but who tells children that God will go on being willing to wake them every single morning, tirelessly, over and over, even though the children almost daily commit a horde of offenses that give God ample reason to get fed up in the end and finally not to wake them as he has done every other morning but to turn their restless sleep into a deep and then an eternal slumber? Nothing is impossible to God, nothing is impossible under his sun, this sun that will no longer shine on me ever again, that's what the sobbing, nail-pierced child thinks while lying in bed—I remember. Instead he or she will get stiff and rigid and dead, and lie unwakened and unwakeable in a coffin—one of those that are displayed in the window of the coffin store, little white children's coffins—and the mother's tears will flow copiously while the coffin is nailed up with big coffin nails, and never again will the mother tell the child, "You're a nail in my coffin"—not even as a joke, no not even as a joke, and never again will she tell the child not to take everything so hard and so seriously and so literally because the things people say aren't really meant to be taken literally. They always say things aren't really meant to be taken literally, the child thinks—I remember—until finally we decide to get down to brass tacks, and make nails with heads on them.

Or hammer nails into heads.

That wood sculpture from the Congo, that genderless head of black ebony wood that is densely coated with nails driven in from both sides—cheek, ear, neck. The mouth meanwhile is half open as if to cry out (or to moan, or exhale?), in any case passing air from the inside to the outside, and the left eye has been kindled to a yellow fire next to the flat yet expressive nose. Does the eye reflect a source of light? Like the first rows of the nails that have been hammered unevenly into the head, "*nails that help to articulate light phenomena*"? Nails that are mysteriously intended to mediate between the living and the dead, "*ritual devotions using hammer and nails,*" the nail as "*pure fetish*" that protects the innocent and punishes the guilty—that's what I read—an artificial inanimate object that is venerated and to which magic powers are ascribed. So it's nail magic, I think, misshapen nails of differing length and thickness, perhaps not machine-made, each of which, I hear, holds a message. Its own story. "*In the beginning was the nail.*" The bent, brittle, pathetic nails in the museum showcase, dated 800 B.C. Whereas the talon, the claw with its thin horn-plated nails on the outermost finger and toe joints of vertebrates, must have been capable—I am thinking—of gripping, clutching, holding, scratching, ripping, clamping, carrying things off a long time before there were pegs of wood, bronze and iron—isn't that so?—and for the first time it occurs to me that without those long, firm, pointed nails, neither the birds nor our early relatives the primates would have survived; but why, I wonder, do the little white spots on my left hand appear only on the last three fingernails? They are supposed to be a symptom of something but I forget of what. Calcium deficiency?

"He begrudges her the dirt under his fingernails": scraps of conversation in the supermarket. Every nail has a story to tell. Believe it not, whatever isn't nailed down these days gets stolen. Of course, our merchandise is guarded by electronic security, and store robberies are reported immediately, aren't they, but who's scared off by that? Early in the last century—so I read in a popular humorist—there were two thieves who "Bagged the fat man in his den / So he couldn't scream or run / And hung him up, oh shame to all /

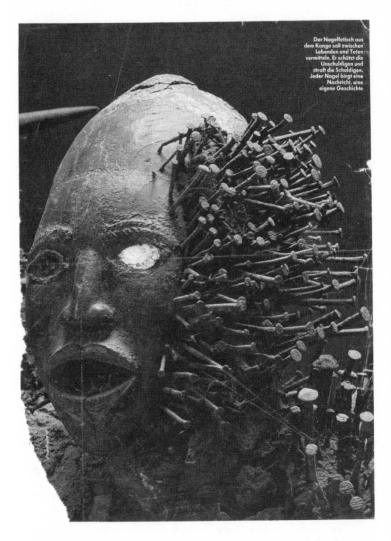

Nail fetish from the Congo. The inscription in the upper righthand corner reads: "The nail fetish from the Congo serves to mediate between the living and the dead. It protects the innocent and punishes the guilty. Each nail holds a message, tells its own story." Private collection, Barbier Müller, Paris.

Upon a nail there in the wall," only to spear each other later on the points of their umbrellas. "Just punishment always comes apace / The umbrella's our instrument of grace." [4]

"*Cultural fetishes with nails hammered all over them, TVs, pianos*"—penetration. I think, forced entry, violation of the idol— and of the participants in the worship? I wonder—destruction of what is precious, of what perhaps is most precious, the forcing of dialogue? "*Dialogue which calls for the preservation of man*," I read, "*art which revolves around the human although it does not depict the human being*." Nail brushes, nail boards, nail trees, nail forest.

Military campaigns waged with nails. Pointed objects, dangerous objects are hammered out, driven forth under cover of a pretended innocence, I take it that this is what happens. "Do not awaken as a jest / The heart that still lies deep at rest / As with hobnailed boots you do not tread / Into the gentle forget-me-nots' bed."

A nail always comes in handy, doesn't it? I picture my grandmother, the long bent nail on which she skewers pieces of newspaper after my grandfather has cut the sheets into quarters so they are the right size for toilet paper; a very particular odor comes into my nostrils, and then I see my grandfather's bearded mouth lined with a thick row of shoemaker's nails that he takes out one after another to hammer them into our shoe soles, once again saving us an unnecessary expense. Isn't that so?—if you look after your pennies, the dollars will look after themselves.

Then there are those acts, costing pain and sacrifice, by which we try to change God's mind about us—God whom we call "our dear Lord" but who in reality is strict and vengeful (and rightly so, rightly strict and angry in view of our transgressions!)—and seduce him to forgive and look kindly on us again. The fakir's bed of nails would definitely fit the bill as an object with which to inflict pain on ourselves; but then you have to work your way up gradually from the little to the great, from the imperfect to the perfect, don't you? And just one nail under your bedsheet presses and torments you so that to your shame you cannot bear it; by morning the nail is lying next to your bed and once again the effort at atonement has failed,

4. The "popular humorist" is Wilhelm Busch, 1832–1908, author of the verse tale "Zwei Diebe" (The two thieves), from the *Münchener Bilderbogen*, 1865–70.

hasn't it, owing to the weakness of the flesh. A nail in your shoe. And besides, in the worst case scenario that we are always eager to entertain along with our popular poet, just punishment may suddenly and unexpectedly overtake naughty and completely disrespectful little boys, like the ones who persecuted the ascetic and philosopher Diogenes in his barrel—in the form of two nails that were sticking out of the barrel and grabbed the boys by their tunics: "No help in tears and cries of woe / For under the barrel they must go / Like pancakes flat it rolls them down / The naughty boys of Corinth town"—so that we also learn to appreciate the deep pedagogical significance of the nail.[5]

And then there are the repeated hammerings of the nobleman smith and guardian of public morals, Count Ludwig, "Grow hard, Count Ludwig!" Hammer in, hammer fine, little Meister Hämmerlein, Old Nick and the sweet hangman.[6] To nail, nail up, nail together. "His mind is closed and nailed shut"—we say that, don't we?—and "that guy's wooden-headed."

You can also be nailed to something. Nailed to the Cross with big strong nails, horseshoe nails? driven in with powerful blows of the hammer—you have to picture a hand, an arm, a strapping man to carry it out, I think to myself—nails whose broad heads painted with loving detail jut realistically from the hands and from feet nailed one on top of the other, and that carry the whole weight of the dangling dislocated corpse, while one of the women down below can think of nothing better to do than wring her hands, and the other seems about to simply collapse. The little lamb prettily raises its right foot holding a little Cross. But no: the nails, the nails of the Cross dominate the scene and the nightmares, so that the message of futility spreading from the central hall of the museum like a numbing miasma penetrates the other rooms where, just to give an example, there is a *Passion-in-progress*—no pain so great that you

5. The allusion is to Wilhelm Busch's verse story "Diogenes und die bösen Buben von Korinth" (Diogenes and the naughty boys from Corinth), first published in the *Münchener Bilderbogen*, 1862.

6. Count Ludwig of Thuringia, a twelfth-century nobleman and stepson of Frederick Barbarossa, reputedly was trained by a blacksmith who enjoined him to "Grow hard, Count Ludwig!"—that is, to be harsh toward enemies in war. Old Nick and the sweet hangman: the German phrase Meister Hämmerlein (Little Master Hammer) is a nickname for the Devil or for a hangman.

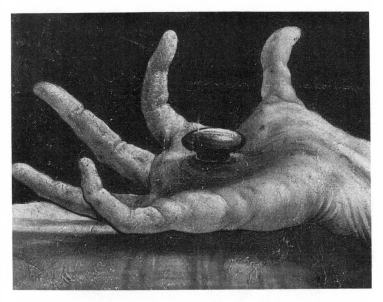

Matthias Grünewald, *Isenheimer Altar* (1512–15), detail of the center panel.
Copyright Musée d'Unterlinden, Colmar, France.

don't find a greater—in a picture of the still-life genre where various objects painted punctiliously in three-dimensional detail—namely bottles and jars of the most diverse shapes and materials, among them a wicker demijohn of a sort that regrettably is no longer in use today—are hanging from hooks, or bent nails, on the back of a wooden cupboard: *still-lifes with books, still-lifes in trompe l'oeil.* There's still a lot left for me to do, I think, and *led by the magic hand of coincidence* I find myself standing in front of Lucas Cranach's *Melancholia* who regards me mockingly, a very young and shapely blond maiden in a flowing red garment who is gazing dreamily into space, see? while she engages in a surprising activity: she is whittling away at a little stick with a little knife that is the only nail in this picture, and turning it into the sweetest little whip. Her ball or sphere has slipped from her and rolled to the foot of the table, where in the foreground the little dog, which is also gray, rests with its paws crossed while in the background three putti are merrily pushing a fourth who sits in a swing dangling from the sky. But in the dark cloud above the landscape outside the window we see a

Lucas Cranach d. Ä., *Melancholie* (1532).
Courtesy Musée d'Unterlinden, Colmar, France.

hunting scene, figures riding on the backs of a wild boar, a drag-
onlike serpent, a horse, and a bull, the dark knight wearing a feath-
ered cap, the naked crone astride the serpent and holding up a skull
mounted on a spear; but facing backward on the bull—and conse-
crated to the bull-god and to the love-god Dionysus?—is a stark-
naked young girl, riding behind a second naked crone and brighter
than all the rest, who so diabolically resembles the other girl, still
demurely wearing her red dress and angel's wings and little wreath,
who whittles artlessly at her little whip. It's true, isn't it, all our good
deeds and desire to preserve our innocence are in vain? The dark
wild hunt has come upon the land, perhaps in the form of our very
own selves, and the steep mighty fortress in the background will be

Lucas Cranach d. Ä., *Melancholie* (1532), detail. Courtesy Musée
d'Unterlinden, Colmar, France.

no defense. On the contrary, the hunt is already upon us with spears
and stakes, and we hear the hue and cry, and hot breath beats on
the backs of our necks, and when we turn around and look into their
faces, we are shocked to see our own image, which we do not want
to recognize, like the faithless chambermaid in the fairy tale who
did not realize that she was passing sentence on herself. That's what
I think, and now I am telling you.

> *The Principle of Hope*
> Nailed
> to the cross the Past.
> Every movement
> drives
> the nails
> into the flesh.

✦ 1 9 9 2 ✦

Is it only Stalinist structures that must be
abolished, is it only corporate interests that
must be pruned for the benefit of society
and the environment? I think not. The evil
lodges deeper. We have too little insight
into the dangers of a rationalistic culture which
views the logical operations of reason, with its
mathematical, digital structure, as the foundation
of culture. We must change our culture of thought
as a whole.

OTL AICHER
was ich tun würde, 1989

On the Road to Tabou

Paul Parin

➤➤ ◄◄

Ladies and Gentlemen, Goldy Parin, Paul Parin:

When I began to work on this "eulogy"—another of the words I feel I have to set in quotation marks—I dreamed one morning about the award ceremony that we have met to celebrate today. (Oh yes, I am brazenly preparing to talk about my dreams—setting foot on the "royal road to the unconscious" in your presence, the presence of a psychoanalyst, and in Vienna to boot!) In my dream I arrived late, so I sneaked in from the back—the auditorium, unlike this one, was brightly lit, square, and bare of decoration—and I saw the densely massed backs of the audience in front of me. In my left hand I was holding a bouquet for you, or, to be exact, a big, straggly clump of green grasses; and to make up some of the time I had lost, I started to hurry along the side aisle toward the front, where an empty podium waited so that I could dutifully give my speech. "Yes, ladies and gentlemen," I said, "I am here to repair an omission— for your sake, Paul, but also for the rest of us—to bring you here,

Speech delivered on May 4, 1992, in Vienna at the awards ceremony bestowing the Erich Fried Prize on Paul Parin. First published in *Literatur und Kritik* (Salzburg), June 1992.

to bring you to us, where you belong." I kept walking as I said this. But then, out of the corner of my eye, I glimpsed two figures who were sitting modestly in one corner of the hall in two little extra chairs. It was you, Paul, you and Goldy. I admit I felt uneasy when I saw you, but only mildly so. What I hoped—in fact I definitely counted on it—was that you would not just go on sitting there in your corner but would come and sit in the front-row seat where you belonged, and where I needed to have you so that at last I could address you as you deserved. And then I saw the back of your head already shining from the place of honor, and I was relieved and felt that everything was all right.

Was I trying to turn you into a split personality, sitting in two places at once? When I woke up I hurried to my desk, and among the notes I had made the previous evening—while I was reading your book on Slovenia, *Untrügliche Zeichen von Veränderung* (Unmistakable signs of change)—I found I had jotted down this observation: "In Parin, the division of labor between the scientist and the writer has not split him as a person." Hmmm. Which of the two parts of your personality did my wicked dream place in the little extra chair, and which in the seat of honor? (And of course my dream was putting things in reverse, as dreams will.) Also, you had written to me the day before about some flowers you were sent—flowers for a prize that had not been awarded yet: I really thought that was great!—but why, in my dream, did these flowers change in my hand into unadorned green grass? The fact that I arrived too late to give public recognition to your work as a writer—well, you know that I have felt for a long time that recognition was long overdue, yet you were genuinely surprised each time I said so. Let me correct that statement: I arrived late but not too late. Homage paid to someone who can still enjoy it does not come too late. But the poem by Erich Fried, which you gave as a token of thanks to those who congratulated you a bit prematurely, does hint at a feeling that things are "too late" and, I am certain, must have colored my dream by a subterranean route:

PAUL PARIN

With the Years

With my experience
grows
my ability
to describe
what I
will describe
no longer

An enigmatic poem. An inability is expressed by way of an ability. Sadness with a smile, and not without self-irony. The undescribed, the no-more-to-be-described, is glimmering on the horizon, but it will never rise up to become the described. There is acceptance of this, and the knowledge that no one else will ever express the thing that is left unsaid. No one else has access to it.

I think I know why this poem moves you, dear Paul Parin. I am just beginning to decipher its first lines, and I would like us to go on talking together about the tension between the powerful, insatiable longing to say everything—even at the cost of the almost inevitable pinch of dishonesty that an invisible hand scatters into our work as we write—and our reluctance to expose the secret hidden in the words "human being," a feeling that is almost equally compelling and may be what drove our remote ancestors to entertain all those rituals, exercises, and imaginings that stem from awe: that emotion which in our century is vanishing forever at a frightening speed.

But I do not have to avoid old-fashioned words when I am in your presence. They fit quite well into your trains of thought, which I believe are up-to-date though not at the height of fashion. You keep insisting that you are "committed to the Enlightenment," yet you have no reservation in claiming that you have "always been skeptical about human affairs." One of your essay collections is called *Subjekt im Widerspruch* (The self in contradiction), and its companion piece is *Widerspruch im Subjekt* (Contradiction in the self). No doubt it was my craving to reread all your books and articles that inspired me to offer you this prize, because of course one

does not make such a choice "freely" or unselfishly but always reveals something about oneself. And so a beacon kept flashing everywhere I looked, as I had both hoped and feared it would, telling me
to "do my thing," and I forgot all about the letter that I had written
earlier to our president, Hans Mayer, asking him to release me from
the duty of serving on the awards jury. And then the moral effort of
examining Paul Parin's life and the aesthetic effort of addressing
his texts overcame any discouragement I felt—which, remarkable
as it may seem, is a common experience. Also I thought, "Erich
Fried would agree with my choice."[1] That certainty gave me something to hold on to. By the way, the first thing Paul Parin said after
he was told about the prize and after expressing surprise and disbe-
lief was, "I think Fried would be glad." For Erich Fried had adopted
Paul Parin as an older brother and was convinced of his authority,
his understanding, and his spirit of brotherliness.

The idea of a "brotherly community" is a basic element in Parin's life and work. It was the goal he worked toward, unconsciously
at first. He felt sheltered and happy whenever he "arrived" in such
a community, whether in the sharing of dangerous activities, stren-
uous work, or adventurous investigations. The group of like-minded
people with equal rights, bound together by a brotherly, sisterly kin-
ship, who struggled together "to make things better"—who struggled against fascism, or worked as doctors among the Yugoslavian
partisans or as psychoanalysts in Zurich or as ethnopsychoanalysts
in Africa, represents the hard core, the practical center of Parin's
utopia. Utopia is a word which, *horribile dictu,* he has refused to
give up even in his most recent writings, and which he *cannot* give
up because his writing stops with the vanishing of his utopia. He
demonstrates this most strikingly in the book in which he describes his time with the Yugoslavian partisans, *Es gibt Krieg und
wir gehen hin* (There's a war and we are going). Besides, he does
not feel that he *must* give up utopia, unlike the hordes of people
today who once held liberal and emancipatory views and now are
hastily abandoning all their earlier insights and hopes in the fear-
ridden wake of postmodernism, and who not only abandon them

1. Erich Fried (1921–88) was a German poet.

but think they must ridicule them as well. Another thing that seems fashionable nowadays is simply to yield to the sense of the vanity of all human activity, an emotion consisting partly of despair and partly of complacency. Parin, I say, does not feel compelled to join in this chorus—just as in the past he felt no need to join in the choruses of rejoicing and assent from people who needed integration, a sense of homeland, and the certainty of "fighting on the right side" and of "helping justice to win in the end" and who found all this in some strictly disciplined, hierarchically structured organization that was held together by quasi-religious emotions. I have learned that needs of this kind can be dissolved and replaced with others that afford more inner freedom and scope for self-determination, but it is a difficult and wearisome process. Parin says his "emotional needs" and those of his comrades were "just the opposite of this" from the very start: "We were disciplined when we ourselves thought it was right. Any command hurt our sense of dignity. We felt we were citizens of the world, in solidarity with all who were oppressed and exploited. For this reason, any homeland was too narrow for us, and the obligation to follow a party line was a chain."

You may be wondering what is the point of my saying all this. After all, we are not here to judge principles of life and action— and God knows I would not be entitled to be a judge if this were the case—but rather we are awarding a prize for literary work. But the problem is that this literary work, whether in essay form or in fiction, springs unmistakably from the same source as the "actions" of its author. Parin's whole idea seems simple. A vision is "real"— for him this means "effective"—to the degree that a person is willing to commit to it without reserve. You must accept the repeated experience of being always "either behind the times or too far ahead of them." Even at inopportune moments, you must insist upon playing a role in society—you must be free to do "what we ourselves thought was right"—even though this role may have been "erased from the life of nations": "People of our sort had become rare to the point of being unrecognizable." Parin did not mind paying the price for a life without reserve, without any anchor in traditional structures; often, it seems to me, he paid it gladly. His life has been a sort of marginal existence. Where Goldy and Paul Parin are concerned—and for over fifty years you could only think of them together—it seems indistinguishable from happiness.

We should also be able to read Parin's works from this vantage point, the vantage point of happiness in times when "compulsions and regressions . . . cripple and maim the individual." I would never have expected a word like "happiness" to figure in my talk. It seems to me a long time since I have even been able to think it, because that "second self" that Parin talks about—the one that does not accept being split in half and "wants to rebel, to act"—was and is captive inside me. That is why I follow Parin's stories with such a feeling of suspense: because whatever their "subject"—and their subjects include a wealth of interesting material, both detailed and vividly presented—their subtext is always the search for deeper fulfillment, for which the outward circumstances merely provide the pretext.

The pattern begins early. As a boy, his longing for friendship is very strong. The son of a Jewish landowner in Slovenia, he lives isolated from possible playmates, but that will change: "Before I was fourteen, I decided to sail my boat, which I had named Vrag, 'The Devil,' along the foaming Savinia river that flowed on its rubble bed down into the wide valley, and to find a friend." An ancient theme, a classic motif of epics, sagas, and fairy tales whose mythical undertow seems to carry the boy quite effortlessly along to his meeting with the "tanned and slender creature" who rises up out of the world of undines, suddenly begins to play with him in a whirlpool, and taking the place of the male friend he had searched for becomes the secret goal of all his desires. In time he finds out her home and her name: Wanda, the daughter of a neighboring landowner. But her fate remains mysterious. She even appears to offer her admirer the opportunity to rescue her, but in the end he is not required to carry out the deed and finally is forced to understand this, after a series of "events that easily evaded conscious attempts to sort them out because of the immature desires that led to them, and because of their humiliating outcome." Wanda reenters his life three years later, still invested with an aura of unreality, and then vanishes forever—thus leaving the young man free to carry out his first real "deed"—namely to help refugees who are fleeing from Austria after its occupation by the German Wehrmacht to cross the river border at night. You should read all this in the book on Slovenia, and let yourself be captured by the unusually dense and graphic description, interspersed with apt self-observations of the kind that Parin always brings into his texts.

("Do we ever really do anything new, do we do it better? Don't we just return again and again to the same place that we did not know how to go beyond when we were children, when we were young men?") And there are short illuminating reflections on the political situation: "We lived in a time that was not great but evil and cruel. Maybe it was difficult to get through, but it was easy to know what one had to do."

I hardly need to point out that a passage like this—one of many such—has the quality of sticking in our minds and of setting off a process of self-questioning and self-examination: When exactly was this statement true of my life too, and when was it more the reverse that was true—that it wasn't especially difficult to get through a time but not so easy to know what one had to do? And how long will we have to go on saying that the times are "evil and cruel"? And how long must we go on enduring them? Certain images arise in my mind and voices are audible, and at the same time a different character forms in another layer of my consciousness, called up by the slightly unreal figure of Wanda: a being from a much later story by Paul Parin whom the first-person narrator calls "La Gioconda," characterizing her only by her smile even though it is the most famous smile in the Western world.

"The novel of a man who found another life after suffering social death," Parin writes in a strange little preface to this narrative, which is only seventy pages long—"it could even have been my life." But it is not his life. All the same, the lure to imagine how a man might live on after carrying out a political murder—to live out his story even if only on paper—may be the strongest impulse in the rich web of relations on which this story is based. After all, in 1938 some students in Zagreb had hotly debated the possibility of assassinating Hitler as a way to avert the impending disaster, but they did not realize that one among them thought he was the only one who could and perhaps must carry out the murder because he was an excellent shot. He was Paul Parin . . .

This story, "Noch ein Leben" (Another life), swings back and forth between two selves, that of the narrator and that of the protagonist, whose real name is unknown but who is called "Giorgio" by his landlady and shelters in a prostitute's room by arrangement with the Party. The room is in Milan. And I, having reached this point in my manuscript, will then travel to this city for the first time in my life and get to know it in the way I love best, which is through the eyes of a writer and one of his characters. I will wonder whether the nameless man in the story hid in one of the houses we are passing; whether in one of these houses I could find the room where the man appointed by the Party to carry out the killing—the man exhausted by this labor and incapable of anything, at least for now—is lying on the bed brooding, in reverie, receiving phone calls from admirers of the woman who lived in the room before he did and whom he glimpses in the mirror one night, a shadowy figure with her peculiar smile, whose appearance he eagerly awaits each night and who each time disappears again as if she had never been there, so that this man who can no longer feel anything but his mounting lack of feeling cannot help wondering whether she is a real woman or a phantom conjured up by his worn-out yet overstimulated senses. I too will stand in the square in front of the cathedral whose overly ornate exterior is contradicted by its simple interior in a way that is quite surprising, while the voice of the narrator, dry but glowing with a hidden fire, echoes in my ear. And even if I am not shooed away by a downpour like the nameless man in the story, I will stroll through the Galleria still frequented by "everyone who is anyone in Milan," "extras in a play they have not read, for they are strangers in their own city." Why do words like this affect me so when I read them in the slim little book back at the hotel in the evening—words that actually apply to other people, to a different time, to an unfamiliar city?

In one of his psychoanalytic essays that is tinged with autobiography, Parin writes that "social death" occurs when customary ties are broken. Many of us have had this experience, are having it today. The nameless man in "Another Life" builds a bridge back into life, partly with the help of books. A very remarkable doctor, who seems not quite of this world, recommends that he read Elio Vittorini. The nameless man finds Vittorini's *Conversation in Sicily* in a Zurich bookshop; I take the book down from my shelf in Berlin. I read what was quite new to me the first time and again comes across as something new today: how the "Great Lombard" thought "a new conscience was needed, and new duties to accomplish, in order to feel more at peace with men."[2]

Parin's nameless man becomes a brother of the "Great Lombard." After killing a man in La Gioconda's room—he kills him just as a reflex, not knowing if the man's visit has anything to do with him and not knowing that he is in fact the fascists' top assassin—he can only relax and begin to feel again as he travels from Milan back to Zurich. Only now, after so many years, does he feel able to "completely separate his conscience from what is written in the lawbooks. Laws simply cannot be relied upon. For one man it is enough to do what he must to avoid going to prison. For others that is not enough. They want more, a proper, great conscience. They want everything to become more just, if possible the whole world. That has nothing to do with the law."

"La Gioconda" also appears to him in Zurich and stays with him for a long time. At last she vanishes from his life, having never solved the riddle of her appearance. The man now finds that he must "write it all down": "I am afraid of forgetting. I must record it all quite accurately, so that my present-day life . . . is not disrupted by all sorts of quirks and peculiarities."

It occurs to me that Parin's descriptions of the things that motivate someone to write are rather like the motivations at the beginning of psychoanalysis: "Only at the beginning was it an effort to sit down at the desk. Now the memories seem to come spontaneously and I do not lack for words." All we have to do is see the desk as a substitute for the couch, and the scene is set for a successful therapy. The "disruptions" that trouble the man and probably scare him disappear as he writes and remembers. "This technique has proved quite successful."

As a psychoanalyst, Parin views with skepticism and reservation the oddities, peculiarities, blindness, the dangerous irrational outbursts of individuals and of whole social classes and nations. As a practical man, he cannot help but be pessimistic. He recognizes

2. Elio Vittorini, *Conversazione in Sicilia* (1946); quoted from Wilfred David's translation, *Conversation in Sicily* (Harmondsworth, U.K.: Penguin Books, 1961), p. 30.

our inertia, our cowardice, the sheer immutability of our unconscious, and our seemingly ineradicable compulsion to conform even
to unacceptable conditions. And yet the existence of people who are
free, or somewhat free of this compulsion, is not a fantasy. The "intellectual climate"—that is, a critical spirit, opposition, liberal-
mindedness—can achieve "a great deal," Parin says. And he himself makes a powerful and sustained contribution to creating this
kind of intellectual climate, while at the same time he analyzes the
contradiction and the resistance that he inevitably experiences in
his efforts. He jokingly calls himself a "moral anarchist" who does
not want power to be institutionalized, yet he remains true to the
commandment of "radical love of mankind," to his stubborn conviction that it is worthwhile to create "islands of reason in a world
insanely threatened by ourselves" by forming alliances of like-
minded people, by civil courage, by dauntless thinking that goes to
the roots of contradictions and conflicts. Besides, what other choice
do we have?

I've just noticed that I wrote all this on the backs of the galley
proofs of my last little book, that much-impugned tale *What Remains*.[3] My right elbow kept hurting me while I wrote it, as if it
were trying physically to prevent me from writing. An all too transparent maneuver, using physical pain to avoid emotional pain or to
make it bearable. This tactic no longer works in the age of word
processors. All the same, at the moment I cannot bring myself to
exchange my old-fashioned writing surface for the screen that
glows at me with a challenging greenish light. It's as if the layers
of writing that are building up on the paper were creating a sort of
palimpsest, as if the urgent question that is being asked, that is
growing more urgent by the minute, were penetrating through the
paper, meeting Parin's sentences there on the back, and stimulating
new attempts at answers. A new text.

I must admit to superstitious behavior about written things. *Zu
viele Teufel im Land* (Too many devils in the land), Paul Parin's

3. *Was bleibt* (Berlin and Weimar: Aufbau Verlag, 1990) is a story about GDR
state-police surveillance of Wolf and her family. Wolf was accused of publishing it only
after it became "safe" to do so, that is, after the collapse of the Communist regime. It
has been translated by Heike Schwarzbauer and Rick Takvorian as "What Remains,"
in *What Remains and Other Stories* (New York: Farrar, Straus & Giroux, 1993).

book about his travels in Africa with his companions, was the first of his writings that he gave me—in 1984—and the last I have read. I was warned against it: it will haunt you, people told me. In those years I apparently didn't think I was up to being haunted, even in my sleep, by insoluble problems, so I avoided the question by not reading the book, whose back cover bears the words, "Doom hangs over Africa. Its amiable people, its black men, women, and children, are victims of a disaster that Europe's missionaries, soldiers, traders, and machines have brought down upon the whole continent. And we ourselves are a part of this horror that no one talks about, and are its belated messengers."

Setting out for another country, making a journey, surviving adventures—these are recurrent themes in Parin. First there is the journey into one's own unconscious, psychoanalysis as adventure (Parin sharply criticizes psychoanalysis, by the way, when it is institutionalized and becomes untrue to its mission of social criticism); then the ever-new journey into the tangle of patients' psyches, with the analyst as companion. This is the road into the depths, to the "Mothers." [4] Traveling this path, psychoanalysis and literature have continually learned from each other in our century, and I believe they are dependent on each other. In a search for ways of life different from the law of white civilization, "which is developing in a way so unsuited to human welfare," Goldy and Paul Parin and Ruth and Fritz Morgenthaler set out to find an alternative, autonomous principle; they head "for the Sahara," for the heart of darkness, for the dark continent of Africa, looking to expand their psyches, to see themselves more clearly but also to "discover what is African in themselves." The two books in which they recorded their experiences in the early sixties with the Dogon and the Anyi (two West African peoples) have meaningful titles: "White people think too much" (*Die Weissen denken zuviel*) and "Fear thy neighbor as thyself" (*Fürchte deinen Nächsten wie dich selbst*).[5] Their studies lead the travelers to conclude that "the psychology of Western man

4. Chthonic mother-goddess figures from the "Dark Gallery" in Goethe's *Faust*, part II, act 1.

5. Translated by Patricia Klamerth as *Fear Thy Neighbor as Thyself: Psychoanalysis and Society among the Anyi of West Africa* (Chicago: University of Chicago Press, 1980).

merely describes one special case within the possible range of human psychic life."

I have now read Parin's book about the devils in the land twice, the first time skimming it, running away from it, momentarily expecting "the horror" to break out from the moving description of encounters with alien people and landscapes; and then a second time, shielding myself with a pencil, tracing the patterns of memory and association that underlie these carefully crafted stories that Parin disguises as travel reports. He creates a web in which clearly delineated figures move at a visible level, while from the depths of it rise the myths of the African nations; a web where landscapes are conjured and the light painted in above them, where villages and towns are placed along the roads and streets, in the middle of the desert or in the rainforest, and where, as the web soaks up the passage of time, we see marks of the mostly disastrous changes taking place in the former French colonies. As always, Parin writes to stop forgetfulness. His anger and pain at the barbarity of the colonizers, who share his own skin color and culture, are fused with the affection and love that he and his companions experience and with the spell that the African continent casts on them, a spell that only intensifies as they learn more about Africa and that reaches its full glory in the description of their journey to Tabou, the center of all longing.

Tabou, a place that does not exist but whose name keeps recurring like a beacon, enticing and seductive, until they feel compelled to set out and search for it; a place which—as is only appropriate—cannot be reached except by the most extreme bodily and mental effort. It is a place that you must first "forget" so that it will finally "approach" you in a "fragrant breath of wind." "We saw the sky glowing blue between the treetops, an unaccustomed breeze stirred the leaves, the plants thinned out along the road, white sand crunched under its edges, there was a hill, a curve in the road, and before us the blue ocean spread wide, the surf and the white-sanded coast stretched into the distance, and facing it, amid groves of swaying coconut palms, lay the little town of Tabou."

This too is a typical feature of journeys to one's heart's desire, and is one of the laws of utopia: the traveler who finally arrives at the longed-for place does not experience anything very remarkable but "only" an intensification of the ordinary, a concentration of the human, a "light" from far away that "illuminates the future, the dark wall of clouds that is rising." This light may reveal itself to someone in an African town with a name like Tabou that is rich in associations, but it does not belong to any one city or continent. Some people, of course, have a special talent for seeing the light. And Paul Parin is one of them because he was born lucky. He says so himself and confesses that before he was born, his mother prophesied: "I will give birth to a son and he'll be a lucky guy." You don't have to be a psychoanalyst to know that neither sorrow nor cruel strokes of fate, neither pangs of conscience nor threats of conflict, can prevail against such a prophecy and that if a person has luck like this, even his deepest doubts will not turn into despair in the end and his own faults, omissions, and failures cannot impel him into hopeless feelings of guilt and self-hatred. And should he become a writer, even his most fearless and most accurate diagnoses— that is, those which are most terrible—will not drive readers to resignation and apathy but will encourage them to take joy in thought and action. So, Paul Parin, in praising you I have to praise your artistry at life—which leads to cheerfulness and self-command— in the same breath with your artistry as a writer—which is nourished by these good fruits and nourishes them in turn. And I must consider it a stroke of luck for *me* that I met you both—you and Goldy—and your books at just the right moment, for they have been and they still are an essential part of my life.

Clinical Findings

➤➤ ◄◄

Now, I said, I have the feeling more and more often—just recently I've had it all the time—that a bush is growing in my
throat; it's growing in the direction of my jaw and is shaped so that
it allows me to swallow almost without interference—I could swallow anything, I said, including tears—and so that my breath can
pass without hindrance through my windpipe toward my lungs, but
not the other way around: at least not when it has to carry my voice,
I said. The bush in my throat is intervening to stop it, I said; it
doesn't let my voice through, at least not in its full strength, its full
vocal power. The first phase was this thinning out of my voice, I
say: the filtering out of its undertones while weakening it at the
same moment, so that by the time it forced its way through the
shrubbery in my throat it was only a small voice, a thin sound, and
I couldn't help being surprised that no one seemed to notice this
change in me; but perhaps that was because I no longer used my
voice as much as before. At first I made many mistakes, of course,
giving in to my habit of talking whenever I felt like it; and then I
had to find ways of concealing the thin tone that struggled out of
me. It's hard to believe how quickly an experience like this produces
conditioned reflexes. Anyhow, the change in my voice moved me,

First published in the German edition of this book.

faster and more effectively than all my high-minded resolutions over the decades, to speak only after careful reflection, when I considered it unavoidable. I worked out a technique of breathing and pressure for these occasions that allowed me, in these rare cases, to simulate almost normal speech, using what was left of my vocal power; and I quickly recognized that no one missed my verbal contributions, which in the past had no doubt been shamefully excessive. But the plant growth in my throat—which I sometimes picture as resembling algae—was not content with this success. It began to censor my speech, preventing me from pronouncing certain words. One of the first words that got stuck in the shrubbery, I remember, and was lost to me forever, was, surprisingly, the word "certain" and all its variations such as "certainly," "certainty," "ascertain," and, of course, "uncertain." I recall that it took me a while to notice the loss of this word from my spoken vocabulary, to recognize that the obstacles to my pronouncing it were not merely a matter of chance, and finally to conduct, so to speak, a series of systematic experiments to—I was about to say to "make certain"—that this word had become unspeakable for me. After that I learned to recognize more quickly the signs that yet another word had failed to overcome the barrier of the bush in my throat, and I also learned to avoid the words that I could no longer say, and managed to devise substitutes for them by the use of imaginative paraphrases. I am saying that there seemed to be no system governing the selection of the words that would be forbidden; and moreover, I would have refused to attribute to the shrub in my throat—algaelike or not—anything like rationality, much less a moral principle, which guided its actions in stealing my words from me. I admit that, after a time, I couldn't help noticing that the words I lost were exclusively from the class of abstractions. I observed—and I confess I was relieved to see it—that I had no need to fear the loss of "man," "table," "bed," and "child" and that "house," "bread," "money," and "washing machine," or "car," "rug," "book," and "chair" were not to be taken from me, even though, as I learned, these words scarcely needed to be pronounced, because if necessary one can point to the objects they stand for. But no, I am being unjust (I say); for could I have pointed to "night," "morning," "weather," to "sky," "moon" and "stars," to "life" and "death," to the "atom" and "electrical waves"—all words that were not taken away from me and are still at my disposal today? Whereas "truth," "loyalty," "love," and "betrayal" were gradually lost, and I may say that I did not give them up without a fight. To start with, I often went to the park or to the open country when a new word fell prey to the tentacles of the bush in my throat, and there, unobserved, I would try by force to gain the use of this word, which I believed I could not do without. For example, I thought that it was impermissible to bar me from pronouncing the word "honest." My attempts to squeeze it out of my throat must have looked to an observer—fortunately there was none—like the convulsive spasms of someone with a severe stomach disorder. It is superfluous to say that all my efforts were unsuccessful and that the number of words I am prevented from speaking has continued to mount and recently has been increasing daily, so that it is becoming more and more difficult to salvage certain parts of my sentences by the use of paraphrase, a technique of which admittedly I have become a master. The removal of a single additional word may cause the collapse of an entire linguistic structure that was still able to support my disguises, and suddenly a whole group of declarative sentences is caught in the whirlpool and goes under. At night, I say, I often lie awake and *think* all the lost words as loudly as possible, but I have given up any attempt to pronounce them. Also, I am no longer so presumptuous as to seek a meaning in the loss of words to which I have been sentenced—reward or punishment would be the probable explanation, I say to myself. I can just sit there and listen to the crackling growth of the bush in my throat, whose branches seem to be growing denser and denser. Everyone will understand my only speaking a little and hesitantly and softly, I think; it's only natural that I should treat the words that remain to me with care, almost tenderly, and that I value each and every one. Besides, in the past, when all words were at my disposal and I used them without thinking, I would scarcely have finished saying something before the noun "lie" rose up like a shadow behind every word, but now I have noticed that every word I can still say, even the simplest—especially the simplest—is surrounded by an aura of stillness that I find comforting. I confess that I have reached the point of no longer wanting to be able to speak all the words that have fallen prey to the bush in my throat and that will probably continue to fall prey to it. For example, what could make me want to say a word like "honest" in a carefree way, and thus willingly expose myself to the torment that inevitably comes from giving false testimony? No. Calmly, almost smiling I let all these words from my past life sink back into stillness and oblivion—I say— where perhaps they may be purified and renewed. I remember them less and less often. When I lie awake at night I no longer hear the bush growing in my throat any more either, because there is no more space there for it to grow, so it has come to rest, it has achieved its goal, and at last it is at one with me in our common silence.

The Multiple Being Inside Us

Correspondence with Efim Etkind

➤➤ ◄◄

Helsinki, April 23, 1992

Dear Christa,

Lew [Kopelew] has given me your book to read.[1] I am writing you while I still feel the very strong impression of this simple and tragic narrative. I have experienced everything you write about ("Are they still there? Yes, the white car is still there . . . What do they want to know? Why are those poor guys parked there?"), only I could not have expressed it so wrenchingly. Another aspect of your book impressed me deeply. On page 81 you write: "I asked the questions one asks, got the same old answers . . . not even leaving out words like 'worry' and 'longing,' since, after all, *those who feel nothing have all words freely at their disposal.*"[2] I could not express this idea better: yes, one can say everything when one feels nothing. I am about to write a book on this theme, it involves Tolstoy, Goncharov,

---

Etkind's letter and Wolf's reply were first published in the *Frankfurter Allgemeine Zeitung*, February 3, 1993.

   1. *What Remains* (see note 3 to "On the Road to Tabou," above).
   2. Efim Etkind's italics.

Dostoevsky, Chekhov: The more one might say and the deeper one's feelings are, the less one *can* express, the fewer words are available to us. The Russian writers understood this well, it is very clear especially in *The Idiot*. I have called this chapter, "On the Ease of Lying and the Impossibility of Telling the Truth" (General Ivolgin — Prince Myshkin).

I was also very moved by what you write about the "self" on p. 57: "I myself. Who was that? Which of the multiple beings from which 'myself' was composed? The one that wanted to know itself? The one that wanted to protect itself? . . ."[3] I would like to express my love and my admiration for all these multiple beings called Christa Wolf.

Yours,
Efim Etkind

May 23, 1992

Dear Efim Etkind,

You will not believe—or perhaps you can imagine—how important your note about *What Remains* is to me. You know that this story was torn to pieces,[4] and as a result I could not look at it again for a long time, much less do any readings of it (besides, I have cut down a lot on my public readings). Among other things I was accused of having wrongfully posed as a persecuted person in this text when actually I was a "state poet." I had to wonder whether the people who said this can't read, or do not want to read; perhaps both. In any case, the recognition that no one wanted to listen to arguments reduced me to silence. There was and is no point in throwing complicated experiences into this witches' cauldron known as "German unification"—it has the same name if one is talking politically or about the arts—when powerful interests, including psychological interests, of course, are taking advantage of this unique opportunity to make their mark. The urges involved are

3. *What Remains*, pp. 244, 234.
4. Attacks from critics in the West were led by journalists Frank Schirrmacher in the *Frankfurter Allgemeine Zeitung* and Ulrich Greiner in *Die Zeit*, both of whom accused Wolf of political opportunism and cowardice in publishing *What Remains* long after it was written.

so powerful and irrepressible that the need for historical truth and justice is minimal by comparison; and people are rather shy about articulating this need, especially in the "new federal states." It is bewildering to watch how extreme opposites manage to coincide in this process, how "right" and "left" no longer apply, given the overwhelming desire—stemming from a variety of motives—to be seen as being on the right side when the "victims" are sorted out from the "perpetrators."

Nothing can be done to stop this process; primal forces will have their way. What really troubles me, when I am able to free my emotions a bit from the pressure of these forces, is this damned question of the truth, which you homed in on in your letter: "On the Ease of Lying and the Impossibility of Telling the Truth." In other words, how is it that the closer you get to the truth—that is to yourself, to the multiple beings inside you, and especially to the one of these beings with whom you would least like to be identified—how is it, I ask, that a tinge of insincerity always sneaks into any text in which you try to track down this being and its truth, somewhere along the way from the head to the hand to the paper?

I want to tell you something. For two or three weeks I have been poring over our Stasi files, though by no means every day. Sometimes Gerd is with me. We go to Lichtenberg, to the former Stasi complex with its gigantic, Kafkaesque layout, where you find one building labeled FEDERAL ARCHIVE, with the emblem on it bearing the federal eagle. A woman who used to work in a market research institute is responsible for the two of us. That is, she read all of our files—43 volumes of them—before we did, and processed them. She gives me, or us, the two or three volumes we want, and then we can examine them in the Reading Room, where of course other "readers" are also sitting looking at their files. You are given forms on which you write anything you want copies of. You must try to write out in full any names you want included on the copies, because names are blacked out to keep people and information confidential. But anyone who works in the Federal Archive can get hold of our files if they really want to. An anonymous woman journalist once phoned us and said that she had the file card for our Stasi files and no longer needed it, and she wanted to know if she should send it back to us. But she ended up not sending it anyway. I don't know by what right these files about me, and about others, were stock-piled and later made available to outside parties for evaluation—except to find out who may have been guilty of past criminal offenses.

Well, those are the outward facts. I am telling you about them so that you can picture something of what is meant by the phrase "examining your Stasi files." (A further detail is that the majority of our files are housed in a green, iron-rimmed, wooden box, which we call the "sea chest" and is stored in a room labeled "Temporary Storage Room.") But what are the inner facts that result from read-ing the files? Why, in the first few days, did I feel so worn out when I finished reading mine that I took the subway to the Alexan-derplatz and went into one of the stores to buy some piece of junk, or to a café where I blindly ate a cream cake, something I normally avoid? (It's the same syndrome I have observed in myself after an audience with a political bigwig from whom I was trying to extract a favor for someone.) Oddly, it's not rage I feel, it's a mixture of hopelessness and humiliation—and not because, as we have now discovered, the two of us together were under close observation from 1969 on in what was called "Operation Double-Tongue" and were considered under permanent suspicion of subversive activity, "PUT" and "PiD" (political subversion and political-ideological sabotage). I observed my reactions pretty carefully, and when I read the first files, which began very early to classify us as potentially harmful to the state, I almost felt satisfaction: at least this govern-ment did not view me as its "state poet." Then we read the tele-phone records (mostly summaries of bugged conversations), and then many incredibly long reports made by one of our closest friends which included material about the private affairs of our daughters; occasional reports of conversations monitored directly from our apartment; records of searches. We found a report stating that some of our friends had been influenced by the rumor that was deliberately spread about me after the expulsion of Wolf Biermann, according to which I had secretly reverted to the "party line" about Biermann.[5] Blueprints of our house and of the inside of our apart-

5. Wolf Biermann (born 1936): see source note to "Rummelplatz, the Eleventh Plenum . . . ," above, note 1 to "Two Letters," above, and note 8 to "Hours of Weakness, Hours of Strength," below. Also, compare Biermann's own article about Wolf's publica-

ment were among the items that hurt me the most. There was a description of "legends" that were invented about particular "IM's" to enable them to infiltrate our circle.[6] And then came an incident that involves you, which was recorded in admirable detail.

Do you remember the physicist from Berlin, the specialist in high-frequency engineering who had studied in Leningrad, then worked at an institute there, and used to visit you fairly often? You first met him in a bookstore where you were selling books. He was a lover of literature (he may very well have been that, *besides* being a spy). I have forgotten his name; I only know his cover names, which were used by the Stasi to refer to him: "Werner" and then "Timur." Informal collaborator "Timur" was given the assignment to visit us—because they knew we had seen you in Leningrad—to give us your greetings and to find out how we would react to the news of your dismissal from the Institute and of your intention to leave the Soviet Union. We trustingly met him in a restaurant in Berlin; then he visited us once more in our apartment and reported in minute detail that we took a great interest in your fate, did not wish to break off our friendship with you on any account, were thinking about how we could let you have some of the money that we had in Moscow, and so on. That may have told the Stasi people some things they wanted to know—but what prompted "Timur" to lend them his services? In this case, by the way, the Stasi were working with the KGB, which was once again keeping a close eye on you; a short document in Russian is included in our file.

Anyhow, we now have a complete record of everything we did for a decade. Our files for the period after 1980 have been almost completely destroyed. But what depresses me so, when I read all this? I believe I object on quasi-artistic grounds: I feel insulted as a person by having been reduced to this yes-or-no question: Is she or isn't she an enemy of the state? It hurts me to have our life so trivialized, made so banal, in these unspeakably silly IM reports. Don't you find that laughable? As if secretly one could expect the Stasi to

---

tion of *What Remains* in "Family Arguments," translated by Martin Chalmers in *The Idea of Switzerland* (New York: Granta, Spring 1991).

6. IM = *inoffizieller Mitarbeiter*, "unofficial" or "informal collaborator." The term was used of ordinary citizens who were recruited by the GDR state police to report on the activities of friends and colleagues.

show any kind of respect for the inscrutability of people who produce art!

Joking aside, I must get a bit closer to the contradictory feelings I have in reading the files. Because one part of my "multiple personality" experiences all this nonsense as something for which I am personally to blame, even though I am the target of it and even though I stopped identifying with the people who did it a long time ago. But I did identify with them once, and an echo of that still reaches me from these files. I have to wonder how many moral systems I have taken on board in my life and partly "internalized," and why it took me so long and I felt such conflicts in separating from them each time. Also, I am somewhat shaken by how much I dutifully repressed. My already deep distrust of my own memory is now intensifying and turning into an increasingly strong distrust of myself, which I can barely overcome when I write. Each sentence seems to me a lie before I have even finished writing it. Is this what the Russian authors you plan to talk about felt? Dostoevsky—he did, yes. But Chekhov, too? I am looking forward very much to your essay.

I will break off now. You no doubt noticed long ago that my letter is addressed to myself as well as to you. I will send a copy to Lew too. Along with this I'll send you a copy of *What Remains*. Do you want copies of "Timur's" reports on you? No doubt you would remember the man, but for what purpose? I too am somewhat at a loss as to what one should do with information of this kind. Václav Havel, after inspecting his files, is said to have remarked sadly: "I hope I have forgotten it already." He is a better person than I am.

Dear Efim Etkind, I am happy that you wrote to me, and I send you warm greetings, from Gerd as well as from me.

Yours,
Christa Wolf

Mood Fit

➤➤ ◄◄

M y body is moving away from me in the same way that time
is moving away from me, though probably not at the same
speed, this sentence occurred to me while I was brushing my teeth,
and at the same time I could not help thinking that I said to you
this evening after we went to the popular movie *Basic Instinct* and
were eating lamb chops later, somewhat upset, in the steakhouse on
the Kudamm, that I well understood Yuri Trifonov's remark that
the libido of writing can be lost as a person ages, and I remembered
how dismayed I was to hear that from him of all people, but you
did not want any excuses, you asked: Was I still thinking of a public
instead of simply trying to gain clarity about myself as was necessary and to write only for myself? and just now I have remembered
that my first impulse was to contradict you as it always is in such
cases, but then to my own surprise I simply said yes and enjoyed
admitting to you that you were right, and in the aftertaste of this
feeling it occurred to me what I could have brought in evidence
against you, Kafka, for example, who before he could write a word
felt compelled, even in his will, to guard against the risk of his
works being published, and who chose as the executor of this order

First published in the German edition of this book.

a friend about whom he could be sure that he would ignore his last will, while protecting himself from realizing this by means of a complicated system of self-deception, and there is nothing to smile about in that, I thought, I at least have absolutely stopped smiling at such transparent maneuvers, I can tell you, and I read with satisfaction that Virginia Woolf, of all people, one day decided it was time to gauge the effects of discouragement on the mind of the artist, because literature is sowed with the wrecks of men who (she says) against all reason gave some importance to the opinions of others; so that I am happy to see that this uncommonly shameful event, namely that I allow myself to feel discouraged by people I have learned to despise and whom I nevertheless permit to harm me to the point of feeling destroyed by them—so that this event, I should like you to understand, is legitimized by the highest authority and this legitimation gives me relief, against all reason, so that the fact that I am *allowed* to be discouraged gives me a wee bit of courage and, as a result, a sort of faint thought can arise that some time or other I may perhaps again be able to wrest words from this persistent suspicion of my own insincerity

or, I wonder, will I never again muster the joy and impudence to take in my stride the distortions and falsifications that inevitably arise during the conversion of experience into written sentences, that is, will my moral reservation, which has long since become dangerously powerful, nip in the bud permanently any frank, free, pleasurable, cheeky piece of writing, judging it as arrogant, as a lie and as something to which I am not entitled, so that the gap that exists between honest, wordless, not-yet-thinking knowledge on the one hand and the written text on the other—this gap that now looks to me like an abyss—will become something that I am finally unable to face?—I ask myself coolly, and also of course I must take into account that my name has been devalued, yes, in part I experienced it as a disgrace, this attempt by others to discourage me, though they would indignantly deny the pleasure they took in it, but their choice of words has betrayed them—so I think this evening, without anger and sorrow, and tell myself that I will no longer throw my name into this encircled field of carnage that is called the literature business and that brews a poison that has destroyed many by disintegrating the substance that fed their writing, namely the remnant of self-confidence they needed in order to write, I think

I,

however, I promise you, my dear, will find myself a new name and, riding on this deception, behind my own back will again smuggle words onto paper, using my false name as a shield I will climb back into the murderous fray, unrecognized and invulnerable and fool-hardy, laughing I will pay them in false coin, that is what I resolve; wearing my cloak of invisibility I will rain blows on the slave-drivers and they will not be able to see where the blows come from, and in the end I will no longer be myself, and that will be good, because then at night I will once again have dreams that will quietly remind me of who I am.

Caught Talking

Otl Aicher

→→ ←←

In May 1988, when Otl Aicher looked at next year's calendar and set the date for us to meet again—September 29, 1989—we looked at each other: Could we stick to an appointment that we fixed a year and a half in advance? Admittedly we had spent two days and two nights at Rotis, but we didn't know Otl Aicher well enough to understand his precision, or the way that he treated time as a unit to measure activity, or the absolute seriousness of his belief: "It is what you do that produces the meaning." All the exalted notions about freedom, autonomy, and self-realization become real only in everyday use.

It seems we only gradually came to understand what we were seeing. And what were we seeing? A property on the fringes of the Allgäu region in the Federal Republic of Germany. Cultivated land, meadows from which strange shapes rise up, buildings useful and beautiful, wood-clad structures with zigzag roofs and skylights: the

First published in Otl Aicher, *schreiben und widersprechen* (Berlin: Gerhard Wolf, Janus Press, 1993).

offices where, among other things, the new typescript was developed in which this book is printed: "rotis."

They were expecting us in the old house, the residential building, the core of that sensitive cluster of dwellings and workplaces which, along with the people who live in them, make up the "Autonomous Republic of Rotis." There is humor in this name they have given themselves, but it is no joke. So there we stood in the "old" house, trying to figure out how the space was divided up; what purpose might be served by the individual areas we could make out, which were often separated from each other only by metal screens that appeared to be the main furniture, supplying shelves and places to store all sorts of objects. Newspapers, books, made up the walls. The angle of the light was carefully planned. Wood. A projecting glass porch with a large table where you could sit, eat, talk while looking out onto the fields as the darkness gradually fell.

We ate simply and well; Otl Aicher did the cooking. Standing in that kitchen, you have to ask yourself: where is the logical place to put a particular cooking utensil, a particular piece of crockery? If you have thought about it properly, you will find the object in that place. White stackable dishes; silverware, ladles, kitchen tools of the most practical sort that Otl Aicher could find after studying cooking and kitchen design and drawing up a design plan for a kitchen contractor to carry out. The chopping board where you can cut things up and immediately push the waste scraps into the opening in the middle. Evidently there is an optimal sequence to every operation, a correct way to perform every task. Gradually we understood that this correctness was something Otl Aicher found out by listening attentively. By concentration and empathy with the operations themselves, he helped them to realize their potential of perfection, that is: to move, to become active. This, among other things, is what he calls design. Of course, we are under no compulsion to organize our culinary activities along the same lines as he and Inge do; but we have seen his kitchen and from now on we will compare every other kitchen to it. We will know that it is possible to grow herbs and vegetables in raised beds so that you don't have to bend down in order to cultivate and harvest them. And at midnight I saw Otl Aicher standing in his kitchen, enjoying it and listening devoutly to find out what sort of food he wanted to snack on and where his tastebuds were headed at that moment.

Gradually the spirit of place revealed itself to us, we were seized by that mood that goes with harmoniousness and unfolds out of exact reflection and cool-headed decisions. Efficiency is not the supreme value. It would have been more efficient to hook up Rotis to the public power grid. But the turbine whose roaring we heard day and night, and which we were permitted to view, supplies more than electricity; it generates technical know-how, a sense of responsibility, a feeling of independence—and also delight in this elegant, natural, technical solution: the cycle that runs back and forth between two streams. Independence is the core and hub of Otl Aicher's labors, which focus not on individual, isolated phenomena but on achieving a way of life worthy of a human being. The "Autonomous Republic of Rotis." A blueprint that is meant seriously, taken seriously.

What did we talk about with our wine, far into the night? About that very thing: How could we—real people in specific circumstances—live in a way befitting human beings? In other words, about whether and how we could change our circumstances. In other words, about politics. Inge and Otl Aicher asked us many questions, were ravenous for concrete details about that other Germany where we lived. So we told them stories, gave examples, life histories, events. We would often laugh grimly at some punch line while they remained grave and thoughtful. The pressure was building up in the GDR, we said, and the protest from the grassroots was not meeting with any understanding from those "on top," so how could it end? Inge and Otl wanted to know who was protesting, against what, when, where, how many. How the government reacted to it. What kind of surveillance measures there were, what they felt like. The press in the Federal Republic was still saying that a reform process within the GDR might introduce gradual change; we said we no longer believed in that. Did we believe in violence? they asked. We shrugged. The regime would not step down voluntarily, but how would the Soviet Union react? The Aichers were troubled. Otl reached above his head for paper and pencils, which of course lay at hand on a metal screen hanging from the ceiling. He began to take notes, to make drawings; he began to analyze the situation in terms of simple, verifiable assumptions. He began to unfurl the possibilities, to label different routes that were bound to lead to different results. It was fun to watch him thinking. It was heartening to test our critical thinking against his. What is now reality in Germany today is a possibility that none of us considered.

Some time that evening I became aware that this was a conversation between Germans. And at least on our side we urgently needed this discussion to expand our field of vision and to sharpen our eyes. During the decades of division and beginning from different starting-points, our views seemed to have moved closer together. I experienced this accord as happiness. Within the precinct of this house one could dream of republican attitudes and forget for hours at a time that in Germany such attitudes had never flourished except in minorities. One of Inge and Otl Aicher's sons arrived, accompanied by a friend with whom he was researching the history of the civil war in Swabia, very close to Rotis. Upstairs, Inge kept the archive of the "White Rose." She brought it out, and Sophie and Hans Scholl, Inge's sister and brother and Otl's friends, were present with us.[1] During the night, with deep excitement, I read unpublished letters written by the Scholl family, parents and siblings, during the time of their imprisonment after Sophie and Hans were murdered. *This* was really the "other" Germany. I dare to say it because Otl Aicher himself used the same phrase. For two days and two nights the Wall had no meaning.

We were at Rotis in May, and we celebrated Otl's birthday with him and his co-workers. There was whole-grain brown bread, ham, sausage, beer; we sat outside at wooden tables, I remember the tender green foliage and the transparent light. During the night I felt the onset of the appendicitis that it took me so long to recognize—almost too long—and that brought me into the hospital all summer and prevented me from doing any work.

In 1988, Otl Aicher wrote a series of political essays, but we had

---

1. Inge Scholl (born 1917) compiled the book *Die Weiße Rose* (translated by Arthur Schultz as *The White Rose* [Middletown, CT: Wesleyan University Press, 1983]) about the White Rose anti-Nazi resistance group, made up of university students, scholars, and artists, that operated in Munich in 1942–43. The leaders, Sophie Scholl (1921–43) and Hans Scholl (1918–43), were imprisoned and executed in 1943. Christa Wolf was awarded the commemorative Geschwister Scholl Prize in November 1987.

not yet read them by September 29, 1989, when he and Inge arrived with a big suitcase at the tiny train station near our home in Mecklenburg ("Only the precise becomes concrete," Otl says). If we had been familiar with his essays, we would no doubt have realized how and why he had set his hopes—for his own nation and for himself too—on the revolutionary movement that was now underway in the GDR; and we would also have understood why he was so insistent on defining the popular uprising at the end of the GDR as a revolution.

But we had read several of his other books in the meantime, *Die Küche zum Kochen* (The kitchen for cooking), *typographie* (typography), *gehen in der wüste* (Walking in the desert), and especially *innenseiten des kriegs* (The inside pages of war), a book in which we found, among other things, a description of his intellectual and political development up to the time when he became a deserter in World War II, and his philosophical credo, which he defends chiefly by reference to the later Wittgenstein, whom he admires for his "heroic" decision to "turn himself upside down" again.

"Thought becomes manifest only in action"; "I always had an underdeveloped capacity for faith but a high degree of confidence in what I saw and could touch. I corresponded with the world through a sort of visual language and a sort of grasping thought; I leaned toward a consciousness that derived from contemplation, from looking at things, and I relied on what could be held, on the tangible." Before we got to know his principles, we had the opportunity to see how he realized them. We could continue our dialogue with exact information about each other.

There is a great difference between the work center at Rotis and our old vicarage in Woserin, and the difference involves more than what Otl Aicher described as our shortage of lumber. We had been looking for a place like this. Increasingly we felt that the Berlin of the seventies and eighties was exhausting and destructive. The many demands that people made on us—with our consent— were getting harder and harder to combine with our work. Also we harbored the illusion that the eyes and ears of the government would be less able to keep track of us in the countryside. We were looking for a free space. But it was a series of fortunate accidents that led us to this particular property, a former church holding, after our first farmhouse burned down. Equally accidental—and far removed from the efficient perfection of Rotis—was the condition of the house and grounds. Fixed up as much as we could manage, given the materials, craftsmen, and time at our disposal, it was an improvised work and, as far as the land was concerned, still largely uncultivated. We ourselves were satisfied with our efforts, but someone who had not seen the house and its surroundings as they were at the start could not really judge the results. What would the severe gaze of Otl Aicher make of our typically Eastern semiwilderness?

He thought it extraordinary that we had so many devices for receiving news into our home, something we took for granted. The pressure in the GDR had built up enormously since our last meeting, and the government was flying in the face of political reason by not opening up an emergency vent. The Hungarians did it for them. But rights granted too late, unwillingly and in the wrong way, don't stop people from demanding other rights, all the other rights—quite to the contrary. The week before Otl Aicher came to visit us, the number of people taking part in the Monday demonstration in Leipzig rose to tens of thousands. We returned to Woserin only because of the Aichers. All our attention was focused on Berlin. We knew the plans of several citizens groups that wanted to achieve their goals nonviolently through dialogue with the government. We knew or suspected that the other side had drawn up scenarios to maintain power that included violence. I notice that now, two and a half years later, as I read Otl Aicher's description of those days—a description that sums up the conversations we were having day and night—even I can hardly remember the suspense we felt then. On October 2, the day of the Aichers' departure, the cry resounded in Leipzig: "We are the people!"

But despite the political situation, we wanted to show the Aichers Mecklenburg, which we love. "The land is beautiful," Otl Aicher writes. "The clouds are the same on both sides of the border." Looking at the land with their eyes, we saw that its beauty stood the test, while the signs of abandonment and decay in the little towns and villages looked more pronounced. We went through the side roads of Güstrow. There was a lot to do there. The Aichers' commentaries were frugal, empathetic, never insulting. Standing beside Otl and

Inge, we saw with new eyes the Barlach statues that we had looked at so often before. I remember pausing for a long time in front of the "Doubter" and the "Man Walking in the Wind," and being especially moved by "The Reunion," a man and woman embracing, although I could not have explained why. Then we saw the hovering figure with the face of Käthe Kollwitz in a dark side niche of the cathedral. The Aichers had never looked at art so far east before. In the museum shop, Otl and I each bought a volume about the Barlach statues, we each wrote down the same inscription, and all four of us signed our names twice, once in each book. Then we exchanged the volumes with mock solemnity. Our self-mockery had something serious about it. We were East and West Germans, meeting on equal footing in the presence of a great German artist. The breath of a vision touched us fleetingly: Couldn't all our meetings be like this, an easy crossing back and forth, unhindered by spiteful border checks, a give and take, a meeting to which each brought what was his own?

A utopia. We have an urgent job to do, we have to form a government—was Otl's view. He worried about the people in the GDR, about the tireless citizens of Leipzig at their Monday demonstrations, about what would happen to Berliners after the national holiday that was just about to be celebrated. "We are the people"— later we would read in his books how deeply he was moved by this watchword, and what far-ranging conclusions he drew from it when he planned a new commonwealth suited to our times.

He wanted to help save this precious German revolution, he didn't want to see it stifled in a bloodbath. The pictures from Tiananmen Square burned their way into us all, we sat in front of the television crying. We realized that Otl Aicher did not fancy having to watch similar pictures of Berlin Alexanderplatz on his safe television screen back at Rotis.

We all knew that the people's movement had to continue and would. But Otl Aicher begged us to be shrewd and cautious and to try to secure a transition to a true people's government, by keeping some of the old politicians in power. We must try to prevent all the alarm bells from going off and making the old guard blow their fuses, he said. He also said: We in the West can't help you, that could mean war, in spite of Gorbachev. Did we realize what a tight spot

Gorbachev might be in if there were a sudden collapse on the western flank of the Soviet empire? Instead we should tread warily, introduce a gradual step-by-step transition.—A ridiculous discussion? Perhaps.

That was not the only time that we drew up a list of hypothetical members for a new government, but it was the first. Concrete memories of this sort testify that hope was truly sprouting. For a very brief moment in history, hope shot up into the air, created active but short-lived institutions, then quickly collapsed again so that today we can hardly believe our own memories of that time. This is the trajectory that Otl Aicher describes in his book of essays (*schreiben und widersprechen*). He experienced it along with us in a way that very few West Germans did, because after the many profound political disappointments he had undergone in his life he once more felt a young man's hope that it was possible to create a democratic German republic, a state which, unlike all the German states that had come after Hegel and Bismarck, would have no "higher idea" behind it other than "the lowliest subject." He thought it possible that the mass movement in the GDR would lead to a new start and would then be in a position to organize change, and itself could generate the "new faces" to govern the country. This did not happen, as we know today and as Otl Aicher too learned eventually. He wanted to take the wish list we had drawn up for a new government with him across the border, through the checkpoints, when he left for home. With Inge's support we were able to take the list away from him when we said goodbye, and kept it at our place.

We ate river crabs and pike, both from the lake by our village, along with cress and lettuce from the garden. In exchange for the nettle soup that Inge had made for us at Rotis, we served sorrel soup. It was a happy moment, especially for Gerd, when Otl said: "Inge, the cooking here is as good as in our house." The dark Mecklenburg rye bread earned praise. The beech forest on the far side of the lake was still green, the autumn colors didn't come until later. We walked along the edge of the shrubbery; I complained to Inge that I had already taught my grandchildren all the songs I knew and I needed some new ones. She understood the problem and taught me: "Poor foreigner that I am, I am weary of marching."

Did they still want to see the excavation of the Slavic settlement at Gross-Raden? we asked. Yes, absolutely. "Well done," Otl
commented in his laconic way, and I noticed that I was tempted
to feel proud of this display of artefacts from a premedieval Slavic
settlement, even though I was not sure whether he meant the
craftsmanship of the ancient Slavs or the way our contemporaries
had presented them in the museum. What interested him most
were the evidences of everyday culture, a wooden plow, ceramic
dishware, wooden tools; the way the pieces of lumber for the worship hall were cut, how they were fitted. We talked about the fact
that things develop differently in different places within the same
time period: the early Middle Ages had taken quite another form
farther west with regard to cultural artefacts, building techniques,
and craftsmanship. Otl Aicher writes with admiration about medieval cathedrals. How silly it is for us to want to transfer our Western
culture to the rest of the world—both its high level of technology
and the destruction of our resources that it entails—or even to use
it as a measuring rod for the standard achieved by another culture.
Otl Aicher urgently warned us not to make the mistake of taking
the living standard of West Germany as the primary goal of change
in the GDR. Back then our skepticism still had its limits, and, as I
remember, we believed that people in the GDR were in a mood to
engage in independent projects and experiments, to "prepare to live
humanly in the world," as Otl put it.

It didn't bother Otl and Inge that it was often impossible to find
a restaurant where we could eat lunch. Warned by past experience,
we brought along a well-stocked picnic basket. Traveling in the
same area a few days ago, we noticed a number of new restaurant
signs in the villages. I gave a reading in the same little Mecklenburg town—and to almost the same group of people—whom I met
in early October 1989, in my last public debate before the uprising
that led to the collapse of the GDR and is now known as the *Wende*
or "turning point."

At the time I much regretted that Inge and Otl Aicher could
not be with us on the evening of the debate, to see how the upheaval
had reached this little corner of the land and how the people, who
were stirred up and at the same time were politically shrewd, spoke
out fearlessly, and in very personal terms, about the need for change.

All this gave me a feeling of confidence during the turbulent weeks in Berlin that followed.

When I returned to this same area a few days ago, the meeting had somehow grown musty. People asked what was going to happen next, whereas two and a half years ago—two and a half years is an age—they asked not others but themselves. Should I tell them what I had just read in Otl Aicher: "What would I do? Reintroduce work as the basis of our existence, of our self-esteem, and of our social credentials."—The region of Mecklenburg–Western Pomerania has the highest unemployment rate in Germany. The revolution that is still dreamed about in Otl Aicher's books was doomed to failure. Future historians will analyze whether it really was a revolution. German unification "is being carried out." How farseeing are the reflections that Otl Aicher recorded in 1990. What disappointment, what sarcasm, what bitterness, what anger, what radicality.

To think that we will no longer, never again, be able to speak with him, never again listen to him, never again see new work produced or be able to read new writings. He was a great teacher. His loss hurts me now as it did on the very first day. His time, I think, is bound to come. Perhaps his pupils are only now being born.

The Faces of Anna Seghers

A Picture Book

➤➤ ◄◄

O nce in the mid-fifties, not long after we met, I was sitting at
the same table with Anna Seghers, who was acting as hostess
at a dinner in honor of foreign writers. (At that time I was a young
editor at a publishing house.) One of the guests got carried away
during a toast and wished everyone present "at least one more life."
I saw a look of shock, almost of horror, on the face of Anna Seghers
and heard her say: "For heaven's sake! One life is quite long
enough!" But then she wiped away the impression that this sentence had made by flashing us one of her characteristic smiles,
which she could make appear and disappear again in fractions of a
second. Her eyes did not join in the smile.

Much later I came to realize that this smile—polite, perhaps
heartfelt, but in any case pacifying and soothing—was one of her

First published in *Neue Deutsche Literatur* 12 (1992) and reprinted in the photo biography *Anna Seghers. Eine Biographie in Bildern. Mit einem Essay von Christa Wolf,* edited
by Frank Wagner, Ursula Emmerich, and Ruth Radvanyi (Berlin: Aufbau Verlag, 1994).
Anna Seghers was the pen name of Netty Radvanyi, née Netty Reiling (1900–1983), a
social-documentary writer. A Jew and a Communist, she fled the Nazis but returned to
East Germany in 1947 and became prominent in the GDR Writers Union.

hiding places. I saw it often, on a wide variety of occasions. I never again saw the expression of shock that I observed on the night of the dinner. But I did not forget it, and I often seemed to see it glimmering through her everyday face, a signal I could not interpret at first and that I only gradually understood bore witness to a life whose tragic features she wished to hide. Anna Seghers would have firmly rejected a word like "tragic." Once she told me I should not always write about "those unhappy women," by which she meant not only "Christa T." but also Karoline von Günderrode, to whom she herself had drawn my attention when she included Günderrode in the same sentence with Hölderlin, Büchner, Kleist, Lenz, and Bürger.[1] "These German writers wrote hymns to their country while rubbing their heads raw on the wall of German society. They loved their country all the same." Then I knew: a person does not write such words unless she herself has been initiated into a particular kind of unhappiness, which she saw as specifically *German*. If Anna Seghers's life left a mark on her face, then what it wrote there was unceasing effort, the signs of excessive strain followed by too great a weariness. She tried with all her might to lift this verdict of unhappiness from herself and her generation. I think she knew she didn't have that power. She didn't talk about it.

When she spoke those lines about the "raw heads" of German writers, she was giving a speech at the First International Writers' Congress in Defense of Culture in Paris; she was thirty-five and had already been driven out of Germany.[2] I studied the changes in her face on the photos taken before that one in Paris where she is wearing a hat. There is the picture of her as a very young woman, really

1. Karoline von Günderrode (1780–1806), a romantic writer, is the subject of Wolf's novel *Kein Ort. Niegends,* translated by Jan van Heurck as *No Place on Earth* (New York: Farrar, Straus & Giroux, 1982), and of her long essay "Der Schatten eines Traumes," translated as "The Shadow of a Dream" in *The Author's Dimension* (see footnote, page 3 above). Bettine (Bettina) Brentano (later von Arnim, 1785–1859) was an author, a member of the romantic circle, the sister of Clemens Brentano, the wife of Achim von Arnim, and a friend and correspondent of Karoline von Günderrode.

2. Seghers was a noted speaker at all three of the international writers' congresses held in Paris in 1935, 1937, and 1938, which helped to mobilize antifascist intellectuals in Europe and brought together socialist and humanist writers, including many Germans who had fled from the Nazis, with opponents of the right-wing forces gathering strength in Spain, Italy, and other nations.

still a girl, with brown hair, a dark dress with a round neck, leaning against a cabinet and showing her profile to the viewer as she did over and over in later pictures—a "pure" profile, a face that announces a perfect and strange beauty. Then there is that other photo which lets you understand how Carl Zuckmayer could have compared the young Anna Seghers to a "Javanese temple dancer," a creature who could not fit in among the "pallid petty-bourgeois clans" and was repelled by them. "Even as a university student I was still very childlike. I was much more of a child than I ought to have been at that age." As far as I know, she never concerned herself with psychological theories; but she may have realized that this kind of prolonged "childlikeness," which often was criticized as "lack of sophistication," represented a gift, an ability to hold open longer than others the gates to her own unconscious, to refrain from letting herself be ruled completely by the reality principle, which kills the practice of art at its root. At that time she would not allow inner dams to regulate and supervise her "torrent of writing." She trusted the "first impression"—a point that she insisted on later, in debates in which art was under attack. The marks of the ordeals she went through are written in her face, and so are the marks of renunciation, of disappointment, of suppressed passions, of suppressed grief and doubt. In the end she was forced to build dams, but in her finest writings she broke through them again and again, right up to the last years of her life.

"Justice" was a word she used as a young woman, and "The liberty of the Marseillaise: liberty, my beloved." Her life had a full sound to it, it was "full up," an expression she always loved.

Anna Seghers: German Jew, Communist, writer, woman, mother. Think about each of these words. So many contradictory identities, some appearing to be mutually exclusive; so many deep and painful commitments, so many target zones, so many challenges and demands, so many ways to get hurt, to be marooned, even to risk death. A person like her, with her conviction and conscience, could not help but become the battleground of opposing forces in this century—forces that were or merely seemed opposed and must often have looked equally strong to her so that each choice she made involved a bitter decision and forced her to close out a

Netty Reiling (Anna Seghers), ca. 1920. © Ruth Radranyi. From *Anna Seghers. Eine Biographie in Bildern* (see page 175, footnote).

piece of herself. To complain about this was forbidden in the times when she had to make her decisions, and increasingly she felt barred from even speaking of it. And with whom could she have spoken? I never heard her talk about what it meant to her to be excluded from the German people, to whom she felt she intimately belonged. We who were born later took it for granted that in her life as an émigré she tried wherever she could to make people see that German fascism was not the same thing as the German people and that the first victims of German fascism were Germans. She never talked about homesickness; she never spoke except in the dispassionate tone of a reporter about the difficulties of her first years in France, when she truly was among the "most homeless of this world." And least of all was she able to talk about the events that affected her the most deeply: the way her mother was deported from Mainz and died in a camp in Poland. Walking through the destroyed city of Mainz after she returned to Germany in 1947—a return that could not be described as a "homecoming" and that brought her to the loneliest, most desolate years of her life—she saw a devastated, "bewitched" country and disfigured people whom she no longer recognized, who knew nothing about her or people like her and who did not want to know anything about them, at least not for the time being. There is a small, full-face photo of her with gray hair. Her expression is one of grief, shock, sorrow. The feeling that she was going to "freeze up." A forty-seven-year-old writer whose most important novel had for years enjoyed international success was unknown in the Germany of 1947.[3] Who could blame her and her comrades for clinging so long to the hope they slowly began to have for this country, for the GDR, long after there were still any reasons for hope?

No amount of imagination makes it thinkable that she could have lived a different life, a life in some other place. In the 1940s the United States barred her and her family from traveling to North America, and the only other country where she could go was Mexico. But the FBI kept her under strict surveillance even there, tracking her activities, her correspondence, and her books, as a Ger-

3. The 1942 anti-Nazi novel *Das siebte Kreuz* (English translation *The Seventh Cross*) was an instant success and was translated into many languages all over the world. It was made into a film in the United States.

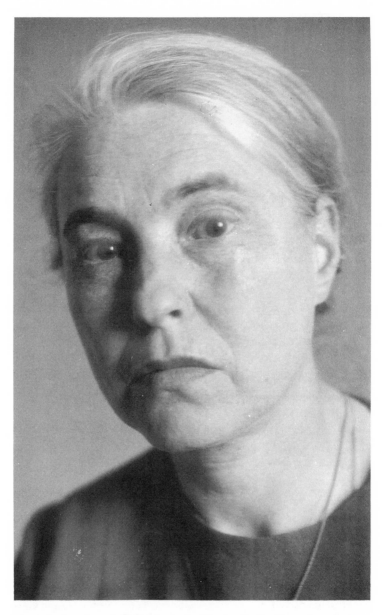

Anna Seghers (1947). © Akademie der Künske, Berlin. From *Anna Seghers.*
Eine Biographie in Bildern (see page 175, footnote).

man scholar learned later from reading her files after her death.[4] And the cold war made her persona non grata in her home town of Mainz in West Germany, where she was frequently the object of political attack while at the same time feeling homesick for Mainz from her new home in the sober city of Berlin.

No, she had no choice. But I'm not implying that she would have wanted one. Her lot in life was to feel responsible for this part of divided Germany and to work to bring the GDR a little closer to the idea of justice that had been her motto since she was a girl. She took on too many tasks that were obstacles to her writing. Another likely hindrance to her writing was an ambivalence that she must have experienced more deeply than we younger writers and that she kept to herself, even though she had been able to speak of it with great vividness and empathy when she found it in her literary forebears. She didn't want to allow herself to feel sadness because her experience told her that sadness would weaken her. "Well, how do you think I feel?" she said once. "At ten o'clock every evening we talk about Stalin." In 1957 she wrote to a friend: "I have a great longing for a particular sort of world in which one can work and breathe and sometimes be insanely happy. At the moment that is rather rare."

We don't know everything about her. We are far from knowing all about her hidden motives and actions, and we will never find out. Almost all the witnesses are dead. She often behaved differently from other people, and differently too from how people expected her to behave. Many times I saw her save a hopeless situation by clever intervention, and resolve complicated problems by sheer persistence. No doubt spontaneity was one of her fundamental qualities, how else could she have been a writer? But she kept herself under a tight rein. She had learned to control herself, and when she failed, she was always aware of it and had a reason. She knew how to use anger and amazement and wit and mischievousness and naï-

---

4. The scholar Alexander Stephan published his book *Im Visier des FBI* (In the sights of the FBI) (Stuttgart and Weimar: J. B. Metzler Verlag, 1995) after studying FBI files on German antifascist writers who had fled to the U.S.A. for asylum during the Nazi period and who were subjected to long-term surveillance by a U.S. government fearful of their emancipatory ideas and their possible influence on postwar German and U.S. politics.

veté, and she could judge when and with whom to use them. No photographer seems to have snapped her picture at any of those moments.

She was not just following fashion when she, as a writer, would spend time with workers. Her photos show her looking inquisitive and attentive, and she behaved in that way toward her readers. She could be taken at her word. She hated self-centeredness. I saw her at times when she looked perplexed, suspicious, haggard, and disappointed—disappointed in me too, incidentally, when I no longer saw a possibility of mediating between irreconcilable opposites. She was afraid we might put at risk the thing she couldn't help but value the most: the continued existence of our commonwealth, where she thought she could see possibilities, however buried, that were worthy of human beings and could develop further, given more favorable conditions. She did not deny the contradictions but she refused to regard them as insoluble. Did she go as far as she could? I ask the question with hesitation. The limits were drawn tighter and tighter; she could not and did not wish to break through them. Her story *Der gerechte Richter* (The just judge) didn't work.[5] The conflict that produced it was one she could not resolve in herself. Her just judge didn't exist, and her longing couldn't create him.

Many of her books met with opposition and reserve, "even from comrades." That did not sway her. Anna Seghers believed that oppressed and exploited people would always set out in search of the "true blue." Life could not wear away this belief, which she acquired not from her own limited experience but from a more remote source, just as she took many of her fictional themes from the faraway, from ancient traditions, from myths and sagas. She had the gaze of the epic writer, which embraces many time zones at once, and she tried—especially in her work but in other contexts as well—to help other people to achieve greater serenity when they were too narrow in their focus, too fixed in time. She was able to take a sovereign view of our unhappy, ragged age, to take it as an image, she was able to laugh. She came sweeping down the stairs

5. *Der gerechte Richter*, a half-finished novella written by Anna Seghers in 1957/58 and unpublished in her lifetime, was printed in fragmentary form after her death (Berlin and Weimar: Aufbau Verlag, 1990) by people concerned that her work was being

Anna Seghers at Wiepersdorf. © Ruth Radvnyi.
From *Anna Seghers. Eine Biographie in
Bildern* (see page 175, footnote).

of her workplace, Wiepersdorf, which had been Bettine's estate,
with the ease of a young woman.[6] Anna cut a figure whom only she
could have described, a combination of entirely earthly traits and
mysterious, legendary ones. Artemis, unknown to all. She did not
particularly wish to emphasize her otherness. She suppressed much
of the magic of her nature in order to adapt to others who were
anything but magical. She was shy, modest, and attentive even
when her mind was on something else. Jorge Amado wrote that he,
Ilya Ehrenburg, and Pablo Neruda had viewed her as their "sister,"
as their "fairy"—"No one in the world had as much charm and

ignored and even banned in the new Germany after unification because of her perceived failure to protest publicly against instances of repression under the GDR regime,
particularly the 1957 imprisonment after a show trial of Communist publisher Walter
Janka (born 1914). The publication of this story was intended to show that Seghers had
in fact been deeply troubled by the Janka case and had tried to write about it in fictional
form, and the accompanying essay by Günter Rücker raised questions about the cultural
purges of left-wing authors and the restoration of fascist authors in united Germany.

6. Bettine Brentano (1785–1851), Bettine von Arnim after her marriage, lived at
von Arnim's estate in Wiepersdorf and made it a center of liberal culture.

fantasy as Anna—so much, so much!" When I read that I thought for a moment: Why couldn't she have come into the world among more generous peoples who would have recognized her, loved her, and accepted her in their way? Why, I thought, did she have to be cast in among us Germans, who feel compelled to smash the fairy tale, the magical, who hardly notice charm and fail to understand when they are shown the vision of something that is completely earthly and yet not quite of this world?

Then I took back this thought. Anna Seghers would not have approved of it.

No, I can't make these pictures of her speak. When I looked one after another at the photos collected in this volume, it occurred to me how often since Anna Seghers's death I have thought I would have to write about her one more time as if I had never written about her before. I thought I would know when it was time to do it. I neither expected nor wished to be "objective." On the contrary, I am sure that detachment and a cool head would no more enable me to do her justice than would that lively, warm interest that I felt for her from the start and that has remained with me beyond her death. Now the great revaluation of all values has caught hold of her too. Now, once again, seems not the time to write about her "as if for the last time." Well, that may be so. We can't form a "final picture" of her yet; she is still stirring, still on the move. Isn't it possible that she may dig her way out again from the debris of history, which has buried her along with others, and that she may bring her best books out with her? Isn't it possible that what her generation achieved will not be permanently consigned to oblivion? That she will not be denied the respect that is due her, and that people will be able to acknowledge the measure of "friendliness" that she won by struggle against truly unfriendly circumstances, and will understand the terrible friction that she converted into energy for her work? And that they will do so generously and not merely with the "indulgence" that Brecht asked for himself?

The suitable view, the just evaluation, the verdict that doesn't keep silent about anything and doesn't gloss over anything—these are not possible yet. The fictional characters in the books of Anna Seghers may include some of the last revolutionaries in German literature. They appear to have cleared off the stage and vanished.

The intense, difficult reality of so many people's lives seems to be fading, all memory of them seems on the brink of extinction. The unease and fervor that filled them are no longer recognized. They allowed themselves to be buried. And yet what would the century be without them?

Santa Monica,
Sunday, September 27, 1992

➤➤ ◄◄

It's 9:45 A.M., I'm sitting in my office at the little computer, I have just made a mistake and deleted three pages of single-spaced type in which I described my first impressions of America the day before yesterday and which unfortunately I did not print out right away. Luckily I still have the pages of handwritten notes that I jotted down Thursday while I was waiting for the three suitcases I had sent by air freight. They arrived around 3:00 P.M., and then I could open the case with the little computer in it and phone Erin at the Getty Center to tell her the voltage so that she could drive downtown and buy the converter I need because the electrical current is not as strong here—but naturally the salesman didn't want to know the number of volts but the number of watts!—and now, God be praised, my little computer can write—and of course it can also delete what it shouldn't delete—but anyhow it spares me from having to get used to the Macintosh computer that the Center makes available to visiting scholars.

This morning I woke up shortly after six. My last dream image was of a blond girl, beautifully dressed, who was holding onto a

First published in the German edition of this book.

brightly painted railing and gazing abstractedly into the distance. No doubt this dream was inspired by an episode of the *Star Trek* series, which I watch devotedly in the evenings here and understand perfectly—though of course I don't understand things word for word, but I get the drift—and which yesterday was about a planet where the crew of the Enterprise met the physical embodiments of their dreams and were able to live out their fantasies. Among their imaginary experiences was a blond-haired girl dressed in old-fashioned clothing, Alice in Wonderland. I admit that the girl in my own dream looked different, and the sentence that surfaced later—"Of course I can't tell yet what depths are being plowed up here, the wheels are rolling and rolling and rolling"— came from a different, earlier dream sequence. I kept my eyes shut and cultivated that casual, absent-minded attention that sometimes allows you to fix the fleeting images of dreams in your memory, and, as I did so, that other, earlier dream gradually surfaced too. A long emigration dream. Gerhard and I were sitting in the car. It was clear that the "new money" was going to come and then we would have to emigrate. We asked a strange man with a broad, fur-covered nose, and he coolly confirmed that we had to go. Would many people "go"? No, we were told, most people wanted the "new money." In the dream, I became very aware that we were outsiders. The man who—our files said—was the "unofficial collaborator" assigned to spy on us for years, played a big role in my dream, as an assistant in our "move." At the end we were sitting jammed against him in the car. We were told we could take more things with us, and two women we knew well helped us to pack the car fuller and fuller. They said nothing and they had sad faces. I was thinking, I still have to telephone our daughters to say goodbye, but they knew all about it and would stay here. Pictures stored in my memory of how we had fled from the Russian troops early in 1945 resurfaced. Everything happened in that atmosphere of messiness, disaster, and homelessness that governs all my dreams.

(Yesterday morning, after seeing on TV pictures of new outrages committed by neo-Nazi youngsters in the former GDR—this is the only thing that people here in the United States see and hear about Germany—I watched interviews with German schoolchildren. Good, normal faces. Intelligent opinions. None of them favored the right-wingers, but no one knew what to do about them either. And what tortures me is that I don't know any more than they do, for I think this tendency of young people to drop out of society and look for a substitute in a pseudo-society—or, in bad cases, to drop out of civilized life altogether—is integral to industrial, efficiency-based societies, is part of their structure.)

I have to force myself to describe the first hours of the day—habits that are just beginning to become ingrained, that I won't remember unless I write them down. I can't rely on my memory even in small things, though I'm positively addicted to the details of everyday life—an addiction that makes me increasingly incapable of inventing anything that has the slightest tinge of the spectacular. But I must say it's hard to see why I want to note down that early in the morning, when I was in bed, I read Dietmar Kamper's notes about his first stay in New York in 1982. What I found illuminating are his reflections about the "displacement of desires" in this remarkable city, reflections emerging from the premise that the emancipation movements in Europe were and are self-deceptions because Europeans have been incapable of clear-cut action since the waning of the Middle Ages, and "knowing what we are doing" has always come after the fact, when it was too late.

So all the time I'm doing my exercises (very cautiously, the pain apparently is in the nerve right next to the spinal column, it's a pain rapidly growing more acute and forcing me, against my intention, to take a pain pill even before breakfast, which seems to have been working now for about an hour; but it wasn't just the overly soft bed that gave me the pain, I shoo away the thought, oh, what will I do here where I'm on my own if I get another slipped disk the way I did last year?), and all the time I'm drawing aside the ribbed curtain at the bedroom window (there's sunshine outside as there is every day, today it will be as hot as yesterday, 90 degrees Fahrenheit, 32 degrees Celsius), and all the time I'm taking a shower, my thoughts keep revolving around Kamper's remark that the quest for paradise has led to the installation of hell on earth. (And in New York, he thinks, it has led to a strange displacement of desires: instead of paradise, the labyrinth). The name Manhattan means something like Isle of the Blessed, but we moderns have not the slightest cause to mock the naive notions that the first settlers may have had about what constitutes bliss, nor to mock the exaggerated hopes of the crew of Christopher Columbus, who right now is the focus of a big celebration here, on the five-hundredth anniversary of his discovery of the Americas. In Communism, the hope of paradise blended inseparably, inextricably, with sober economic thought, and the hope of paradise collapsed long before the economics. I am trying to remember the stages of development in my own thinking, and wonder, not for the first time, what we lived for once the hope broke down and nothing was left but the flat struggle to hold onto power and the moral issues had to be addressed all over again. The same thing is happening once more now to many people in the former GDR. They are experiencing the collapse of a new hope of paradise that it is hard for me to understand—the hope for the "greener pastures" on the other side of the fence, the image of paradise associated with the supposedly blooming economy of the West—and so much depends on where the majority of these people will turn under the weight of their disappointment. And what would it mean, in this precarious state of affairs, if what Kamper says is true: that emancipation and freedom are mutually exclusive?

And what does all this have to do with the fact that I am here in paradise now—I ask myself as I prepare breakfast—and that again and again, whenever I realize where I am, I am overcome by a pervasive feeling of unreality? Should I run away? That would be too easy. Or should I check out the nature of this paradise that now is promised to us all?

While I am eating my breakfast—Quaker oatmeal and a toasted poppy-seed roll with the preserves I bought at the farmers' market on Third Street last Thursday—it just happens that a Sunday morning religious service is showing on TV. I see a giant auditorium packed with people who are avidly following the words of the preacher, a combination of fire-and-brimstone orator, actor, animal tamer, and emcee who is managing the crowd according to the rules of mass psychology, and the whole audience, or most of them at least, both black and white, are playing along; you can see their enraptured faces filled with fervent belief and enthusiastic agreement. Is one reason for this widespread chiliastic hope of salvation the fact that it is the opposite of their everyday lives, in which they are monads? "In God we trust!" is written on the dollar bills.

"You *can* make a difference!" the preacher intones, and at the end of the program comes an announcement that "changed women" are ready at any time to come and visit you and me and everyone.

On my way to the Getty Center, I document all the details with my camera: the Spanish facade of the hotel, the courtyard rimmed with exotic plants and with the little Seville orange tree at its center—though I know that the light and colors which give me a sense of euphoria cannot be captured in any photo. I walk along what is already a familiar route—after only five days! How quickly one adapts—that is, I go left on Third Street down to California Avenue snapping photos on the way, then left again, and sixty or seventy yards farther down at the corner of Fourth Street I press the button of the traffic light and wait until the red hand that warns me not to cross disappears and a green pedestrian lights up; but meanwhile I manage to get a snapshot of the Getty Center towering on my right, a fourteen-story modern office block whose ground floor houses the First Federal Bank, to which I most likely will entrust my fortune.

It occurs to me that the sentence in my dream, "The wheels are rolling and rolling and rolling," could have a different interpretation than I had first thought. Yesterday I traveled about three hundred miles north along the coast road toward Santa Barbara with Martin R. from Stuttgart, who is now the director of a large and famous institute in Dresden. First we drove past the expensive estates of Pacific Palisades (yes, I remembered the first time we saw them, ten years ago), then we made a loop into the Santa Monica mountains, which R. is very fond of and which immediately fascinated me too. There were rocks in every shade of ocher, stretches of land empty of people, with now and then a ranch, horses, giant cars outside wealthy houses, which, I was told, the men used to drive to work in Los Angeles. And the light—my slight intoxication comes from the light, and I will not be able to describe it. Then we went back for the first time to the coastal highway, we had the Pacific Ocean on our left, a magical body of water, its shore lined with low rows of buildings including restaurants and cafés, and on our right were the towering bluffs. R. says he envies me because for nine months I'll be able to see this coastline as often as I want; it's his dream landscape. Tomorrow, that is today, he has to leave. In Santa

Barbara we went strolling through a quaint Spanish town center and ate under parasols outside a Mexican restaurant—tortillas filled with cheese and chicken, beans—after I finally got to enjoy a margarita. Because the first question the waitress asked was, "Would you like a margarita?" and to R.'s amazement I enthusiastically said, "Yes, I would!" I recognized again the taste I had found nowhere in Europe—tequila and triple sec with lemon juice and crushed ice. At noon and in this heat, but that didn't matter to me, we drank an espresso at the next corner and talked about the thin American coffee, then went on to the Spanish mission, which before 1600 became a base for Spanish monks who went out to convert the Indian population. Until 1848 California belonged to Mexico, which to its great misfortune refused to sell New Mexico and California to the North Americans, who consequently had to acquire these territories by war. We saw evidence intended to prove that the Indians were "content" about their conversion to Christianity; but the early photo of a converted Indian showed him looking anything but contented. On the contrary, he looked furious. We read about the draconian punishments meted out by the Christians to the heathens: a hand was cut off for theft, a leg for an attempt to escape. We saw the quiet cloister garden, full of exotic trees and strange blooming flowers, a place of meditation sequestered from the world, where you heard nothing but the splashing of the fountain and you couldn't help saying, How beautiful it is! (In the same way, on the first morning after I arrived in California, I stood looking down on Santa Monica Bay from the steep bluff little more than two hundred yards from my hotel, and said to myself out loud over and over, It's glorious, glorious, glorious!) I saw so much beauty—pure illusion unaware of itself—but only today when I'm not under its spell can I express it. Columbus is said to have written the words "God" and "our Lord" fifty-one times in his ship's log, but he used the word "gold" one hundred and thirty-nine times; and what use are all the confessions of guilt and repentance that Christian churches are making to the native people today now that their tribes have been wiped out and their culture destroyed? At the same time I am aware that my anger, my melancholy, are not for the Indians alone.

We walked across the relatively small cemetery where thousands of Indians, and whites too, are said to have been buried over a period of generations. Today only a few large gravestones of Spanish-American families are still standing. We tried to picture how the layers of time and culture lie one above another in this place in the form of human skeletons. While we were walking, driving, eating, R. and I never stopped talking about the typical structures of colonialism, R. always showing signs of a guilty conscience, no doubt wondering if I counted him among the colonizers; but I did not. He is obsessed with his job and seems to be the right man in the right place, because often a West German can save an East German institution more easily than an East German can if he personally identifies with it. But in the darkness of evening, when we were already driving through the outskirts of Los Angeles, one tiny particle in the many-eyed dragon crawling toward the city that we had seen glowing bright red in the sky for a long time now—R. asked me if I believed that one of the typical features of colonization was the replacement of elites in the colonized nation. I said yes, and he asked whether I thought this feature was motivated by the victors' desire for revenge. I said that a need for revenge, often unconscious, can play a role. Probably the victors feel the need to get even for their fear of the defeated side over a long period of time, even though their fear is now revealed as unjustified. In any case, getting rid of the elite groups in a conquered nation and replacing them with a new elite is among the most ancient and indispensable strategies of domination and is practiced by every new power. It's obvious, I said, that the former political elite must be pushed out. No economic upper class had existed in the GDR because no one was able to accumulate a fortune in the capitalist sense. Therefore the new property-owning class in the East would also come from the West—and all the more so because West Germans were claiming that they had previously owned even the relatively modest residential properties that GDR citizens believed belonged to them. Moreover, I said, it was no accident that, in the intellectual sphere, the first Western attacks were aimed at GDR writers, and, as for the university professors, a major overhaul was now in full swing. Of course, I doubted that they could all keep their posts or even should, I said; but those making the decisions ought to have been people who knew the academics in question and whose motives were not

influenced by the burgeoning struggles over the division of spoils
between West and East.

R. and I wonder how this western part of America may differ
from the comparatively desolate industrial zones of the East. R. says
that here in the West, settlers from the very beginning had a kind
of idealistic vision of nature that led them not to destroy it (except
through settlement itself, through the big cities), but instead to set
aside parks for recreation and to create an industry that did not
pollute the air. And, in fact, despite the horrific pictures of traffic
jams that one sees on TV here every evening, the traffic does not
seem to me as aggressive as in Germany because of the lower speed
limit, which people generally observe.

"Where are you going, ma'am?" the guard downstairs in the
Getty Center asked me. I had to sign in because today is Sunday and
the building is almost empty, and they want to know the location of
anyone who may need to be rescued in case of fire or some other
emergency. When I got into an elevator on the wrong side of the
aisle, the guard started to sing a sort of musical scale on the word
"no": "No no no no no"—until I understood that this elevator is
not used on Sundays. Then up I went to the fourth floor, where
everybody has to go first in order to get into the Center because its
many valuables make it a high-security zone. "Hi!" I said to the
second guard, whom I found sitting there as I came out of the elevator (I believe the guards' chairs are the only seats that blacks get to
occupy here); I took my personal security card—photo I.D.—and
two small keys out of a little cabinet, and because it's Sunday and
the elevator is not in operation, I climbed the back stairs up to the
sixth floor, where no one was around today except for two girls and
a young man—all of them black or brown—whom I ran into right
at the start and who were cleaning the place. Once a guard walked
past my door, which I left open as is the American custom; otherwise I was alone. Once I fetched a cup of water from the kitchen,
once a yogurt from the refrigerator, sometimes I looked out for a
long time across the parking lot and between the skyscrapers at the
sea, which was smooth and sparkling in the sunshine, bordered with
palm trees; and I often looked at the clock and figured out what
time it was in Berlin. But I made a mistake anyhow when I finally

phoned, because instead of counting eight hours ahead, I counted eight hours back. G.'s voice sounded very close, I heard my own with a little echo.

In one of the German newspapers hanging in the lounge I found an interview with the American sociologist Amitai Etzioni, a member of the Communitarians, a new nonpartisan political and philosophical movement which aims to move away from blatant individualism and to recall social values that are binding on everyone, such as a stronger family, the emphasis on duty, and responsibility for society as a whole. The American economy, this group says, should model itself on the socialized market economy of Central Europe and work to become a cooperative enterprise, which the United States has failed to achieve so far, except for the Pentagon in the war industry. The lack of family ties and other forms of social bonding is one of the main reasons for the drug problem in America, the Communitarians say. Also there is a need for apprentice training, and the morale and qualifications of American workers are shockingly low. Americans can no longer afford their wasteful way of life, says Amitai, and he fears that the huge deficits in social policy could lead to the disintegration of American society.

It's one o'clock now, I'm tired and hungry, I will go home and make myself a mushroom omelette and then lie down and read. But first I'll print out the pages I have just written, warned by the mishap I suffered early this morning.

Monday, September 28: I didn't manage to print out the pages yesterday because I could not get any ink out of my ribbon. I tried for a half an hour, unwilling to believe what I saw—or what unfortunately I did not see. Gretchen struggled with the ribbon this morning, and then a young man of Japanese appearance arrived a little while ago, an excellent computer specialist, but he has given up too ("Such a simple thing!"), and now he wants to try to find a branch of the company that manufactured my little machine. Probably we will have to telephone Germany, he says. (This has turned out not to be necessary. Twice I traveled a long distance into the city with Daisy to a repair shop where they found the little part that was broken and mended it for forty-five dollars.)

So yesterday I returned home; the pancakes tasted rather strange—I had made them with the slightly sweetened "Swedish pancake meal" and oversalted margarine—and then I lay down and was glad to be in my quiet bedroom with its big screened window, which is shady with vines at that time of day. I read more of Dietmar Kamper's notes about New York, and for a reason I am well aware of I was captivated by his reflections on the increasing feeling of unreality in modern life, caused in part, he says, by its increasing uneventfulness ("Life here unfolds, so to speak, with deadly security in well-established paths. That is why the craziness gets to you"). If you often leave the radio and television running, as I do, you get the impression that Americans believe there is a solution for everything, a remedy for every ill, relief for every pain, a cure for every disease, and don't want to recognize that this very expectation eventually produces a feeling of unreality, in fact of uncanniness. I, on the other hand, am conscious that I am on vacation from reality. What happens to me here is not "real." Actually, nothing is happening to me. Encounters with people, whether pleasant or annoying, don't lead to commitment, ties, obligations. The relief I feel makes it clear how much pressure reality put on me "back home."

Kamper quotes Steven Spielberg, the creator of E.T., that remarkable imaginary creature who actually is monstrous and yet is endearing and who captured the emotions of both children and adults for months on end: fantasy, Spielberg says, is the only way to escape the uneventfulness of modern times. It seems anachronistic to regard fantasy as a means to expand and solidify reality, or at least as a part of reality. Anyhow, Kamper thinks that the "surplus of the fantastic" has penetrated to the heart of social life and now "occupies the place that once was taken up by the gods." The unicorn on a "real" medieval tapestry is for him the symbol of imagination, although "really"—that is, in the time of matriarchy—it was a calendar sign composed of a number of female animals, and the unicorn itself was a phallic symbol, so that in these tapestries, which tell the story of the hunt for the unicorn, the hunt may be not about imagination but about the pursuit and capture of the "feminine principle"—and wouldn't that amount to the same thing? And what would this imply about Medea, toward whom all my thoughts gravitate if I let them go where they will? Medea the goddess, the healer, who also healed through the imagination—is she vilified, persecuted, and condemned by the man's world in Cor-

inth because of her surplus of imagination, among other things—
given that she did not kill her children as Euripides claims? Evidently he needed a strong motive to explain the enormous hatred
that pursued her through the centuries. So I would have to rewrite
history to explain it. Medea the sorceress who makes men afraid,
including Jason. Who brought from Colchis values different from
those of Corinth. Who ultimately was meant to be colonized.

I slept until four, took my time dressing, packed my swimming
clothes; punctually at five-thirty Kurt F. phoned up from the lobby
to say he was here, and we drove the short distance to the Forsters'
beautiful house on Montana Street. Françoise greeted me by saying
she had already known me for a long time through my books; we
felt no sense of strangeness; they showed me to their daughters'
bathroom—their daughters no longer live at home—so that I
could change and swim in their lovely oval swimming pool among
exotic plants. I found everything in the house spacious, practical,
perfect—a word that occurs to me so often here. It's as if people
had discovered the most practical way to do something and then
acted on it.

We sat outdoors at a simple wooden table, ate radishes and nuts
with a very good Italian dry white wine, and then began a long
conversation about the Getty Center, where Kurt F. has been director for eight years—that is, he helped to found it, helped determine
its structure. I began to be fascinated by this materially well-
equipped outfit, which is dedicated to both the collection and the
production of art. I can already see how often I am going to talk
with a variety of people about the problems that are bound to arise
in a structure like this: the tension between the laws of bureaucracy
and those of art production. The Forsters told me about the superb
collections that Kurt managed to convince the Getty Trust to buy,
among them the libraries and archives of German émigrés, in fact
a lot of German material. The purpose is to document the creation
of works of art. I find it incomprehensible how such a quantity of
material could be assembled in only eight years. (I was just up on
the fourth floor with Kathleen, where I got some idea of the capacity of the library and the possibilities of obtaining books, and I
admit that they are overwhelming.)—Françoise has done a lot of

work on Adolph Menzel in East Berlin,[1] she is familiar with the history of the National Gallery, and she is devoted to several women colleagues there, with whom she was able to collaborate in a personal way which, she says, is not to be found in museums in the West. She laments that the merger of the National Gallery with other galleries and museums has now made it virtually impossible to continue her work effectively.

We eat salmon, rice, and mushrooms, the conversation stays lively, Françoise tells me that she comes from a Hamburg family that was a thorn in the side of the Nazis. Several members of her family collaborated in the assassination attempt against Hitler on July 20, 1944, and were saved because the leader of their subgroup committed suicide after he was arrested so as not to betray anyone. She fears a possible repetition of conditions in the Weimar Republic. (This morning it was reported that neo-Nazis have set fire to the Jewish barracks in the former concentration camp of Sachsenhausen, which triggered a counterdemonstration of perhaps four hundred people.) "But you do intend to go back?" the Forsters asked me. "Yes, of course," I said. We talked about the old question that particularly bedevils intellectuals: How much can we integrate into our society without losing our integrity? This question is now taking a different form following unification of the two German states— or to put it more accurately, after the collapse of the one state made it possible to restore a German state with substantially expanded borders—a different form than the question took for us in the GDR. It is now no longer acknowledged that any such question existed there, that it represented a problem that might have given people some trouble to try to solve. The behavior that came out of a sum of conflicts, errors, illusions, wishful thinking, and faulty judgment, and in the end from insights that were growing increasingly realistic, is now being dismissed as a simple choice between "right" and "wrong" as in a computer game. Once again, I get the impression that the whole of German history comes up and plays a role in almost any conversation one has here.

Everywhere people are talking about the American elections.

1. Adolph Menzel (1815–1905) was a painter and graphic artist who was born in Berlin and worked in and around Berlin.

Françoise hopes Clinton will scrape through even if the only good that comes out of it is that a different party will finally be at the helm again and will wipe the slate clean. Both the Forsters think highly of Al Gore, Clinton's vice-presidential running mate. They weigh the qualities of Clinton and Gore against the deficiencies of Bush and Quayle. Kurt fears that Bush will win by a narrow margin. The Democrats would hold the majority in both houses, and the government and the president would be in stalemate.

They drive me home at ten o'clock, I am very tired, maybe I have not yet gotten over my jet lag completely, or it's simply a strain for me to maintain the tense alertness with which I am taking in all the new impressions. Lying in the dark I suddenly hear the three musical notes—a triad—which, when I hear them back home, always induce a perfect stillness. I feel comforted to know that they have accompanied me here, across the ocean. Quickly I fall asleep.

"Free, Ordered, Inconsolable"

Heinrich Böll on the Occasion of His
Seventy-Fifth Birthday

++ ++

Dear Heinrich Böll, what have you been feeling, thinking, doing in these past few weeks? That is what I would be writing to you now, if you were still alive. There is no voice I have missed as much as yours in recent years. I would like to be able to tell you that. When you died, I was inconsolable. And now I have found this same word again in your Wuppertal speech about the freedom of art. In your speech you say that art is inconsolable. "Free, ordered, inconsolable." [1] Which is not the same as "desolate."

I would like to be able to ask you what kinds of things in the world today leave you feeling "desolate"? Would you feel desolate, as I do, to know that a Jewish university student studying at Berkeley in California is not sure if it's safe for her to come to Germany? Unfree, inwardly torn, and desolate seems to be the condition of united Germany. I am sure you would not be among the people who are surprised to see this. This quality of the state, its tendency to

First published in *Wochenpost* 53, December 21, 1993.

1. See Böll's essay "Die Freiheit der Kunst" (1966) from *Essayistische Schriften und Reden* 2 (Cologne: Kiepenheuer & Witsch, 1979), p. 230.

"become ever more futile, ever more shapeless," has filled you "with horror" for a long time. I know of no one who warned more persistently, more courageously, more alertly against undesirable political trends in the Federal Republic of your day than you did. I assume that you would not have stayed silent in the past three years either. Unlike most West Germans you knew "the East," including the East of Germany. You knew the dull resentments which in East and West alike continued to smolder in German hearts under cover of their conformity, and you had no illusions about how quickly civilized behavior can turn into barbarism when it is based on nothing more than a sense of propriety, or what in plain German we call "good manners." I must admit to you—because I assume that you would not spare us the need for self-examination even though you would not make it difficult by treating us with arrogance, egomania, and ignorance—that for a time I *did* have illusions, and that this self-deception led me in turn into several other self-deceptions. Not until 1988, when I was adviser and interviewer in a DEFA documentary about "fringe groups" among German youth,[2] and I sat opposite a seventeen-year-old who was proud of a yellowed photograph of his grandfather dressed in a Nazi storm-trooper uniform, did I realize that a number of our young people have sustained a total loss not only of social ties but also of the values that are important to us. The director called this film "Our Children," and it belonged to the critical and enlightening tradition of GDR literature and art. Nonreaders cannot be "enlightened" through books. You, Heinrich Böll, argued over and over that there is no substitute for involvement and participation in the living process of society, a process that had been brought to a standstill in the GDR. About that we had no illusions. The reasons for the mass exodus of young people starting in the summer of 1989 were clear for all to see. On the other hand, masses of young East Germans demonstrated nonviolently by walking through the streets of downtown Berlin on the nights of October 7 and 8, carrying candles and being terrorized by the police. Was it naive to count on them to shape our future? Even today, I don't believe those young demonstrators became members of the youth gangs that are roaming our streets now.

2. DEFA was the GDR government-run film company.

Yet these too are "our children." They have seen and heard all sorts of things in the past three years, years in which they grew and matured.

In your last interview, Heinrich Böll, a few weeks before your death in July 1985, you say that our historical experience has been that Germany always moves to the right in a crisis, never to the left. And how much truer that is if the "left" has disappeared as a reference point, if many of those who called themselves people of the left have lost their memories and are pointing their fingers away from themselves and at others because it's uncomfortable sitting on the losers' bench, and if only a few still subscribe to their former slogan: "Learn from the underdogs!" It is understandable that "right-wingers" are overjoyed by all this. I could imagine that you, Böll, would spoil their fun again if you were here, by listing the dangers that lie in a lack of alternative views.

To my surprise, in that last interview you gave, you refer to the Ahlen Program of the late 1940s, which you imagined could be the "blueprint for a possible political future for Germany," for a "Christian, socialist Germany." You regretfully observe the vanity of such hopes, which leads me to assume that you would have raised your voice in the triumphal coda of German newspaper columnists bidding farewell to utopia, and might possibly have asked us to consider that man does not live by bread alone. You, who described "bread" and all it stands for in so sensual and concrete a way. And isn't utopia the core of poetry as you see it? "Poetry is dynamite to all the orders of this world."[3] Is this perhaps why it is once more being treated as suspect? Is this perhaps why, in the more refined aesthetic circles, the word "convictions" has become a postmodernist term of abuse? How I would have liked to hear your sardonic cracks about the journalistic crusade against the "believer aestheticians"—a term that includes you too, of course. Would you have been able to predict, two years ago, where this would lead? To the neat division of intellectuals into victors and vanquished—along

3. The Ahlen Program allowed Germans a measure of self-determination and reflected their critique of capitalism. Adopted by the CDU in 1947, it called for the nationalization of key industries and other socialist measures in the western-occupied zones, but the CDU party of Ludwig Erhard, architect of the FRG's "economic miracle," rejected it in favor of the socialized market economy. The allusion to bread in Böll's

with the rest of their society—so that they are turning their defensive guns on each other instead of tackling together the cynical nihilism that is spreading like a contagious disease because it has found a social and intellectual breeding ground to nourish it?

In your last interview you say that you would not have believed it possible for the old property and power relations to be restored after 1945. You are very radical in this final interview. "There is a blatant expropriation of property going on in the GDR," you say, "and a new takeover of power here [in Western Germany], and the same people are carrying out both." You didn't want either of these things to happen. I must say that for too long I hoped the petrified society of the GDR, stifled though it was by government surveillance, was capable of reform because of its noncapitalist approach to property. Is the old system simply being restored now, after a painful forty-year detour? And wasn't this detour the price that one part of Germany was forced to pay for the Nazi past that belonged to all of Germany? Isn't it possible for us to admit this instead of making Germans in the East go on paying for the rest of their lives, and, on top of that, heaping them with abuse to cover up the shortage not of money but of any genuine feelings of solidarity? Is it so hard for us to think a little bit about our history?

I'm asking questions. I have many more questions than answers, dear Heinrich Böll. I am wondering what message these shameless and heartless youngsters are trying to deliver along with the stones and firebombs they throw into foreigners' homes, and from whom they learned this message? What have they learned in our society in the past few years? That it is terrible to be weak. That the stronger can impose his law without compunction. That adults are cowards and will bend to whichever way the wind blows. Isn't that bound to make children afraid? With every blow they strike against a foreigner, a handicapped person, a woman, they are striking at their own fear, and the fact that their fear can't be killed intensifies their rage and their hatred of everything that is strange to them. The fact that they are strangers to themselves does not exonerate them from responsibility for their crimes. So, is it too late

---

work is frequent; see especially his 1955 novel *Das Brot der frühen Jahre*, translated by Mervyn Savill as *The Bread of Our Early Years* (London: Arco Publications, 1957).

to stop them except with police violence? Can they no longer be brought to their senses?

I am asking. What would you, Heinrich Böll, say about the fact that some of our colleagues, allying themselves with conservative critics, are now expressing a delayed regret that no blood flowed in that people's rebellion of autumn 1989 which many are calling a "revolution"? If blood had been shed, there would have been a lot of it, and not theirs but the blood of others.

If ever any man devoted his life to safeguarding humaneness in everyday German living, it was you, Heinrich Böll. I often think about the picture of the Roman chapel that accompanied your funeral procession from the Catholic church to your gravesite. For you there was no question of giving up. "Prometheus—whose name means 'the one with foresight'—did not fetch fire from heaven just so that hot-dog vendors could make a living."

→ 1993 ←

On the victors' side we lived, safe and separate,
until the unity that knows no mercy hit.

GÜNTER GRASS,
Bei klarer Sicht, 1993

What I never had is being torn from me
What I did not live, I will miss forever.

VOLKER BRAUN,
Das Eigentum, 1990

Hours of Weakness, Hours of Strength

Correspondence with Günter Grass

→→ ←←

Friedenau, February 9, 1993

Dear Christa,

I intended to telephone you, as your husband suggested, but he didn't give me the phone number and that's fine, because after all a letter's a letter.

Peter Rühmkorf and his wife visited me in Behlendorf recently, and a few days later Jurek Becker came. Naturally we talked about what people here call "the cases."[1] You should know that you are not isolated here in spite of all the hostility and self-righteous condemnations. I even believe, because of the extremism of the attack,

---

These two letters were first published in *Akteneinsicht Christa Wolf. Zerrspiegel und Dialog. Eine Dokumentation*, edited by Hermann Vinke (Hamburg: Luchterhand Literaturverlag, 1993).

1. Peter Rühmkorf (born 1929) is a West German lyric poet; Jurek Becker (born 1937) is a GDR author who emigrated to West Berlin as a protest against Wolf Biermann's expatriation in 1976. The "cases" are those of GDR intellectuals accused of collaborating with the Stasi.

that the mood is becoming more objective. (Recently Herr Greiner, after shooting off all his ammunition, said he wants the Stasi files to be sealed: the pinnacle of hypocrisy.)[2]

In the past years, and rarely as we saw each other, you and I often held opposing views back in the time when there was still a GDR. My view was that you ought to express clearer and more demanding criticism of the political party of which you were a member, without fear of earning applause from the wrong side by doing so. You, on the other hand, occasionally felt that my criticism of Leninism/Stalinism was too harsh. I remember the PEN Congress in Hamburg in the mid-eighties when, in my introductory paper on the theme "Literature and History," I talked about Communist terrorism during the Spanish Civil War, citing evidence from literary eyewitnesses (Orwell, Regler). Our differences of opinion did not prevent us from continuing our dialogue, particularly because the criticism I voiced at that time did not entitle me to pass any absolute judgment about your life in an ideologically closed society.

But I am competent to judge the argument that *Der Spiegel* and other publications have presented in the form of quotations from documents which, they allege, prove the case about the fateful three years at the end of the 1950s.[3] These confidential reports on writers and their writings are no different from the readers' reports that were commonly drawn up in GDR publishing firms and in quite a few publishing houses in the West as well. God knows, this material is not pleasant to read, but all the same it didn't put anyone's head on the block. What I can condemn categorically is the method used by the Gauck Commission in both your case and others, in which they turned over Stasi files to the press while they left the accused person uninformed.[4] There is recognizably an attempt to use this episode, which lies more than thirty years in the past, to discredit the critical attitude which you demonstrated over decades, and to

2. Ulrich Greiner was a columnist who, in his commentaries in *Die Zeit* on Wolf's novella *What Remains?* was an initiator of the Western press attack on Wolf.

3. The time when GDR intellectuals, including Wolf, were being accused of collaborating with the repressive state-security policy, the Stasi.

4. The Gauck Commission, a West-German-run body named for its head, Joachim Gauck, was set up at the time of unification to investigate cases of suspected collaboration with the Stasi.

discredit your literary work along with it. That must not happen. But to stop it from happening, people have to come out clearly against it. For my own part I had the opportunity to express my views as I have stated them in this letter when I gave readings recently in Frankfurt/Oder, Wittenberg, and Oldenburg. In no case did anyone voice serious disagreement, in either East or West, during the discussions that followed the readings.

Without wishing to pressure you, dear Christa, I nevertheless ask you not to regard yourself as an émigré. There is no cause for that, or, rather—and this applies to all of us—there is no cause yet. Heinrich Böll—whom you cite as an exemplary figure in the article you wrote about him and sent to me—had to put up with the worst hostility and abuse for years, and with police searches of his home and lawsuits. We might continue to take him as an example.

For me things are a mixed bag. On the one hand I'm permitted to be happy, even if only for moments a time, because since January 2 I have been working on my manuscript and am conversing with fictional characters who are slowly beginning to come to life, that is, to talk back at me. On the other hand, we have the current situation: Mölln is six miles from our house.[5] I did manage to respond to the amorphous state of affairs in Germany by writing a cycle of thirteen sonnets entitled *Novemberland* during the months of November and December, though the reason for my success is hard to define; and also the candlelight demonstrations in almost all the big cities have made a clear sign, despite their powerlessness, and have changed the emphasis. Nevertheless, I still have the feeling that we're at the beginning of a development that neither politics nor society in their Western European form are prepared to meet, and that will affect more than Germany alone.

On February 20 we'll travel to Cuba, and after that across the Yucatan to Mexico City, with our youngest son Hans (twenty-two years young), and then head west again via Portugal, where we'll spend an uninterrupted interval in our house there. We'll be back on March 26. (My work on my manuscript can stand a break.)

On our way back to Behlendorf I will take part in a debate with

---

5. Mölln was the site of neo-Nazi atrocities following unification.

Regine Hildebrandt for the *Wochenpost* on that coming Friday. I like that woman. If we had a dozen of her, a small area of this world would look like a different place.

I hope I have shown in this letter that I am looking forward to your return in the not too distant future.

Regards,
Günter

P.S. Recently, to my regret, I found myself compelled to leave the SPD. Their resolution on the rights of asylum-seekers could no longer be justified.

Santa Monica, March 21, 1993

Dear Günter,

Knowing you would not be home until the end of March, I composed several trial letters, discarding some parts again as I went along. This letter, I expect, will be a condensed version of all of them.

You may have heard that I have now resigned from both the Berlin academies. Certain remarks and (non)reactions from Walter Jens convinced me—perhaps erroneously, though I'm still not sure—that I was no longer considered a very desirable member,[6] and then the German public began to worry again about the Stasi-infiltrated membership of the East Berlin Academy, so I thought it best to set things straight. I only hope that the records of the East Berlin Academy will be analyzed eventually, because shorthand notes were taken of every section meeting. Günter de Bruyn too has now found an IM incident in his files.[7] Things are slowly turning tragicomic. Perhaps even those with closed minds are gradually realizing that a file of this kind does not, by itself, say all there is to say about the life of the man or woman who is marked by it. Anyhow, the disclosure about de Bruyn has apparently been greeted by an embarrassed silence, which is different from my case. It is not

---

6. That is, of the West Berlin Academy of Arts.
7. IM: see note 6 to "The Multiple Being Inside Us," above.

exactly easy to be present at one's own public vivisection and not to have access to the means by which to reply, namely that accursed file. We plan to publish ours along with the whole debate that surrounds it; that's probably the only way to stop the speculation. The material in question consists of 136 pages, 52 of which are my "personnel files": my curricula vitae, IM reports about me, inquiries, questionnaires, extracts from the record of a talk I gave, and so on. The Gauck Commission removed 32 pages from my file because they involve "nothing but the rights of third parties"; another 6 pages contain an additional summary of the information the state police had collected about me. The core of the file, that is, the reports that Stasi people made about meetings with me, consists of 20 pages. In 1959, meetings took place between me and two men in Berlin on three occasions; they claim I must have known and have remembered that we talked about my collaborating with them. Then in 1960 there were three meetings with a Stasi person in Halle, who didn't clarify the nature of the contacts between us, and then one meeting in 1962. After this my file was closed, and again there are several pages of records about this. Among other things I am said to have not shown "the proper devotion to the business." The all-important memories, namely, that I had a cover name, that I once met these people in Berlin in an apartment used for undercover work, and that I composed a handwritten report—things for which it is hard for me to forgive myself—have not resurfaced. I can neither confirm nor deny whether I made the statements attributed to me in the Stasi reports, which are written in what Heiner Müller calls "Stasi prose." I break out in a sweat when I read this kind of language, but I know it's how we used to talk back then. I didn't tell those people anything they couldn't have heard in any public meeting.

This phase of my life is keeping me very busy right now, independently—or almost independently—of how the media exploit it. The Germans have such a need to wipe out other people. I can still hear the rabble-rousing tone of those articles, which are not concerned with unbiased reporting or making people reflect and perhaps reflecting along with them; they are after moral annihilation, and I responded by feeling annihilated. Freud said once that a person with a mild depression is quite capable of writing, so my depression appears to be mild because I am writing in order to get close again to the person I was thirty years ago and to get rid of this feeling of coldness, of being a stranger.

I am writing this to you so you will see that I'm not fit for public appearances at the moment, nor, I believe, will I be for a long time. This time I seem to have received an overdose of whatever it is; it has been crammed into me, and my organism has to deal with it first. I have written to Joachim Gauck, warning him against operating the same way in future cases as he did in mine with respect to the files, because things could turn out badly. I have not received an answer to my letter.

But I don't by any means feel I'm an émigré, Günter. Notwithstanding reports to the contrary, I am of course returning to Germany in mid-July. Moreover, I am not so foolish and presumptuous as to lose perspective and compare what is happening to me with the fate of the émigrés from Nazi Germany.

I still want to write a few lines in response to your comment that I ought to have voiced my criticism of the Party more clearly, even at the risk of making this letter too long. I did voice it very clearly, Günter, and after 1976 I stated that I wanted to be expelled and would no longer attend Party functions—nor did I, and I told every Party functionary on every level why, from Honecker on down.[8]

I told many of them in writing. I did not give my statements to the Western media, that's true—not because I wanted to avoid applause from the wrong side but because we had decided to stay in the GDR and to have an influence there, which would not have been possible if I had pranced around too much in the Western media. I took part in discussions with West German politicians in which we spoke quite openly, and in the end we were always invited to stay in the East.

After the Biermann affair there was a moment—one of those moments a person never forgets, I could still tell you exactly where I was and when—when I realized: If I succeed in freeing myself

8. A number of GDR intellectuals emigrated or made other protests when the GDR government stripped the dissident poet and singer Wolf Biermann of his GDR citizenship in 1976. Christa Wolf too considered emigration at that time, as described in "Reply to a Letter from Volker Braun," below.

from any dependency on "them" and manage to write in an uncompromising way, I can stay in the GDR. If I don't succeed, I'll have to go like the others. It was a difficult, conflict-ridden process. I did write without compromise. We were able to help a large number of people in a variety of ways. I found it's not always possible to act in a way that is both "moral" and humane. When I realized that, it was clear to me that I was in a dilemma that I couldn't get out of without conflict—and yet I couldn't do anything else. For three years I have been thinking about this, and about what I would do differently if I could correct my mistakes.

A good acquaintance has just sent me the copy of a letter I wrote to her in June 1979. I will quote part of it to you:

Besides, the time of complaints and accusations is past, and one has to go beyond grief and self-recrimination and shame if one is not simply to keep slipping from one false attitude into another. "The flags jangle in the wind"[9] no matter what color they are—so what? So they jangle, but why are we only just noticing that?—Where does the future lie? There's no way of knowing, and it is true that the old patterns—death, madness, suicide—have been used up in the past one hundred and seventy years. So we must live by following an uncertain inner compass, and without a suitable morality; only we must no longer deceive ourselves about our position as intellectuals, we must not pretend to ourselves that we are working for others, for "the people," the working class. Those people don't read us, and there are reasons for it. Still, when all's said and done, they are the ones who pay us, so that we can afford our inner (and outer) conflicts, which have nothing to do with them. I can't picture how all this will end; we are digging in a dark tunnel, but dig we must. And part of the job is to articulate our own position, as a temporary post along the way.

So this is the letter I mailed out, which went from one apartment that was under surveillance to another apartment that was under surveillance—what a joke! Anyhow, it's not that I lacked

9. A line from Hölderlin's poem "Hälfte des Lebens."

awareness of things, and I did express them. I thought quite pragmatically; if possible, I didn't want to vacate the position I held. Our plan was not to run onto every knife blade in sight, but to try to get my writings published in the GDR as well as elsewhere. I had enough prominence so that I was usually successful in this attempt. What happened to my manuscripts behind the scenes is something I was able to read about in the 42 volumes that contain my "victim" files. And shall I tell you something else? Right now, when I leaf through the books that I wrote and got printed in that time, I think it was worthwhile.

I loved this country. I knew that it was coming to an end, because the best people could no longer find a place in it, because it demanded human sacrifices. I described this in *Cassandra*, and while the censors poked around in its companion lectures,[10] I waited in suspense to see if they would dare to understand the novel's message, that Troy must be destroyed. They didn't dare, and published the novel unabridged. But readers in the GDR did understand it.

I know that you have to act in a different way. You come out in public everywhere when you see your political or moral standards being injured. I respect that position, it has to exist, and you are the one to fill it. I believe I know too that it is not so easy for you to recover from the wounds you bring on yourself. I admire your courage all the more for that.

In hours of weakness, how much I envy all the innocents who were on the right side at the right time, who don't ask themselves questions and are not questioned by anyone else. I must just try to concentrate on my hours of strength. I hope we talk more about this together. Thank you for writing me.

Best wishes,
Christa

10. The companion lectures appear in *Conditions of a Narrative* (see note 1 to "Cancer and Society," above).

One's Own Contradictory Life

Volker and Anne Braun to Christa Wolf

➤➤ ◄◄

February 25, 1993

Dear Christa,

We have always known that the *Other* grows out of one's own contradictory life. From the unendurable has come a different life and writing: this is your thirty years of work, whose importance can only now be gauged fully. Sad as it is to confront the sorry figure one cut in the past, you gathered strength later in a way that is exemplary, and people know it. And the fact that the Otherness turned out to be a new contradiction (as Fühmann told us) is still exclusively *our* problem. We like you precisely because you were able to free yourself in your great vivid narratives about our fate. They are a dwelling-place from which you can speak without reservation, and to our relief you are doing so. We read your interview in the *Wochenpost*, and it made us feel quite light-hearted. Müller had and has a different way of relating to himself and us: "I don't want to

First published in *Akteneinsicht Christa Wolf* (see source note to "Hours of Weakness, Hours of Strength," above). The files referred to in the letter are Stasi files; "Saint Just," etc., are code names; and "our friends" who complain are Stasi friends.

know who I am." — I have taken the first peeks into the stacks of my files. Total surveillance, "Saint Just," "Watchman," "Romeo," and so on, many weeks no day passed without a contact, a life marked in secret code. We are such stuff as files are made on. Our friends merely complain to Officer Girod that I never opened up to them completely. But I did open up to my real friends. And that is why we are waiting for you to come back, and are looking forward to another good gossip with you and to the good time that is due us. Hugs and kisses, dear Christa,

Annelie and Volker

Reply to a Letter from Volker Braun

➤➤ ◄◄

We have always known that the OTHER grows out of
one's own contradictory life

Yes Volker but which OTHER
               and what does it mean to always know something
Until when did we call our knowledge faith
      VERILY I SAY UNTO YOU, TODAY YOU SHALL BE WITH ME IN PARADISE
Do you want the dates of the process of erosion
     1953   1956   1961   1965   1968   1976   1985   1989
              and until when
                        was how much faith
mixed with how much knowledge
Do you want percentages
(Or did we never express THE SCIENTIFIC AGE in numerals
and was it one of our mistakes not to do so)
And from what date
        were we allowed to call faith hope
        and raise it to a principle

First published in the German edition of this book.

HOPE IS WHAT HARD-PRESSED PEOPLE CALL
PRESENT CERTAINTY BEHIND THE WALL

But
    how often and when
                    was hope self-deception
        HOPE LAY IN OUR PATH LIKE A TRAP
And why was it so hard for us
                        to free ourselves from it
Why and how long
                did we insert the made-up questions
of the worker who reads, into the mouth
                of the worker who does not read

To phrase the question differently
            Who built the building-block-shaped Hoyerswerda
            Who raised the standard in freight-car construction in
            Ammendorf
What occurs to you are faces   names
I see gestures   gazes
Wide-open expressions in the public meeting
There was something important at stake
Or
        is all that supposed to have been nothing
        self-deception and hallucination
        Paule Bauch   Rolf Meternagel
        the People's Own Natural Gas plant in Schwedt   the People's
        Own
        Freight Car Construction in Ammendorf
At least we achieved that
                        so we thought
At least we can point this out
                    to those who come later

But
        the People's Own means rubbish to our grandchildren

(WHAT WAS MINE IS NOW IN YOUR CLUTCHES)

And

THE PEOPLE OF HOYWOY slap foreigners around

I write this Volker in the City of Angels with a sore brain which is
circling faster and faster is running hot but regrettably does not
consume itself so that it does not stop uttering sentences like this
one to learn from one's mistakes is the hardest way to
learn how much easier to learn from one's successes
but that was not granted us and when I sleep if I sleep I
sleep dreamlessly fortunately because these dreams whose bits
and pieces trouble me would be something more to remember
Although
One night my limbs are cut off one by one and at last my brain is
cut off in slices My name remains, glowing Finally it too fades away
When I am thrown out of sleep I say my brain is already awake and
on this night too it diligently recorded I know not how many yards
of cassette tape so that it is almost an accident, at which extract of
text I catch it, at a piece of life in me like a cave that is
completely sealed off Who will believe me But that is not the
point It is seven on the radium dial of the electric clock on my
night table it's eleven pm where you are You are watching the last
television news I am beginning my morning exercises which bore
me and plague me because I am defenseless against the brain machine but I force myself to exercise certain muscles because here
where I am alone I am not allowed to be sick After breakfast I swallow 500 mg vitamin C obeying the controversial prescription of Li-
nus Pauling Sometimes my heart rhythm gets off the track otherwise I am healthy or neglect the symptoms

*Müller had and has a different way of relating to himself and us: "I
do not want to know who I am"*

Do I want to know
                    Can
                    I really want to know

Müller did you confidentially
                    read its diagnosis
                    in the *Frankfurter Allgemeine Zeitung*

CORONARY VESSEL

NOW YOU KNOW WHERE GOD LIVES

WHAT YOU DID NOT WANT TO KNOW TIME CAN RUN OUT

"Now I have to keep on my mask of cynicism"
Now
     the last mask drops from my face

From the unendurable has come a different life and writing: this is
your thirty years of work, whose importance can only now be
gauged fully

And which
        that was the horror
             melted away from me in one second

I have never written one line
I will never again write one line
at the moment when in the government office behind the federal
eagle
          I ran across a picture

when my
       hair stood on end
         so such things exist
               because it was unrecognizable
This *"unendurable"* with which we are so familiar Volker
              was something different
That was the contradiction of how we thought for too long
which had to be built into the dialectic anyhow
That was how we were then forced to see
          the abyss that lay between them and us

WE AND NOT THEY

      ah Volker
the meaning of this line too
      has been twisted in your mouth

(and your whole text becomes incomprehensible)
Because "they" was the others

                      in the costume of our comrades
That was the pain

           that was unendurable

                    and that did not wane
And writing meant

          FOLLOWING THE TRAIL OF PAIN
and every step on this trail

              was a phony line
(So that it just occurs to me that one could say we had it easy For
set upon this trail once and for all How could we leave it)

NO PLACE All right We weren't the first
and for dear life's sake

              we diligently trailed our forerunners
July 1979   From a letter

    "The flags jangle in the wind," no matter what color they
    are — so what? So they jangle, but why are we only just no-
    ticing that? — Where does the future lie? There's no way of
    knowing, and it is true that the old patterns — death, mad-
    ness, suicide — have been used up. So we must live by fol-
    lowing an uncertain inner compass, and without a suitable
    morality; only we must no longer deceive ourselves. I can't
    picture how all this will end; we are digging in a dark tun-
    nel, but dig we must. And part of the job is to articulate
    our own position.

Ha, we sometimes thought we were suffering

                  though we had just dipped
a toe

    into the dark water

               (Will this statement hold true)

Sad as it is to confront the sorry figure one cut in the past

Much obliged for the "one," Volker

          ON THE DIFFICULTY OF SAYING "I"

      (But we already went through that Didn't we)

REPLY TO A LETTER

I read that there is
             a human right to error
Is there a human right to an IM file

Overreaction
        I know
My mother, from whom I get it, already told me that
        You mustn't always take everything so hard

It ought not to have happened to me
                        Why not to me
                            I am like everyone else
Day and night I tell myself my story

In a mild depression
            says Freud
                one is quite capable of writing

        So I have to call it mild
In fact everything is a matter of how you regulate language
            (But of course we know that)

Here in the City of Angels I read the political mood of people I
meet from the word they use to describe last year's rebellion of the
black population in the poor districts of the city "Riots" is the official term This helps the white non-poor population to calm their
fear and avenge it Whereas other words — rebellion uprising revolt
insurrection — would concede to the rebels a trace of justification
for their actions which however cannot be forgiven because they
were directed against private property But hasn't it always begun
this way And when it is over the inviolability of private property is
reinstalled before all else
            (But of course we know that)

        ALTHOUGH WE KNOW YOU'LL THREATEN
        US WITH GUNS AND CANNON THEN,
        WE THINK TO LOSE OUR LUXURY
        SCARES US MORE THAN JUST TO DIE

Ah, Brecht
Do you remember how they died
                              like flies
Weiskopf Brecht Fürnberg Bredel Becher Kuba[1]
in the fifties and in the sixties
their names (apart from Brecht)
                              expunged not only from the street signs
but from textbooks, too
                    I'D LIKE TO GROW OLD LIKE AN ANCIENT TREE
Ah, Louis
The rupture of the aorta
                    was the rupture
                              that went through the man
Overstrained lives
THE SKIES OF SPAIN
                    but also
                         HMM, STALIN WILL SAY AND TWIST HIS BEARD

Moreover I have seen you too lying
                              incredibly pale
under a marvelously beautiful tree
                              in Denmark
(Is it really true that your doctor spied on you)

I was impelled into convalescent homes and hospitals
     Can you perhaps explain to me
     why your immune system has broken down
Yes Doctor
     I could
          It was in the summer of '88

The bad thing is
               We loved this country
(Director's notes call for: Roar of laughter)

1. Franz Carl Weiskopf (1900–1955) was an antifascist writer who settled in the GDR. Louis Fürnberg (1909–57) was a writer of poems and accompanying music that became popular songs; he is the "Louis" mentioned six lines later, and the capitalized lines are some of his songs. Willi Bredel and Johannes Becher: see note 3 to "Two Letters," above. "Kuba" is Kurt Barthel, a friend of Fürnberg's (see note 8 to "Rummelplatz,

One time you know in the train from Dresden
      which was not heated well enough by the way
you said after we had talked for two hours
        So we have to leave this country
But we stayed
    along with every Tom, Dick, and Harry, every Hinz and Kunz[2]
        in niches, under observation
in the small catastrophes of the
          TRANSITIONAL SOCIETY
among people
      who did not know
            that Troy is falling

And the fact that the Otherness turned out to be a new
contradiction is still exclusively our problem
    yes
    as Fühmann told us[3]
Fühmann who
      said he had failed

        That the Otherness
          was not ours
    that we could not make it ours, either
     that was and is our problem, to be sure
        Overstrained lives
        We had no choice

I Volker would have had a choice back then
        Why did I not refuse
I no longer know

---

the Eleventh Plenum . . . ," above). All these figures are part of the antifascist tradition of the GDR.

2. The German phrase *Hinz und Kunz* corresponds to the English "Tom, Dick, and Harry," but the phrase here is also an allusion to works of fiction that Volker Braun wrote in the 1980s about two characters called Hinze and Kunze, a GDR functionary and his driver, who reflect attitudes of domination and subservience in a repressive milieu.

3. Franz Fühmann (1922–84) was an antifascist author in the GDR noted for his writings about the Nazi regime as the defining experience of his generation, as in the story *Das Judenauto* (The Jew car).

Memory
       is a malicious filter
I myself could hardly believe that I could forget that

Attempts at answers   I did not yet see them as THE OTHERS
                         I did not trust my own feelings
                         I believed that I owed them information
                         Anxiously I believed I was helping THE CAUSE
                         I did not know what to do
                         I was afraid

Somewhere in the network of these sentences
               and in the imprecision of my mixed feelings
the answer must be caught

But you didn't put anyone's head on the block
          Not true
              My own

They feel out
         your weaknesses
and use them
         as a way to get in
They test you to see how far they can go
   I took my own name and spoiled it
   I wrote the report
   I went to the strange apartment
I was thirty   How
           slowly we grew to be adults

Alienation
      is the coming of the alien
                into yourself
He will look at you
          when you look into yourself
that is
    what the Christians call diabolical

Saying no has come hard to me
            I learned it case by case
When I was able to do it

(You admit it was a mistake
No no no no no)
They lied and turned my contradiction
into agreement
and served it to my friends
as betrayal

(When I read that I wanted to murder someone)
WE WHO WANTED TO PREPARE THE GROUND FOR FRIENDSHIP

Was this the wickedest trap
the most ingenious self-deception
. . . WITH LENIENCY

O no there is no pardon
The scale of the vengeance
shows
the scale of the former fear

. . . that you were able to free yourself in your great vivid narratives
about our fate

Certainly
I entrusted myself seriously to language
which opened the doors for me
to those inner spaces
into which *they* had not penetrated
and in which I
to my own surprise
found such boundless grief
Thus any other speech was forbidden to me
in set phrases accusations prefab parts
and I forgot that I had ever spoken that way
(Did not forget entirely Forgot when where with whom and
about what)
Gradually I thought
I got rid
of the stranger in me

it was a male person
by plucking up courage
to watch him
(What is any fear compared to the fear of self-knowledge)
did not kill him
but as much as possible
changed him into me
And what was left of him
I tried to accept
Easily said It was my life
Now all that counts for nothing

(THERE IS NO PAIN SO GREAT THAT THERE IS NOT A GREATER ONE)
The stranger
has risen again
and wants to overwhelm me

. . . *your narratives are a dwelling place from which you can speak
without reservation*

If only it were so
Do you hear the hue and cry Do you see the faces Do you feel
the craving
(But of course we know that)

To speak without reservation To whom
I know it's the weakness that asks
But
now that everything is possible are there also
courses in further education that teach you
how to survive your public vivisection
without losing your cool

The finger on the wound
but there are so many fingers there already
The NEW MAN seems
to be the glass woman

I SEE THE SALAMANDER GO THROUGH EVERY FIRE

NO SHUDDER PURSUES HIM, AND NOTHING GIVES HIM PAIN[4]

Something must be wrong
                        with my skin Volker
            It is so hard to be hated
Sometimes like this evening
                        I am woken up by the racing of my heart
and hear a voice
But you were a different person then
and at the same time I hear a countervoice
                        Lazy excuse
I know
            it is the old struggle
The stranger in another form
Grinning he brings up an old debt
                                    and presents the bill
Or is he deceiving me with a cold smile and
                                    I have already paid
In the City of the Angels Volker will it ever be customary as in
heaven to take and give according to one's just deserts Every two
weeks I get a check on which I live well and of which I pass on
small quantities to the homeless people God bless you says the
man who crouches next to the moviehouse and looks at me I run
into the hotel crying A person should not have to look at another
person that way Such a look Volker I have never seen in our country Or was I simply not there when *they* manufactured humility
and subservience Yes I was there A friend asks So do we only have
the choice between the two sorts of humiliation It seems so And
the choice between two sorts of guilt

*I have taken the first peeks into the stacks of my files; total surveil-
lance, many weeks no day passed without a contact. A life marked
in secret code. We are such stuff as files are made on.*

---

4. "I SEE THE SALAMANDER," etc.: a line from Ingeborg Bachmann's poem
"Erklär' mir, Liebe," which Wolf discusses in detail in chapter 4 of *Conditions of a Narrative: Cassandra* (see note 1 of "Cancer and Society," above).

Objection Your Honor
That dreams are
                    transformed into files
                                        but we knew that
Also that they wanted to make our lives
                              into the plaything of their sick dreams
I know, if anyone does, the torment
                    that every little instance of playing ball with them
                    costs today
But the only cards
                    they were able to mark
                                        were the marked ones
That is an irrevocable law
And you Volker whatever anyone could say against you
                    you have never played with marked cards
                    and you can build on that and plead your case on
                    that basis
But I   this is new for me
          cannot cite anyone or anything any more
My saints went to pieces
          and the authority
                    with which I would need to register my vocation
is accepting no proposals from me
The case
     which I have brought against myself
     is one I must pursue without an advocate
                    The outcome is uncertain
I have the notion
               that being in the wrong
                                   can do me good
that I do not have to accept
                         the verdict of others
and that this language too
                    of bureaus and authorities
                                        will fall away from
me
Until then I have hidden these lines inside me

REPLY TO A LETTER

HOW WRONG I WAS AND ALWAYS FAILED THE TESTS
BUT NO I DID PASS THEM TIME AFTER TIME

Three days went by tonight in my dream
a hurtling fall through layers
of increasingly dense consistency
air water mire debris pebbles
getting stuck I was in danger of suffocating
Then suddenly underneath me rock
and this voice
You are on firm ground
To weep is permitted in a dream

*Our friends complain to the officer that I never opened up to them
completely. But I did open up to my real friends. And that is why
we are waiting for you to come back, and are looking forward to
another good gossip with you and to the good time that is due us.*

Yes and the sorrow that is due us
                                    I am coming   Soon

        Santa Monica, March 26, 1993

Berlin, Monday, September 27, 1993

➤➤ ◄◄

I wake up at 5:45 A.M., unable to retain a scrap of my dream. For too long now I have not been dreaming. I am no longer tired. G. wants to talk with me about Alice Schwarzer's book on the death of Petra Kelly and Gert Bastian, which he is reading and which disturbs him because it does not admit of any other interpretations but the author's.[1] I remember how I was affected in Santa Monica last year when I heard the news of this ghastly double death. Something about it seemed to me typically German. I wondered why I felt compelled to think over and over: what a German couple they were, an uncannily German couple. An uncannily German couple. The material in Alice Schwarzer's book tends to make you feel that way, only it is too prejudiced and judgmental for my taste, there is too much pleasure in evaluating and condemning, too little empathy and sisterliness. I get annoyed by the condescending, disparaging adjectives, and the perhaps unconscious ill will that she brings to her investigations. Yet the relationship between these two people definitely merits detailed investigation and description, which of course does not need to be uncritical, in fact ought not to be so.

First published in the German edition of this book.

1. Petra Kelly, peace activist and founder of the West German environmentalist Green Party, who was found dead with her companion in October 1992 and is presumed to have committed suicide, though there were speculations that she was murdered.

But a somewhat superficial Freudian psychology and a rigorously applied feminism seem not to take us any farther. The old question arises: do we portray people more accurately by dissecting them with a scalpel or with a sympathetic eye that reflects knowledge of our own weaknesses?

Read the newspaper at breakfast. In *Freitag* I read an article about where the West might expect to find friends in the former Yugoslavia—certainly not among the official politicians. I resent our inaction and my own feeling of helplessness, as I always do when I cannot avoid contact with this topic—feelings not excused by the fact that they are shared by most of the people around us. I have the impression that the number of problems I do not understand and therefore cannot evaluate is increasing, and my uneasiness about this is increasing too. For example, I am reading about the "Moscow coup" in which Yeltsin dissolved the parliament last week, and since then there have been two presidents, Yeltsin and Rutskoi. (At breakfast later, G. will read to me what Falin writes about this: the German view of the most recent events in Russia is mistaken; this is not a struggle for power between the "reformers" and the "antireformers" but a struggle between two factions both representing the market economy: Yeltsin represents the "free" market economy, Rutskoi the "social." Only 6 percent of the population say they feel content under Yeltsin, compared to 26 percent, who for the most part were content under Brezhnev. No comment.) The "Heitmann case" is preoccupying Erich Kuby, *Freitag*'s "news reader." He makes fun of the way "the scandalmongers in Bonn" are discharging the job of "turning a Saxon preacher into the president of a federal republic." I wonder which would be worse: if the federal chancellor and those who are defending his candidate really believe this candidate is being criticized because he comes from the East, or if they are using this argument purely as a demagogical tactic because what they really want is an easy-going, clumsy president who would present a conservative image of Germany at home and abroad. A government's loss of reality is expressed through different areas and problems in different political systems.

"Eastern Germany Is Not Yet the Promised Land" is the headline of an article by a research group from the German Society of

Applied Economics. The article begins: "Three years after the formal establishment of a unified economic system in East and West Germany, it is becoming increasingly apparent that the economic policy of unification, which is based primarily on market forces, has failed. Even now, a self-supporting economic upturn is not yet in sight." What is needed, the article says, is a "build-up program" which would guarantee "reindustrialization and a policy of encouraging an active labor market." Very likely right, I think as I shower and dress. And yet something about it is not right, because all the rescue proposals aim to restore the old monster, the industrial society, to its former glory, that is, to restore its priorities and values and thus its alienation effect as well, which led people to define themselves and to find value only in work so that the prospect of more leisure time was experienced not only as a social threat but as a threat to their survival. It took industrial society generations to create this perfect, serviceable worker. How much time can it spare to move work out of the center and into the periphery of most people's lives, before the "breakdown of society" that we are hearing so much about gives rise to new dictatorships?

I am standing in the kitchen door, a light has entered that is new to me, a pale autumn light, now less filtered than it was before because of the thinning of the poplar leaves outside the window. Suddenly I see the pale new bench and the kitchen table as if for the first time, it is as if all the light from all the kitchen tables in my life were gathering on this one; for the blink of an eye, all the members of my family and all the guests who ever sat at our kitchen table are united at this table and I am among them, a shifting and aging form. Over time, many pairs of eyes have gazed at each other here. Some have closed for good, others have turned away in permanent shame, estrangement, hatred. New eyes have come, have been welcomed. The glow on the table remains, there is a burst of laughter, a sense of intimacy. How alive we were. How innocent. How gay, friendly, generous. How curious. Oh, how unprepared. Betrayal, at our kitchen table? We didn't want to believe it. We tried to hold on to the fugitives. Meanwhile a malicious hand put out one candle after another. Who guided its movements? The others? I myself? A blink of an eye. I am standing, leaning against the door frame. The glow has gone out. All day long I can't forget that I saw it. That one moment glutted with reality sharpens my perception of all the other moments in this day.

Later, when we are having breakfast—G. is eating his beloved smoked salmon and I my crispbread with plum jam, G. is absorbed in the newspaper, it says the night passed peacefully in the White House in Moscow—later, I wonder where the glow came from. It is overcast outside, the mood is autumnal, the too cool, too wet summer is ending too cool and too wet. I must get busy unpacking the giant carton, from an environmentally friendly shipping firm, which has been standing in the corner for days. I have ordered all sorts of boxes and folders, hoping that perhaps I may get the paper chaos in my room under control for once. I have been trying to do this for decades, I remember, continually varying my strategy with scant success. No doubt I should permit myself the consolation that the fault lies not in me but in the flood of paper that pours over me, only part of which really has me as its source. But next week I will put things in order from the ground up. Right now, the first thing I must do is record in my notebook what happened last week. It's another of my quirks, I realize, that I'm always hoping to use my time better if I note down how I have spent it and for the most part failed to put it to use. A friend phones from Hamburg wanting to know how I'm feeling. Not bad, I say: one keeps running into sensible people. "Yes?" he says. "Let's hope you're right, maybe there are still a few bright spots left."

It's 11:00 A.M.; I sit down at my little computer to start writing the notes for which I have set this day aside, and I already know—I have been carrying on this practice long enough that I can't help but know—that the moment I begin to describe this day at 11:00 A.M., the question will arise: Is this text swallowing up the day, is it determining how the day goes? Is the day being lived for the sake of the text, and the text written for the sake of the day? In short, does self-observation lead to falsification? But what doesn't lead to falsification? I forbid myself to fall into the trap that is always waiting, fully installed and ready to snap shut, at the bottom of my consciousness. I want to stick to the concrete.

The telephone. It's my publishers, about the texts to be col-

lected into a smallish volume next spring. And while I listen—
expressing agreement, reservations—I remain superficial and unconcerned, it's still a long way to spring, I don't know yet if I really
want this little book, if I even want the eyes of strangers to look at
what I have written, if I really want to put up with it. So far it's all
just a game, a trial balloon; everything is open, what does the chat-
ter about the book jacket, the number of pages, the blurb on the
cover mean to me? G. says I am always like that, apparently I need
the self-deception, he comes back from his morning walk earlier
than I expected, the potatoes aren't in the oven yet and he does it, I
stir the cottage cheese. A woman editor phones from the radio station; against my principles I gave her an interview recently, which
as always got longer than had been promised and which as always
did not finish when I noticed it was going on too long—she has
passed on parts of it to another station, which is why she is now
asking me for more exact details, which I don't want to give, and a
newspaper would like to print the interview too—the usual media
mill that I always get caught in when I break my rule, so that in
the end I have no one to blame but myself, until I stop blaming
myself, because it just isn't worth it.

So we eat baked potatoes, cottage cheese, the savoy cabbage left
from yesterday, drink milk, talk about the conference on Friday at
which G.'s publishing house, Janus Verlag, presented Otl Aicher's
book. We tell each other anecdotes about the evening, which oddly
enough never occur to us until several days later. Once again we
find what an advantage it is to share an experience. It takes on an
added dimension, greater density. And even our judgments about
people, which often differ and in the past could lead to bitter quarrels, are things we now accept so that we can each let the other's
view blend gradually with our own view—a process we don't notice
until long afterward.

Before my midday nap I read the conclusion of Alice
Schwarzer's book, which makes clear that she is working off an old
personal injury and old aggressions through the case of the couple,
Kelly and Bastian. I think it would have benefited the book if she
had made this obvious to readers. Probably the long years in which
she experienced the merciless way women are treated when they

criticize the patriarchy and neglect to hide their own weaknesses has made her suppress her vulnerability, or at least the expression of it. So once again we are right back where they want us—another of those vicious circles that I think a lot about now.

M. arrives. He tells us he has just written an indignant letter canceling his subscription to *Taz*, which claims, in a review whose main aim is to vilify me, that Otl Aicher's concept of the culture of the commonplace is "barbaric." It's incredible. We laugh, and yet it's a crying shame. This is an instance of bad manners by those who consider themselves on the left but whose views are based on ignorance, stupidity, and arrogance. One could ignore it, except that increasingly there are signs that members of the left-wing spectrum are once again indulging in mutual recrimination and factionalism while right-wingers, cheerfully growing in strength and meeting no impediment, are busy networking, merging their diverse groups and centers of ideas.

Five o'clock, time for me to change clothes, black pants, yellow silk blouse, black silk jacket; I put on makeup, pack my handbag, G. is already standing impatiently in the hall while I don't know yet what shoes to put on—a situation that recurs over and over; sometimes we can laugh about it, today we can't. It's after five-thirty when we leave, what time we arrive in Potsdam will depend on the traffic situation. We head down Wollankstrasse, as always now when we go to "the city." For a long time Schönhauserstrasse has been virtually impassable inbound because of the construction works; how much longer is it going to take, we ask again; I catch myself thinking that very likely I won't live long enough to see Berlin become a city whose streets are once more open to traffic. West Berlin begins right behind the curve of the railroad, the bumpy road surface smooths out, we stop several times at streetlights, I open my eyes wide and try to memorize this route that I have already traveled dozens of times, how strange West Berlin still looks to me, how difficult it still is for me to find my way around many districts, I seem unable to store these new localities in my memory. I wonder whether this is partly due to an unconscious resistance. This evening we are making speedy progress. I stick to the sky, it is dramatic, great dark patches moving rapidly northeastward, sometimes a sickly yellow appears in between, even a pale orange. As we curve onto the city highway behind the ICC[2]—which I have never set foot in, by the way—the news starts on the car radio. Schäuble is supporting Heitmann for president—how long will we still remember who he is?—the FDP seems inclined to support Frau Hamm-Brücher after all, and peace reigns in and around the White House in Moscow.

The trees at the edge of the road are beginning to change color, and it's getting dark earlier now that the clocks have been moved back an hour; a dense row of lights comes toward us from approaching cars. On Dreilinden we drive past the monstrous, now decaying border installations of the GDR. A war was still going on there, we say. Those are legacies of war. Is this peacetime? (The onslaught of Abkhazi troops has driven Shevardnadze out of the Sukhumi district, where he wanted to hold out until the Georgian population had been evacuated; so once again a hundred thousand people are fleeing, and Sukhumi, the "Pearl of the Black Sea," has been destroyed. We make no comment, no doubt we are both seeing the same images: once we took a seaplane from Gagra to Sukhumi. The city, the white pearl, was set in turquoise blue and agate green: the sea and the hills with their groves of orange trees. The harbor bay, dusty streets. For us it was the South. The photos I took then could help out my memory now. I forbid my imagination to conjure up the images of flight, misery, destruction.)

And what if the exactness that I require of myself on a day like today is no use for anything except to make me aware that I am tied into a chain of repetitions, and have been for a long time now? The road to Potsdam, which I drove along so often to visit my father— it all comes back into my mind, his apartment in the new apartment block that we are driving past, his gradual decline, which he tenaciously resisted, the few belongings he had managed to amass in a lifetime of over ninety years. The former Hans Marchwitza House—which of course is no longer called that—is closed. From a side entrance we walk into the "Bacchus Keller" at the same moment as Hermann Vinke, whom we had arranged to meet. He has come from Bremen, we sit down in an alcove and begin to review

2. ICC = Internationales Congress Centrum, a gigantic conference center with numerous meeting halls, which symbolized West Germany's belief in its economic future.

the evening's program one more time, a cheeky young waiter comes over and suggests that we order a mushroom dish—he says that this autumn there are so many chanterelles in the Brandenburg woods that you can mow them down with a scythe—so we eat steak and mushrooms along with the inevitable little potato balls, drink spritzer; then the two book dealers arrive, the ones who organized this evening, W. and R.; they are even younger than I had pictured, one has a bald head, round metal-rimmed eyeglasses, and a narrow black scarf tied in a knot around his neck, the other man, his friend and companion, has a curly mop of hair; of course they both are sporting jeans and leather jackets and are quite willing to tell the story of their lives as book dealers while they relish their beer. W. says that he twice began to study in the GDR, was expelled twice from university, then got along doing odd jobs until an elderly Potsdam archivist who knew about his mania for books took him on as a trainee. This had been his apprenticeship. R. had left the country and had returned after the revolution. They both bought up books, which could be had for a few pennies each or even for nothing because they were going to be thrown out. On the day of the currency union, they stood in the market square with an upholsterer's bench full of books—they claim they sold ten books even on that day— and 1990, which other booksellers refer to with sheer horror, became a dream year for them. When Treuhand announced that the August Bebel Booksellers was up for sale, R. and W. applied and— once a frivolous speculator had been unmasked and sent packing— were actually awarded the contract, along with a bank loan. They were then offered the chance to buy the building that houses the bookstore—"an immense sum, of course it brought us to our knees," W. says, "what did we know about money?"—but they got the bank loan, and after renovating the building they rented out some offices to a wine dealer and to several attorneys and are now using the rent money to pay off their loans. Oh yes, the bookstore is a success. Where seven people used to be employed there are now three and a half, including the two of them; we would see. They're a pair of lucky devils.

Before eight we go to the Stauden Gallery, which already existed before the changeover—we were often here before—and now has been taken over by younger people. A long narrow room,

Mecklenburg landscape paintings hang on the walls, two hundred and fifty people have come, I doubt whether a discussion will be possible here, which is what matters to me. Vinke and I have to climb onto a podium; of course, I am once again plagued by doubts whether I ought to have agreed to this enterprise. What am I doing here? I think. Isn't this just another case of pure arrogance? You have to talk loud into the microphone to be understood at the back of the hall. Our subject is the volume *Akteneinsicht* (Inspecting the Files on Christa Wolf) that Hermann Vinke has published. He and I take turns telling people what it's about, I read excerpts from the letters I wrote in Santa Monica, which are included in the book, it was only six or seven months ago, I still remember it all, it has been graven into me, and yet it is a finished chapter, I feel that already I am no longer able to convey to the public the emotions I experienced at the time. Or is the detachment I am experiencing now a protection I have built up unconsciously against being flooded again with uncontrollable feelings?

The discussion begins rather awkwardly. A man asks me about the line in *Cassandra* that says Cassandra is ashamed for earlier having thought, I want the same as you! Does this line apply to me too, he asks. I confirm that it does, I talk about how, during the campaign against my book *Der getrennte Himmel* (*Divided Heaven*), I always used to start out by saying, But I want the same things you do! And how, with considerable difficulty, I had to learn that I was mistaken.

Someone asks me to describe how I have developed since looking at my files, especially my IM file. I try to speak as openly as possible about the various stages; about the initial shock, the horror at myself, my despair because, given the universal Stasi hysteria, it was impossible to count on the public to draw distinctions; about the risk of my identifying with the public image that was painted of me; about the therapy of writing and the gradual process of getting out of my depression; and about my current state, when I believe I can fit this episode into the history of my development even though it will always remain a painful spot and a dark one. While I am speaking, I realize that I have overrated my abilities, that I am still too thin-skinned for such forums, but now there is no way of getting out of it.

An older woman gives a lengthy description of what she gleaned from my books before the 1989 revolution. In particular, they made it clear to her that we are living in a man's society, she says. She claims to have no interest at all in this business of the files, and will I continue to write about women's themes? I say that all I have known and perceived is still part of me, and that there are structures which were basic to the GDR regime just as they are basic to the Federal Republic: both were and are patriarchies, both were and are industrial societies. These matters will form the background of my writing even if I don't treat feminist themes in the narrower sense.

One man talks about the appeal "For Our Country." He has read one of my letters thoroughly. In it (he says) I explain that in *Cassandra* I claim that Troy must fall because it is demanding human sacrifice; but then in the "For Our Country" appeal I apparently called for the preservation of the GDR. Wasn't this a contradiction?[3] I welcomed the chance to clarify this. In our appeal, I said, we were not thinking about preserving or restoring the old GDR. For a very brief moment in history we were thinking about an entirely different country, which none of us will ever see and which is an illusion, as I already knew at the time. For a moment I feel once again the atmosphere of that time four years ago which otherwise it is almost impossible for me to recapture.

Then suddenly the whole complex of problems associated with the Stasi comes up. The question arises, is it important to keep going back to that complex and struggling with it? Various opinions are expressed. I feel little enthusiasm for the topic and try to keep a close watch on this feeling, because I am not without bias. So when the word "reconciliation" is voiced, I say there can be no reconciliation without knowing the facts. And even as I say it, I am wondering if I really think this or have only read it. This is one of the growing number of subjects about which I have no definite opinion. I say I would like to hear whether people want to confront their past. (Or can you actually "want" it if it is embarrassing and painful? Is it a typical instance of German Protestant rigorism to assume that

3. The "For Our Country" petition, signed by intellectuals on November 18, 1989, declared that there was still a chance for the East to develop a socialist alternative to the Federal Republic.

confession and repentance are followed by forgiveness and catharsis, when the course of events in history thus far has not borne this out?) Several people say that indeed they would like to reflect about the past, only they do not want to confront it in the way that is dictated by the West, without sensitivity or the ability to discriminate. The practices of the Gauck Commission in my own case are brought up as proof that the Stasi files are being used for political ends. I try to say that, on the other hand, you really must reach the point at which you can account to yourself for your life, regardless of how difficult other people may make it for you, and regardless of how much guiltier other people may be—but I know these are expectations that have nothing to do with the real life of vast numbers of human beings. As the discussion shifts back and forth, I get the impression that once again people are expecting me to come up with easy-to-remember slogans about what will happen next. I understand each impulse and counterimpulse from the audience. It is as if I had never been away, it is as if, in the time I was gone, they went through the same process of change as I did and I now have to protect myself against their attitude of expectation, which I do not want to go along with. I ward off any form of GDR nostalgia that allows a person to gloss over what he or she said or did, or usually did not do, in recent decades. I mention occasions when we—I say "we" and mean a small group of friends—were pretty much on our own, until finally, when the signs of national disintegration became increasingly apparent and the risks grew less, more and more people struggled with themselves and finally joined the opposition. That was the normal course of events, you could not reproach anyone, I could least of all. But neither could I forget how desperate I often felt in the last years of the GDR, and no one could get me to approve of the manner and the speed with which everything connected with the GDR was liquidated, considered suspect. But even as I am saying this, I see us with the eyes of people looking at us from the outside: we are housed in a barracks under quarantine, infected with the Stasi virus. For the first time, I believe I really can understand the psychological advantages that lie in looking at things this way: since you don't have to get involved with these infected people, you can protect yourself by not letting them come near, and obviously you can dispose of them as you like. Then I get an inkling of the kind of damage that this way of "processing" information is causing to both sides; and I hear myself say in a more impassioned tone than I intended that it takes two to cause humiliation and to dismantle a society. Why didn't we resist? (But how? a countervoice asks inside me.) Why did no one join the people from Bischofferode when they went on their protest walk through the country?[4] (The moment I spoke these words, I realized that they were the ones the newspapers everywhere would quote, and next day I saw it confirmed.)

Someone asks the splendid question: Are the Stasi files the guilty conscience of our nation? I say: No, only in Germany could people get the notion that files can replace conscience. After reading my files I knew that they did not contain "the truth" either about the person they were set up to observe, nor about the people assigned to fill them with their observations. They contain what Stasi people saw or were supposed to see, were compelled to see, were allowed to see. They reflect a growing paranoia in the smallest of minds. The very language they employ is not suited to the reception of "truth"; the very way they pose questions reduces people to objects they make use of. You can glean a few pieces of information from them—often information that is out of date even when it comes to the informers themselves, because the files don't allow them to show any development but fix them at a point that they may eventually have gone beyond. (For this reason we were not interested in decoding the identity of the many IMs who surrounded us in earlier periods.) I am very glad to be able to say this quite impartially, because I had my own IM files published. I say: No, "the truth" about this time and about our lives must come from literature.

Of course people seized on this point: Where was this literature? For instance, why hadn't I begun to speak publicly again long before this?—asks a woman with a mop of hair. Someone wants to know what I meant by leaving for America: was I running away? I insist on my right to speak when I choose but also to keep silent, I resist

4. Members of the Bischofferode plant in the GDR protested, by means of a hunger strike, the economic results of the absorption of the eastern states into the new Federal Republic. See "Parting from Phantoms," below.

the role of counselor that they want to assign to me again, I realize that they are partly right, but I list the things that I and others nevertheless did say and write, without their being widely noticed. I remind them, as I always do on occasions like this, of how many years passed after the Napoleonic Wars before Tolstoy wrote *War and Peace*. I urge them to grant writers, as well as others, a pause for reflection. They answer yes, yes, but I feel that inside they are still insisting on their demands. I can feel in a physical way how strongly they are pressing their claims again—or perhaps they never let up.

After that, book signings, individual questions. A young woman reminds me that she came to visit me once, but I can't remember. She wants to tell me what her life has been like since she saw her Stasi files. She knows now who in her circle of colleagues was spying on her, and she feels so ashamed for these people that she can no longer look at them. Those who now know that she knows creep around quietly when they are near her. When she speaks to them directly, all she gets is apologies and self-condemnations which don't satisfy her. She simply does not know how to deal with this problem, she says. She is now working with a women's theater group and wants to invite me to their next production.

A man in his mid-fifties with a funny crumpled face speaks to me. He wants to apologize to me at long last, he says.—What for?— For the fact that, back when my book *The Quest for Christa T.* was published, he followed what looked like the trend and called me a "stupid cow" and a "dumb bunny." He had been a teacher, he told me. Then when *Patterns of Childhood* came out, he said Oh well, hm ... But a long time later he reread *Christa T.* and felt as if the scales had fallen from his eyes: he realized how wrong he had been about me earlier, and that's why he now wants to say he is sorry. I laugh and reply that a lot of people thought and said the same about me but he was the only one to tell me straight out.

When we are in the car, driving in a wide arc through Potsdam in almost total darkness, I reflect that the problem of the young woman and that of the man—both of which are my problems as well—are complementary. In part, perhaps, they even answer each other. How much time had to go by before this man could voice an apology for a comparatively harmless misdeed, which nevertheless troubled him. If this case reflects some kind of law, then in ten, fifteen, twenty years the spies and informers of the past decades may perhaps apologize . . . I don't know.

We go to W. and R.'s bookstore, which we knew well back in the days when it was still called the August Bebel Booksellers. We are surprised at the successful renovation of the building and offices, which seem more spacious, more open, more modern than before, especially the view into the romantic inner courtyard. The two book dealers explain their clever, well-thought-out technique of presenting the books so that customers don't have to bump into the most superficial stuff the minute they enter the store. The demand for authors from the former GDR is as high as ever here, which is why they can't get very far with the Western bestseller lists. They tell us that it has just been reported in the press that people in the new eastern states of the Federal Republic still read considerably more than people in the West. We climb the steep spiral staircase to the upper floor. Cheese canapés have been prepared, there is wine, there are six of us: a West German man, a West Berlin woman, a young man who left the GDR and came back, and three citizens of the former GDR, all obsessed with literature and all in the business of writing, manufacturing, publicizing, or distributing books. Everyone seems to think it's a good combination, we talk, laugh, tell jokes and anecdotes.

Midnight in the empty "pedestrian zone" in the center of Potsdam, spectrally lit by whip-shaped lampposts. For a few seconds I have an intense feeling of déjà vu: I've stood here before in the same light, have exchanged the same parting words, the same hugs. But that's impossible, I'm just tired, I sleep through most of the journey home, G. is tired too but the driving keeps him awake. We don't talk much; once I say, "I couldn't do that again." G. says: "You don't have to." I've brought a book home from the bookstore, one that people are talking about now, I've leafed through it, a completely invented story, I envy the woman who wrote it. When will I—or will I ever again—be able to write a book about a distant, invented character? I myself am the protagonist, there is no other way, I am exposed, have exposed myself.

Before falling asleep I read some of an essay by Erwin Chargraff, *Zweierlei Trauer* (Two kinds of sorrow), which begins with the sentence: "A mute sorrow has descended over the world." That's true, I think—sorrowfully. And then I find a quotation from Kierkegaard's diary, dated 1849: "A single individual cannot help or save an age, he can only express the fact that it is sinking."

Insisting on Myself

Christa Wolf in Conversation with Günter Gaus

+> <+

"We were born in the same year, 1929,
but in the East and the West, and that
makes a difference . . ."

Günter Gaus

G ünter Gaus normally does not have to travel halfway around
the globe to record an interview for his television program
"Zur Person" (In person). His interviews almost always take place
in the Federal Republic. But to get Christa Wolf in front of the camera, Gaus had to travel in late February 1993 to Santa Monica, California, where Wolf was spending a number of months as a visiting
scholar. The journalist brought with him the files on the IM case of
"Margarete," thus enabling Christa Wolf to study them for the first
time, weeks after they had been read by others.

Gaus did not go straight to the point, the question of Wolf's

First published in *Akteneinsicht Christa Wolf: Zerrspiegel und Dialog. Eine Dokumentation*, edited by Herman Vinke, © 1993 by Luchterhand Literaturverlag GmbH, Hamburg. The introductory paragraphs are by Hermann Vinke. This interview did not appear in the German edition of the present book.

work as an informer for the Stasi, but began by interviewing her about her background and the stages in her development, and only then asked precise and persistent questions about the main issue.

For over an hour the camera focused almost exclusively on Christa Wolf, who replied with sincerity, self-possession, and remarkable calm. By the date of the interview she had already gone through the worst of the experience, and she commented with relief that "I can now talk quite openly with everyone about [the files]."

During the long interview Wolf said things that hint at what she went through: "I think nothing else can ever hurt me so much again. Now I don't have to avoid pain any more." At another point, she spoke of the danger that the Stasi might be dictating her public biography, assisted by the West Germans who hold her files: "One of the obscene results of the way my file has been described in the press is that they've taken over the Stasi's characterization, the Stasi's language, and are applying it to me as I am today."

The text of the following interview reproduces the version printed in the May 1993 issue of *Neue Deutsche Literatur.*

GÜNTER GAUS: Christa Wolf, in your book *The Quest for Christa T.* you write about a young Communist woman, Christa T., who dies of cancer, but before that she is already destroyed by conditions in the society. I quote: "When her name was called: 'Christa T.!'—she stood up and went and did what was expected of her."[1] Did you also mean that as a description of yourself as you were then?

CHRISTA WOLF: My first impulse now is to simply say yes, and that would be my whole answer. But I believe that would be taking the question too lightly. First I'll say something that concerns me about your question. You say she died of cancer but that she was destroyed by conditions in her society. I would dispute that, I disputed it at the time. Many reviews focused on that point—

GAUS: In the GDR and outside the GDR?

WOLF: In the GDR and in West Germany. In West Germany the response was positive: Aha, so here someone is dying from condi-

---

1. Quotations from *The Quest for Christa T* are from Christopher Middleton's translation (New York: Farrar, Straus & Giroux, 1970).

tions in GDR society. In the GDR that was the main point why the book wasn't allowed to be published for three years. Back then I said—not for tactical reasons but because I really have a different understanding of failure, of destruction—back then I said that this woman lived a full life, she didn't collapse, she experienced a great many conflicts. But your question about whether I was describing myself: yes. Yes, if you continue the quotation. I happen to know how it goes on, it says more or less that she heard her name called and wondered is it really me who's meant or is it only my *name* that's being used, counted in with the names of who knows how many thousands of others. Should I just slip away leaving the shell of a name behind? If you take these self-doubts into account, then I would say yes, that is also a description of my situation at the time.

GAUS: But the passage goes on from there, I remember now.

WOLF: Yes, what do you remember?

GAUS: It goes on to say that this—standing up and saying here I am and I'll do what's required—even though she wondered if it was her real self that was meant—that Christa T. did this at a time when many people were already trying to escape from it all.

WOLF: Yes, that's right.

GAUS: So now I'll ask again: is that a description of yourself?

WOLF: Yes, especially if you add that extra line, because "escaping" doesn't just mean going away physically, but also turning yourself off inside.

GAUS: Continuing to sit there and no longer really standing up.

WOLF: And being cynical.

GAUS: What's good about Christa T.'s readiness to do what's expected? What's bad about it?

WOLF: "Good" and "bad"—again those are concepts that—today I would still consider it good for someone to do what's expected, what's expected of me, provided I expect it of myself too, provided I can bring myself to expect it. That's a broad area. You can make a lot of mistakes.

GAUS: Did you make mistakes?

WOLF: Yes.

GAUS: What's bad about it?

WOLF: What's bad is when it's the other way around: if I, or someone else gets to the point of doing only what is expected and stops asking what he expects of himself.

GAUS: Christa Wolf, what led you and enabled you to make that kind of commitment to a cause, the cause of socialism, even to socialism in the actual form that was defined in the GDR—to a cause that you felt called to, even if you had to overcome inner resistance?

WOLF: I would have to tell you the history of that commitment.

GAUS: Go ahead.

WOLF: Oh no, that would take too long. But I'll begin at the beginning, what led me to it at the beginning? In 1945 I was very far from committing myself to anything related to socialism, and of course I didn't know anything about it. Anyway, the postwar period was a shock for me, when I learned what *we* had done, we Germans, and had to accept that it was true. For months, for years I was in deep despair and didn't know how to go on living with it. Then I went through a short, very intensive phase of trying out Christianity. It didn't work, and then—I was still in high school at the time, I was a bit older than my classmates—

GAUS: In Mecklenburg?

WOLF: No, in Thuringia, I took my high-school graduation exams in Thuringia.

GAUS: At the end of the war you were in Mecklenburg, and then you went to Thuringia.

WOLF: Yes, because my father got work there. It was there that I came into contact with Marxist writings for the first time. And I found them convincing, they made sense to me. Actually that was the first step. For years I was firmly convinced—it was then that I joined the Party—that it was the direct opposite of what had happened in fascist Germany. And I *wanted* something that was the direct opposite. At all costs I didn't want anything that could be like the past. I believe that was often the case in my generation. That was the source of our commitment, and that was the reason why we clung to it so long. Actually we didn't have to overcome inner resistance. And even later I still didn't see any alternative. And then there was another factor that affected our generation, my—

GAUS: We were born in the same year, 1929, but in the East and in the West, and that makes a difference—

WOLF: A big difference, yes. A factor that made my generation take such a long time to grow up. It's that back then, in the early 1950s when I had finished my university studies and was working in the Writers Union, we met comrades who had come out of the concentration camps, out of the prisons, back from exile, impressive people—today I still believe they were among the most interesting people you could meet in Germany at that time—and our guilty conscience about them was another big reason for our commitment to their cause.

GAUS: Okay, so today, after everything you've experienced in the meantime, would you say: I'm still happy with this commitment— aside from its specific content—because without it I wouldn't have become the person I am?

WOLF: Well, I wouldn't have become the person I am, that much is true. I think a great deal about that, but I've never been able to imagine inventing a different life for myself. Whether I'm happy about it—

GAUS: You still feel that way today?

WOLF: Yes. Whether I'm happy about it or not isn't the question as far as I'm concerned, it's all at a much deeper level than that now. You know everything was very much a matter of chance. We were refugees when we left Landsberg/Warthe, which today is called Gorzów, and crossed the Oder, and we stayed on in Mecklenburg because the Americans were coming from the other side and the Russians from the East, so we were in between, and then we were occupied by the Russians, the part I was living in. Of course we wanted to make a mad dash across the Elbe, we really wanted to get to the Americans. In two more days we would have crossed the Elbe, and my life would have been completely different. But instead it has turned out this way. The fates of Germans depended on where we happened to be.

GAUS: I'll get back to the central themes of your life, as I understand them. But first I want to return to the subject of the young Christa Wolf. I mentioned that we were born in the same year, 1929. You've already talked about what 1945 meant to you, as a watershed year. I want to ask you about something else: Do you have the same sweet memories as I do of that enchantingly beautiful summer of 1945 when planes would fly overhead and you didn't have to go down into the cellar anymore? Did you have that same powerful sense that peace had come?

WOLF: The sense of peace—yes. I experienced the end of the war as a time of great danger. During our trek we kept being attacked by low-flying planes, and naturally I was delighted that after May 8, no low-flying plane would come down on us ever again. But I didn't feel the summer was enchantingly beautiful. We were jammed in together on farms, in barns or in attics, and the feeling I had that summer was more one of great hardship and depression.

GAUS: When did you lose the feeling of hardship and depression, and why?

WOLF: I think it went away a few years later when we—

GAUS: Years is a long time.

WOLF: Yes, it lasted for years. Then in 1947 we moved to Thuringia, where I finished high school and I came in contact with a lot of younger people—everyone in my class was younger than I was, and only a few were refugees—and then I suddenly realized that there was such a thing as an easy life. I'd had no experience of that, I didn't have any youth. With these two or three younger girls I sometimes had an almost carefree feeling again.

GAUS: Did you think, back in 1945 and the years that followed, that fascism and the war had plunged people so deeply into poverty, misery, fear, and crime that now we were bound to come to our senses, to turn away from all that once and for all? Did you count on things changing?

WOLF: Not in 1945, but I would say in '48, '49, when I had fully realized what had happened back then. And when I saw the danger that something like it could happen again, I didn't think that was possible, I really thought the experience would lead to deep, to fundamental self-examination.

GAUS: At least during our own lifetimes?

WOLF: Yes, yes, naturally I thought so. I never thought it possible that I would see a swastika again on the wall of a German house. If someone had told me that after the war, I don't know what I would have done.

GAUS: We know now that the hope that many people of our generation felt after 1945 was a delusion, a self-delusion. Apart from what you and I individually may have hoped for then, we had that hope in common. So, putting it in general terms, what does it mean to you to realize that people can't pass on their experience, that the next generations demand the right to make their own mistakes, including terrible new disasters?

WOLF: It really knocked the wind out of me the first time I realized that, years ago. I wasn't just depressed, it made me feel desperate. That's changed somewhat. I do think there may be something for people to learn from our generation, not in the sense of imitating it but rather learning what not to do.

GAUS: That would be quite an achievement!

WOLF: Yes, it would be an achievement, but at the moment it seems they're resisting that too. I've reached the point of somehow accepting it now because I see that the younger people really are learning from their own experiences. I don't think they are stupider than we are, than I am.

GAUS: You aren't afraid that they'll harm someone—not you but themselves—harm that you'd like to spare them?

WOLF: Yes, I am afraid of that.

GAUS: Doesn't it drive you crazy not to be able to share anything, to pass anything on?

WOLF: Not any more. It used to drive me crazy. But—

GAUS: Is it a step toward resignation or toward wisdom that it doesn't drive you crazy any more? Or are they the same thing?

WOLF: No, they're definitely not the same thing. On this point, what I am is resigned.

GAUS: Without bitterness?

WOLF: Yes.

GAUS: In recent years have you doubted whether you were allowed to feel sad or unhappy?

WOLF: Yes, I think—May I ask you something? No, I suppose that isn't appropriate.

GAUS: Actually I'm the one asking the questions here, but go ahead and ask.

WOLF: What prompted you to ask me that?

GAUS: I can't say. I don't want to say.

WOLF: All right, I accept that. You're right—in thinking what your question suggests. First, as a child I was taught a double message. On the one hand there was the Hitler Youth, which aimed to make children hard and tough. On the other, there was the Protestant upbringing I had at home, which didn't much lean to tender feelings either. And then later, in the early days of the Party, of course it was the same thing: You really have to be happy, you're obligated to be happy, now that we're soon going to have paradise on earth—

GAUS: After studying the subject of Christa Wolf, that's exactly what I thought, and that's what moved me to ask the question.

WOLF: Yes, I realize that. Now that we're going to reach paradise, to build it in our own lifetime, why shouldn't we be happy right now! Of course all that changes if you love someone, if you have children. You get softer then, and then you get unhappy too.

GAUS: We've come back again to the theme we discussed earlier when we were talking about Christa T.: the fact that you often made yourself live in a way that was against your nature, for what you thought were good and compelling reasons. Did that need for self-control make it hard for you to be natural?

WOLF: If things had stayed that way, no doubt I would have felt inhibited and confined, but they didn't. It's true that I used to push crises away from me, or tried to solve them rationally, for years. But then came a real eruption, an outburst of sadness, when I wrote the book *The Quest for Christa T.* You could look at my first three books as stages along the way to that outburst. In *Moskauer Novelle*, everything ran along conventional lines. In *Divided Heaven*, the girl broke down, but she managed to pull through anyway. But Christa T. doesn't pull through.

GAUS: But she isn't destroyed.

WOLF: She isn't destroyed, but she doesn't get through it either. There's a great deal of sadness in that book.

GAUS: Yes, one can say that. It's a great book if I may say so.

WOLF: Anyhow it's a sad book. Back when I wrote it I always used to deny that, to some degree, but in fact it's very sad.

GAUS: But let me ask you again: you say Christa T. isn't a failure, that failure is something different. What is it?

WOLF: Failure is not having any crises but hanging tough, bulldozing straight through things that aren't really you, that are extraneous to you.

GAUS: Having no crises?

WOLF: Having them or not having them, but in any case doing what is secondary to you, your whole life long. You can be tremendously successful that way, you could become a prime minister and I don't know what else, but you couldn't be a writer. For me, that would be failure.

GAUS: What had to happen to Christa Wolf, wanting what she thought was a great new society—what had to happen to her before she could write this book about Christa T., this young woman who, as you say, wasn't destroyed but was caught between her willingness to work for a great cause and her need for personal self-realization? What had to happen before you invented this character Christa T., your spiritual stepsister? Was inventing her a substitute for action, a substitute for real life?

WOLF: Just the opposite. Inventing her *was* action, and *was* life at long last.

GAUS: But what had to happen to you before you could do it?

WOLF: In your question you said I wanted a great new society. Actually I wasn't so much concerned with the new and great. Instead I took the idea of what I really wanted from Marxism and socialist literature, and from everything I studied at university, and I believed that this society and this idea of things would achieve what I wanted: the self-realization of human beings. And when I understood that something different was happening—it was like this: you already mentioned that I was a candidate for the Central Committee of the Socialist Unity Party, and in 1965 the Central Committee held a plenum, the notorious Eleventh Plenum, which they turned into a meeting on the arts, that is, a punitive action against artists, especially filmmakers and writers but painters as well, and I was present and gave a speech, a speech in *opposition*—

GAUS: And in fact you spoke very courageously—

WOLF: But I couldn't help seeing from the inside how the machinery worked. And then it became clear to me that it wasn't working properly. It wasn't moving in the right direction. When I left the plenum—I still remember exactly what I was thinking as I walked down the stairs: hands off the machine. I wrote about it too. That was what I felt back then. And when I wrote about Christa T. it wasn't to find sanctuary in the book, but rather I understood that writing it was my way of taking issue with what was happening. But the book rescued me anyway.

GAUS: That makes it urgent to ask the question that's bound to occur to people, here and in other instances: Why did you go on standing by the flag?

WOLF: Which flag?

GAUS: The flag of the GDR, the flag of this alternative society that you thought was the right response to what happened before 1945—that's what I mean by flag.

WOLF: Yes, of course I have to *write* about that—

GAUS: Are you writing?

WOLF: I've been thinking about it nonstop for three years, nonstop, truly day and night. I believe you have to bring history into this question. Because my standing by the flag, as you call it, of course was very soon viewed as absolute desertion by the people who thought they were holding the flag. I was able to stay there—I mean not only in the GDR but beside the flag—because I was surrounded by so many people who were going through the same development, and for a while we still thought that *we* were the ones who would really put this country on the right track. And it wasn't just writers; back then there were economists involved and intellectuals from other professions; and when I lived in Halle back in 1963, or even before that, and was working with a work brigade in the railroad car plant, I saw the same thing among workers. There was a broad movement in the GDR that wanted the same thing I thought we should want, and I didn't want to leave, even though I knew from 1965 on that I would have nothing to do with the party apparatus.

GAUS: When you read your Stasi files last year—more than forty volumes describing how you were kept under surveillance—you discovered, to your own surprise—because you say you must have suppressed the memory—that from 1959 to 1962, that is, over thirty years ago, you were an IM, an unofficial informer for the Stasi.[2] You had conversations with Stasi officials, you gave them reports about colleagues you knew from your work as a writer and literary editor, partly in Berlin, partly in Halle.

2. IM: see note 6 to "The Multiple Being Inside Us," above.

"They want to turn everything around"
Extract from Christa Wolf's speech at the Eleventh Plenum of the Central Committee of the Socialist Unity Party, 1965

My impression is that this conference, which is justified in criticizing features that have truly gone wrong, is exposing us to the danger not just of taking a more aggressive line—which we may have to do—but of halting or even retracting certain achievements in literature and aesthetics that were gained through the Bitterfeld Conference and the foundation it laid. And I would like to warn you of this danger, which I observe in many institutions.

Comrades, the same people who had an overview of all these features—unlike each of us individually, who only see particular details—the people who saw the trends and either let them continue or promoted them, or followed a policy that shifted from moment to moment—I am referring to the arts division of the Central Committee—never once invited us to talk with them, never once asked us to prepare arguments, or accused us of anything specific. These people now want to make a 180-degree turn. They want to turn everything around. They mean not only to cover up every bare neck on television but also to view any criticism of any government or party official as damaging to the party. They're doing it already. That's how things are. It isn't right to use these negative features in our arts policy to put people on the defensive, to force writers into a defensive position so that all they can do is keep on saying "Comrades, we're not enemies of the party." . . .

What I believe is that this institution, which I have already named a number of times, will prove to be very timid on the next points that come up as well. It has been said often and by everyone at the Bitterfeld Conference, in the newspapers and elsewhere, that art is not possible without risk taking. That is, art raises and must raise questions that are new, that the artist believes he sees, even without seeing the solution. What kinds of questions do I mean? Not naturalistic, economic questions in the narrow sense. What I have in mind is this: When I came back from West Germany, I was deeply preoccupied with the problem of human types, which are evolving very differently, not only in the GDR but in both German states, within particular social strata, among young people, in particular professions, and so on. This is a typical example of a question in literature. We have very little help when it comes to such questions, because our sociology and psychology afford little material for generalization. We have to study the issue and make experiments in our field, and it still happens—no doubt it will happen to me or has happened already—that one generalizes about something that isn't worth generalizing about. That may be true. But I would like to say that art in any case is based on individual cases and that art now, as ever, cannot give up being subjective, that is, understanding the handwriting, the language, the mental world of the artist.

Extract from *Kahlschlag. Das 11. Plenum des ZK der SED 1965.* (Berlin: Aufbau Verlag, 1991, pp. 340, 343).

WOLF: I think I have to be more precise about this file and the files in general. I didn't personally read this file until two days ago, when you brought it to me. Everyone else who has used it had access to it before me. Now I have analyzed it for myself. It's true it was a shock for me, when I read my so-called "victim files" in which I was the object of Stasi surveillance, to find a mention that there was also an IM file on me. My hair stood on end, literally. I would have sworn that there could be no such file on me, and I have to explain why. In 1959—I knew this, I hadn't forgotten it—there were three meetings between me and two men who asked me about things I no longer remember in detail but which had to do with my work as an editor of *Neue Deutsche Literatur* and in the Writers Union. What I no longer remembered was that I had a code name and that I myself had written a report. That is, I had very effectively suppressed my knowledge of events that could have led to an IM file.

And after that, in Halle, there are four reports about meetings with a man whom I remember quite well, but who must have played a double game both with us and with his bureau. He doesn't write in his reports that my husband was always present, but talks as if he were meeting me on my own, carrying on with the semiconspiratorial rendezvous his colleagues had with me in Berlin; and he didn't tell me what he was writing either. The meetings took place in our apartment. He only reports what suits him, and in very brief form, not the critical things we happen to remember we said to him, for example about censorship.

In a file 137 pages long, I found twenty pages that contained reports on these meetings. All the rest is investigations or reports about me, or personal bios on me or by me, and bureaucratic stuff from his office headquarters. I simply have to say that here, because the newspaper reports gave the impression that there was a file in which 130 pages were taken up with reports about my cooperation with the Stasi.

GAUS: Before I come back to my basic question about all this, I want to ask this: Seeing how you just described what's in your file, and now that so much has been said about you and your Stasi files, do you want to comment on the way Stasi files are being handled in general?

WOLF: Now of course I'm not in a good position to say anything critical, I realize that. But my impression is that the procedure has to change. In my case, there are forty-two volumes of so-called "victim files"—a phrase that I don't claim applies to me—that report on me up to 1980. The files from the last nine years were almost completely destroyed, which means that we might have had perhaps eighty volumes of files if they had all been preserved. We were under intensive surveillance from 1969 onward.

GAUS: You and your husband?

WOLF: Yes, Gerhard and I. And then there is this one IM record from more than thirty years ago, the one I just described. By law the press has the right to apply to see the IM files of people suspected of IM activity. A journalist told me they had been given clues that there might be an IM record on me.

GAUS: Only the Gauck Commission could actually have supplied such clues.

WOLF: I don't know. Then the IM record can be published, which in my case happened just at the time when I had my article in the *Berliner Zeitung*—

GAUS: —in which you yourself report what you discovered when you read your files.

WOLF: In which I reported it because I saw what was happening to Heiner Müller, and I thought now I have to talk about it too. Of course it could be a coincidence that it was at that same moment that my file was given to various newspapers—though not to *Der Spiegel*, which didn't get it from the Gauck Commission, at least not officially. Anyhow, I think we should consider whether it is acceptable to turn over a file of this kind to the press without any commentary, without the person involved being told anything about it, and when, as in my case, there are so many files of the opposite kind that the press are told nothing about, and the person himself is not allowed to see the files. Those were the rules of the Gauck Commission as they were explained to me by the woman who worked on our files. At first I didn't want to make any clear statements saying that this woman colleague of ours had let me look briefly at my file; she wasn't actually allowed to do that. Recently I learned that she has died, and that's why I'm talking about it now.

GAUS: She wasn't allowed to show it to you because it was, so to speak, a file of criminal evidence against you, Christa Wolf, code-named "Margarete." And you *were* allowed to see your victim files—

WOLF: —where our code name was "Double-Tongued"—

GAUS: —but not your file as a criminal suspect.

WOLF: Yes, I really wasn't allowed to see that. I was very disturbed and asked this woman colleague to show it to me anyhow, and she said: "But there's nothing in it!" Then she did give me a brief look at it, as I said. The reports from Halle weren't in the file yet and so I couldn't make any reference to them, and I was very much criticized for not doing so, by *Der Spiegel* for instance. I could only quote what was said in my "victim files" and what I was able to get photocopied from there. Following an application to the Gauck Commission, I received a copy of the file three weeks after the journalists had it.

You can destroy a person that way, I know what I'm talking about. If I'm regarded as a "Stasi collaborator," reduced to the two letters "IM" wherever I go, even in other countries, as far as *Die Zeit* and *Der Spiegel* can reach—and I foresaw that this would happen—all I can do is repeat: you can destroy a person that way. And we have to think about whether this part of the Gauck Commission's work can continue to be handled in this manner; whether the law on this point needs to be changed, whether it has to be managed differently. I don't know. But we have to give it some thought.

GAUS: I'll come back to my basic question. Why, at the time, did you get involved in this kind of collaboration?

WOLF: It's hard for me to answer that question because of course I didn't have any memory of "collaboration," but that's how it must have been at the time. What I remember—memory for me is very often of feelings that accompany actual events but not always of the events themselves—is that I felt deeply uncomfortable at the three meetings that took place in Berlin. I'm only talking about Berlin, what happened in Halle was somewhat different. It appears I got into it for two reasons: first I felt I was in a jam and didn't know how to get out. And second, I wasn't convinced yet that this was something I absolutely had to turn down, because I didn't yet have the attitude to the Stasi that I began to have a short time later, when they couldn't have gotten anywhere with me no matter what they did. I reduced my contacts with them to the minimum—I think that's clear from the file—but all the same, yes, I did get involved with them. Now I am trying very hard to trace the reasons. I have no choice but to resurrect that whole period, because I can understand it all only in terms of the time when it happened. Which makes me think about the fact that the highpoint, or lowpoint, of my commitment, or rather my dependency—that's the right word—on the Party and on Party ideology was already behind me; and actually it was in Halle that I began a different development, when I first encountered major criticisms of my work, which had to do with my attitude to the Twenty-Second Party Conference of the Communist Party of the Soviet Union.

GAUS: That is, with your attitude to de-Stalinization.

WOLF: Yes. This happened as a result of the Twenty-Second Party Conference, which of course had been a deep shock to me. At the Twenty-Second Party Conference, the divergent standpoints of Sholokhov and Tvardovsky were very interesting to me.[3] Tvardovsky was the editor of *Novy Mir*, which had been first to publish the work of Solzhenitsyn. I supported his views at the Party conference and was criticized for it. I am only trying to say that I had reached the phase when I was beginning to think critically. I have to reflect more about how it was all connected; what stopped me at the time from just saying no to the Stasi.

GAUS: You spoke of the discomfort you felt about the whole business, your memory of a feeling, the way you tend to remember how you felt about an event. I read your file when I was preparing for this interview and in fact I did have the impression, for example, that you tried to avoid everything that savored of the conspiratorial. In this connection I want to ask—but please, I mean it in a general sense—Do you by nature avoid conflict, not from lack of courage,

3. Mikhail Sholokhov, 1905–84, winner of the 1965 Nobel Prize for Literature and best known for *And Quiet Flows the Don* and *The Don Flows Home to the Sea*, was an exponent of socialist realism. Aleksandr Tvardovsky was from 1958 to 1970 the editor of the influential monthly journal *Novy Mir* (The new world), printed in Moscow as an official organ of the USSR Writers Union, which published many censored authors and was itself the object of repeated censorship.

which you've displayed in abundance on other occasions, but simply by nature, and were you concerned, or are you still concerned, with establishing harmony almost at any price? Was that one reason why you didn't pull out of the arrangement?

WOLF: Do you mind if I really hit the ceiling?

GAUS: Go ahead.

WOLF: I mean, really. Because what you just said reflects what's happening right now. The things in this Stasi file, the way IMs and Stasi people characterize me in the file, is being taken as a valid description of my character in all the newspapers. (Of course I could get examples of just the opposite characteristics out of my "victim files.") So they talk about "intellectual timidity," that's making headlines now. If you read it in context, you could also interpret it to mean that I tried to hold back, to pull out of the whole business, not to get in any deeper. One of the obscene results of the way my file has been described in the press is that they've taken over the Stasi's characterization, the Stasi's language, and are applying it to me as I am today. It's unbelievable. I know you didn't do that, but the reason I reacted so violently to your question is that I have been stunned to watch this technique they are using.

But I want to give more attention to your question about wanting to avoid conflict, I want to think that over. The situation with me is that I've always avoided conflicts, or not let them play a crucial role, in cases where I wasn't quite sure I was right. I don't necessarily think that applies to this case, but your question was more general. I come from a lower-middle-class background, to use that fine-sounding phrase. In the Party they always said: look at it from the class standpoint. I was often uncertain about that; in the 1950s I often used to think, well are they really right about that or aren't they? I had tried to internalize that system of values and withdraw from the other system. That's a pretty big subject, I can only touch on it here. But it was precisely my inner conflict that often led to my avoiding outward conflict, in the beginning. When it became clearer and clearer to me that I don't want what they want, and they're wrong, or at least I'm right too, right in my case, then I no longer had any fear of confrontation. Or I did feel fear and I overcame it, for example at the Eleventh Plenum, and on many other occasions that were less spectacular and weren't reported in the press. So, I'll continue thinking about whether I'm wary of conflict, but I can say that if I did hold back, that had to do with doubting whether what I thought and felt was really tenable, and wondering if I would cause damage by supporting it. That was an important consideration for me then.

GAUS: Turning to the present, of course it can be an easy way out to accuse yourself and express remorse. As I understand it, you haven't reproached yourself with anything, but you have examined yourself. Self-reproach can be a cheap response. Now that public-opinion makers are demanding it from you, are you still daring to contradict them, to say—in fact you've already said it—What happened was so complicated, and no one came to harm as a result of my actions that would make it necessary for me to apologize now, and the Cold War was on, and I believed I was working in a good cause; so that simple, one-dimensional reproaches and self-reproach wouldn't do justice to the complexity of that time—is that the message? Are you taking the risk of refusing to salute the banner that has been raised by the new trend-setters? Are you saying: I refuse to blame myself as current opinion demands?

WOLF: Of course it's absolutely clear to me that I could ease my position in certain quarters if I would display remorse and feelings of guilt. But I don't feel them. It's much worse than that—or better, depending on how you look at it. When I realized that this file existed and got a brief look at it, and then when I had a chance to really read it, the feeling I had was something quite different. I was looking at a stranger. That isn't who I am. And that's a feeling I have to work on. It's really harder than simply saying: Yes, I'm sorry, I regret that. I don't have any guilt feelings. My guilt feelings have been melted away. Guilt feelings often are something a person uses to hide deeper insights, and what I'm doing now is trying to get at the deeper insights. Who was I really, back then? A terrible feeling of alienness comes over me when I read the file. Naturally I also wonder what it was that pulled me out of it again, because that dependency—I was threatened. When I read the language that the Stasi people use, that they use to characterize me, but also when they quote things I supposedly said—Heiner Müller calls it Stasi prose—yes, but I do still remember that was how we used to speak—I must try to climb back down into that shaft and take a look at it, a look at myself, and find out the details of how things got to that point, and also how I got away from it again.

GAUS: You prefaced your book *The Quest for Christa T.*, which we've mentioned several times in this interview, with a question from Johannes R. Becher: "This coming-to-oneself—what is it?" You've begun to answer this question here. So I'll ask a follow-up question: what is this coming-to-yourself, Frau Wolf? And to what extent have you come to yourself?

WOLF: I don't think I can answer that, at least not the last part, and it's a hard thing to define. I talk about my own case.

GAUS: Yes, that's our only concern. Christa Wolf in person.

WOLF: In my case, things have always come about through crisis, through what in part were life-and-death crises. For example, after the Eleventh Plenum in 1965, I was in a deep depression for a long time, in a clinical sense. It cost me so much effort to take that stand that afterward I went into a sort of collapse. It went on for a long time. And then I sat down and wrote *The Quest for Christa T.* and worked my way out of the depression, and out of my self-doubts too. And it's happened again each time. I've always gone through crises when I recognized: that's something I absolutely don't want, and when I also recognized what I really do want. For example, in 1976 after the Biermann affair, when you really had to stand up for something against the pressure. After that I wrote books and did things I could never have done otherwise. I went through clear-cut stages. My life hasn't unfolded in a steady, even way. There are clear breaks in it, so I can say "before that" and "after that." And each time "after that" I'd moved a bit farther along the road to myself, and I think I was able to show it in my books, too. The same thing is happening now. Of course, I'm in a crisis now too, and I have the impression that it's helping me to gain more freedom. First, I naturally feel relieved—

GAUS: Relieved about what?

WOLF: That I no longer have to hide this business, which of course has troubled me, this file; that I can now talk quite openly with everyone about it. And, second, I have a feeling of greater freedom because the only question facing me has been: Am I going to go along with the demagogues? Will I internalize this image of me that is being handed to the public? I knew I'd be lost if I did. Or, I wondered, if I call on my whole life history, everything I've written and done—can I insist on myself and go on from there?

GAUS: Have you a rough idea what kind of person Christa Wolf may be in this next stage?

WOLF: I've an idea how I'd like her to be.

GAUS: What kind of idea?

WOLF: Skinless, very sensitive.

GAUS: You can't want that.

WOLF: No, but that's how it is. Open, very open, more tolerant toward other people, and also more modest. I certainly won't climb up on any high horse. But I'll be harder on myself, less considerate. I think nothing else can ever hurt me so much again. Now I don't have to avoid pain any more. I've noticed that I haven't been able to write especially well just recently, and now it's clear to me why. I wanted to avoid the pain. And now life goes on.

GAUS: Are you writing?

WOLF: Yes. I can let in the pain, the shame, all of that.

GAUS: Is conformity a human right?

WOLF: So here comes your special question—

GAUS: You mean the question I ask in all my interviews?

WOLF: Too bad. I'd been hoping you were going to ask me what you occasionally ask—

GAUS: About old Adam and old Eve? Do old Adam and old Eve have a human right to conform?

WOLF: My dear Herr Gaus, old Adam and old Eve are the first patriarchal couple, and Adam had another wife before Eve, Lilith, a troublemaker who didn't conform, and that's why she was demonized and banned; and that's how it's gone for the female part of the patriarchy ever since. And since the patriarchy has continued or even intensified its drive to get rid of, suppress, push aside, ban, and demonize the female part—including the female part in the male, of course—right down to the present day, we need to grant the necessity of adjusting to each other, being considerate of each other. It appears that there were other social orders before ours that lasted for many, many centuries, where people were more at home with the group they lived in. But that's far in the past, and the conditions we live in today require that we make some concessions to each other and show each other forbearance, because the pressures would be unendurable for most people if we didn't conform.

GAUS: Is conformity a human right? The right of the weak to conform? A right that you don't want to grant yourself? And that one should give up if one has the strength and there's a worthwhile cause? Is nonconformity ethical, but is conformity a right?

WOLF: I can't answer that yes or no.

GAUS: Have you conformed in your life?

WOLF: By the time I noticed I was conforming, I usually had already reached the point of stopping. Definitely I conformed, now in this area, now in that; I certainly think so. But actually I always broke out of each adaptation. You know, in 1989 I saw people who had adapted for so long—and others who hadn't adapted to start with—who suddenly wore a different expression and showed what they had inside besides conformity, namely, a great longing for a life that fulfilled them. And just to mention this in passing: of course this was an experience that made me very, very glad that I had stayed in the GDR and could live to see it. But it also showed me that one shouldn't be in too much of a hurry to grant people permission to conform. One should also credit them with the ability to give up their conformity when it will no longer cost them their lives to do it.

GAUS: It's not always a question of one's life. It's a matter of losing one's job, of the many varieties of dependency that are different in different systems, but at bottom they exist everywhere, in every system. Isn't that so?

WOLF: Yes.

GAUS: Isn't there a risk facing intellectuals, writers, politicians, the political and intellectual class—don't they run the risk of viewing their needs and standards as the needs and standards of the general public, of frail, fragile, weak human beings, men and women alike? Isn't there a great danger of that?

WOLF: There is a danger.

GAUS: Haven't we just been in that kind of danger again, going by what you've said?

WOLF: I really don't think so. Because my starting point truly was those people to whom I grant their right to conform, and I grant it honestly at this very moment, when they are afraid for their jobs. But I'm unwilling to deny them the possession of the spark that some time or other can turn into a blaze.

GAUS: I'm not trying to deny anyone a spark. I just want to allow people a recess where we don't intrude with our different breeds of agitation. Joachim Herrmann and the *Frankfurter Allgemeine Zeitung* both are agitators, although they have agitated along different lines.

WOLF: Yes, I allow them a recess.

GAUS: And agitators of both sorts to carry on too?

WOLF: Yes, certainly.

GAUS: What would you say happened—judging by your experiences and impressions—what has happened to the people you observed during the turning point at the end of 1989, those you realized had a need to be subjects rather than objects, to be persons with self-determination and not objects at the disposal of others?

WOLF: Various things happened. You're right—we talked about that before—the pressure to adapt is very strong, and many people are adapting. Also there is a great—yes, a feeling of disappointment, or of sadness. But just now I'm also detecting something else. It seems that this summons, this pressure to forget one's past life when the occasion calls for it—that people are no longer accepting it so completely. Nowadays I'm receiving a quantity of letters related to this damned Stasi file, including some from the former GDR, and there are some very reflective letters among them. I see that people—the people who write to me, who of course are a tiny minority—seem prepared to examine themselves again too, if there is an opportunity. I don't think it has anything to do with GDR nostalgia, that would be awful, but it has to do with the fact that you can't develop an identity or acquire a new one if you simply throw the old one away. This gives me some hope.

GAUS: What is your main criticism of the majority of West Germans, or rather of the majority of West Germans in public life, since the turning point? What are the main things we did wrong during unification?

WOLF: I said earlier that I'm chary of offering criticism right now. Besides, I've had different opinions about it during different phases in the past few years. There are two things that seem to me really regrettable. One is that West Germans don't know about life in the GDR. There's no one to blame for that. West and East Germans are complete strangers to each other. The second thing is that no attempt is being made to recognize this fact, to accept it and then to take cautious steps to get to know each other, but instead—not everywhere and I really don't want to generalize, I know so many West Germans whom we can't get along without now—instead, many people who don't know us and weren't familiar with the GDR are assigning guilt and hurling reproaches, so that a lot of people from the former GDR may feel they are actually being asked to deny their lives. And that's dangerous in the long run. You can't work through things that you exclude, that you can't admit to. You can't be really honest when you are living under the conditions of a tribunal; I know that from my own example. But honesty is what we have to achieve.

GAUS: At the moment you are in California on a study grant, you're writing here. In interviews you've given recently, you said that here in California you've seen evidences of the Germans who emigrated to the United States during the Nazi period—Thomas Mann, Lion Feuchtwanger, Germans who were driven out of Nazi Germany—and some people in Germany thought you intended to draw a comparison between their emigration and your time here as a visiting scholar. Do you want to comment on that?

WOLF: That is a dreadful misinterpretation, which has bothered me a great deal in the last few days when I realized that the misunderstanding had occurred. Of course, I wasn't able to see the television interview in question. I don't know whether some things were edited out, whether something I said was taken out of context, or whether I expressed myself unclearly. Right now I am further than I have ever been before from presuming to compare or equate myself with the Germans who were shut out or thrown out of Nazi Germany. I'm glad to have the chance to say that here. It really is a misunderstanding.

GAUS: The socialist system—perhaps not the idea of socialism but the socialist system—has collapsed around the world, apart from some small remaining outposts. One can see that the victorious system, the capitalist system or the free market economy, is less and less able to cope with the new problems. Do you think this will result in some kind of socialist idea redeveloping at some time in the future?

WOLF: No, I don't think so. I don't expect things to result in any idea or ideology.

GAUS: Not in our lifetime or for a considerable time to come—

WOLF: Not at all.

GAUS: But not ever?

WOLF: No, I think—

GAUS: Where hope is concerned you're back where you were in 1945, a conclusive change has occurred. But there is no such thing as a conclusive change.

WOLF: No, you're not seeing exactly what I mean. What I mean is, something could change, but as I see it now it probably wouldn't originate in an idea or ideology again, and of course I wouldn't want that anyhow; it could only come from the grassroots, from people's circumstances and their dissatisfaction with them. It could only be something practical, perhaps beginning quite small; practical attempts that affect how people live together and that might gradually increase in scale. That's the only way I can picture it.

GAUS: Is that the only hope, or is there another hope that you haven't given up?

WOLF: Sometimes I have little hope; but I still can't imagine that the younger people who are growing up now, and who want to live, aren't capable of blocking the drive to destruction and self-destruction that seems to be governing mankind at present. Of course, the task is terribly difficult because it means fundamentally changing our needs, the false needs that are now satisfied in a false way. I had hoped that socialism would change those needs, but it hasn't at all and it can't; it's done the opposite. The question is whether there is any chance of achieving it gradually, starting at a grassroots level, with groups that are small at first and maybe based on an awareness of the great danger facing us. It has a lot to do with giving things up.

GAUS: Are you afraid of developments in Germany?

WOLF: Not afraid, but I am very concerned.

GAUS: Permit me one last question. Are you doing well at growing older, so far at least?

WOLF: Sometimes yes, sometimes not so well. At the moment

I'm in a situation of such turmoil. I didn't expect to go through such fundamental upheaval again at my age. And that may make a person younger, to the extent that she calls herself into question again in her entirety in the way that only younger people do as a rule. But I'm not afraid of growing older. I'm looking forward to watching my grandchildren grow up.

The Symbols of Nuria Quevedo

➤➤ ◄◄

From the roaring, bellowing road jammed with traffic and construction machinery, from torn-open Berlin into the elevator,
rising again at last to the eighth floor on Karl Marx Avenue to Nuria
Quevedo's studio, to the gray November light that painters love, and
to stillness and concentration. The first picture that catches my
eye—no doubt it is meant to do so—begins to preoccupy me at
once. I'll ignore that one for now. It's remarkable, I think. A still
life. Down below, on the left, is the picture of the woman with the
fish, I'll leave that for later too. First let's look at the series of heads
and hands that I have already seen in black and white, in the form
of charcoal drawings repeated tirelessly over and over, which I now
learn evolved out of the Don Quixote cycle—Nuria too seems to
have realized this only gradually—and represent a quest—for
what? I am seeing this theme in color for the first time; immediately I am captivated by the earth tones bordering on Venetian
red that underlie and surround the black charcoal outlines, sometimes in multiple layers: charcoal and tempera on unprimed canvas
treated only with sizing glue.

Don't you smell the sizing? It's really strong. Now I smell it, I
ask if she developed this technique herself. Not oil under reflective

Speech given at the opening of an exhibition of Nuria Quevedo's work at the Technical
University, Berlin, December 7, 1993.

glass but a rough surface that doesn't conceal the strong pattern of the canvas, that draws you almost irresistibly to touch it with your fingertips. To touch it the way the hand in one of the pictures—it's . the first in the series—lightly touches the body of the other figure. It appears to me to be the hand of someone listening. Not really curious, and definitely not claiming possession. Waiting, shy. Listening. Then again, the palm of the hand cradles the head—its own head. Now the head is not a listener but a watcher, reflective, concentrated. It remains reflective and concentrated throughout the sequence. Tiny nuances in the brush stroke, in the shift of light and dark in the face, nuances to which I could not even give a name, change the expression slightly. Head and hand in the tension between thought and action, a pause between the last thought and the next action. Now the fingers are held behind glass while the head watches to see what happens. The refraction of the light is shown as a fracture of the hand. The head is not surprised, the long, narrow, angular head with its big sad nose and its eyes, which perhaps never close. What does it really want, what is its persistence aimed at? I think it wants to see what *is*. It has something behind it that has moved it to think about the interplay between head and hand, perhaps to distrust this interplay. Something that has made it still. "Life Is a Dream," one part of the earlier sequence is entitled. I cannot imagine this head speaking, calling, shouting. Not laughing either; barely smiling. Pensive. Now the hand is held up to the mirror, so that the head sees the back and the palm at the same time. Searchingly. Quevedo has not kept to the laws of physics, the hand in the mirror is breaking away; this is not about naturalism. These works lie somewhere between drawing and painting, the color values are as important as the brushstroke, which has grown sure from years of practice but not routine.

In one image from spring 1989, Nuria Quevedo has made the left hand hold onto the right fist—a fist that is no longer clenched in the pocket and seems to want to hit something. The currents and storms of time strike Nuria directly. Her responses, as a printmaker and painter, are becoming more indirect, more symbolic. Behind the everyday eruptions of passion that blind the eyes of many, she sees what is permanent in human life. Basic themes, basic emotions, basic gestures.

Every evening when I sit at the dining table, my gaze falls on a picture that shows a plaza in front of a row of buildings—I love paintings of houses and urban landscapes. This picture is of a place in Barcelona. Nuria's native city. (Once she painted her grandmother's room, which may tell more about her childhood than many stories would.) To paint this picture she must have sat with her back to the fantastic, unfinished Sagrada Familia, the church designed by the architect Gaudi which is one of the symbols of Barcelona. When I saw the picture for the first time, the row of houses behind the desolate plaza looked familiar to me. By chance I had stood once at the same spot in her city taking photos, some time after she had painted her picture. But when I was there, you had to cross through a rather sparse park to get to those houses. It turned out that the park was a later addition, meant to dress up the neighborhood. Nuria saw and painted the plaza when it was bare, painted it yellow ocher; her Spanish yellow dominates the image. A lamppost. A single human figure: a man, very small, with his hands folded behind his back, in the large expanse near the left-hand rim of the painting. Is he looking up at the row of buildings? They must look unapproachable to him too. A facade of towering cubes, ranging in hue from pale green to pale yellow. Rows of narrow windows with bits of washing hanging out here and there. No faces. Down below, a dark, threatening area and no entryways. The shadows of the man and the lamppost fall toward the left, it's an evening light. The sky a clear yellow without any conciliatory admixture of gold. House, man, square, sky—as concrete as possible. Austere like most of her works. And at the same time, symbols of a house, man, square, sky in their relation to each other and in their lack of relation.

When she visited the prehistoric cave of Altamira in Spain, Nuria Quevedo found that the Stone Age wall drawings are made up of the same, simple elements that she uses in her work: charcoal, pigments taken from the earth. She must also have seen the outlines of hands in the cave.

It's noon now, the sun has come out, if you look out the windows you can see as far as Neukölln and Kreuzberg, to the place on the new map of Berlin where a blue dotted line traces the former route of the Berlin Wall, of which there is no longer any trace. We turn around. There is the still life I saw before, now bathed in the full

Nuria Quevedo, illustration to Karl Mickel's *Kants Affe* (1993).
Courtesy Edition Balance.

light of noon. What do you make of it? Nuria asks.—A woman rising out of the sea, I say.—You see a woman in it?—Yes. A woman
rising out of the sea, grieving so much at what she saw there that
she is almost frozen with grief. A mermaid. The snake above her
face is a female symbol too, and so is the shell in the foreground.

Or isn't it? But that's a man. Definitely a man. The mask of a man. A lizard is crawling over his face, he is rigid with terror. Grief, you say? I think it's terror. The picture ought to be called "The Event." This man doesn't know what is happening to him. It's a joke. Or maybe not?

Sign reading. Is there just one valid interpretation? I become absorbed in the nuances of color: compare the pale pink of the real shell lying on the window sill with the deeper, almost sultry mauve in the inside of the painted shell; note the cool green of the lizard on the face. It's running over his face, I think, says Nuria. It horrifies him.—I had thought the lizard belonged to the woman, was the woman's animal, the woman wouldn't mind if it rested on her face. A different terror had turned the mermaid mute. As a child I used to play with lizards, once one of them sunned itself on my stomach when I was lying in a potato bed. Now I have to look at the picture for a long time before I too can see the man, the male mask, help-lessly shocked by the symbols of the female. What should the pic-ture be called? Still Life with Mask, says Nuria. That's it. To me this picture seems something new, special in her work, effortless, summoned from the unconscious, a time-sign.

The woman in this brightly lit picture has by no means taken the fish out of the water as one might think at first. Instead, she is carrying it across a wide Spanish plain—colored Nuria's Spanish yellow. Her Don Quixote has already walked across this kind of plain, accompanied and sometimes supported by Sancho Panza. The woman with the fish looks familiar too, or, at least, her counter-part in dark colors: the woman by the sea, a profile, black, contem-plating a fish. She almost seems not to believe that she has managed to catch it. (A different woman, or the same woman from the same period who stands beside what very likely is the same sea, has picked up a star with her fingertips; or is it a starfish she has taken out of the sea?) Loaves and fishes are biblical foods, representative of food in general. This woman, this fish, appear surrounded by a swimming, almost liquid air. Maybe the woman came from far away, maybe she still has far to go. She has no doubt that she must go. She is bringing food. Among the early Christians, the fish was the symbol of Jesus of Nazareth.

Once Nuria Quevedo painted several versions of a man walking.

Nuria Quevedo, illustration to Karl Mickel's *Kants Affe* (1993).
Courtesy Edition Balance.

His upper body naked, he walks through water, perhaps a follower of the one who could walk on water. She calls the painting "Walker on the Sea," but the man is sinking, the water is rising above his knees, he is using his lifted arms to keep his balance. The year 1987, when the picture was painted—though its roots reach back farther, there are studies from 1985—was for me a symbol of despair and of desperate hope. The painting shows someone attempting the impossible. Everyone must interpret the paintings however they need to, Nuria Quevedo says.

Nuria Quevedo and literature—that's a topic that merits looking into, all on its own. Her study of printmaking—she says that as a painter she is self-taught—suggested to her the idea of working from literary texts. She has never produced illustrations in the strict sense but is happy when her own formulation of a question coincides with an author's formulation—as happened with Franz Fühmann, with Volker Braun, with Karl Mickel. Her studies on the theme of "knowledge" in the late 1970s blended easily into her "Cassandra" studies. She always aims to reduce things to the essential: woman confronted by man; a couple; birth; violence; pain; death. Each theme always preoccupies her for years, she generates motifs by which the theme can be treated exhaustively, she traces it back to the roots of our culture, extracts the authentic and timeless line which of course continues on into this century and which can be found by a woman—perhaps only by a woman who has rubbed up against two cultures, who has worked to integrate herself into two cultures, who loves both and takes from both what is her own. In her Cassandra cycle she is not concerned with individual psychology. For studies of the individual one must look to her portraits, for example, the large painting "The Émigrés," which she produced in 1967. But in the Cassandra series the focus is the creation of woman and shows the effort involved in becoming a human being, an effort visible in the brushstrokes and in the heaviness, almost clumsiness, of the figures.

And finally there are the images that accompany the text montages of Immanuel Kant and the Marquis de Sade, two writers who were contemporaries and who embodied the opposite poles of thought and emotion in 1800. Karl Mickel calls his literary collage "Kant's Monkey," and, in fact, one sees the monkey behind the curtain as de Sade rips it away, and one sees Kant wrenching his arms out of their sockets while he is thinking, betrayed by his body language. Best of all is the centerpiece of this series, a great discovery for me: a triptych that really speaks to me, that tells me more than I could express. On the left is a woman, who of course does not appear in the texts written by those two men. But here she is very much present, striding forward, almost rushing, unstoppable it seems, and, I should add, wearing a sun mask—the same mask I see hanging on the wall at Nuria's place. It creates some tension in this figure if one knows that in the Romance languages the sun has a male gender, *el sol* in Spanish, whereas in German it is feminine (*die Sonne*). What does it mean that this woman with her female form, her flowing motion, has put on this bright, almost luridly shining masculine mask? May we ask whether—at least in this cycle—it is the woman who sets out tenaciously and without illusions on the never-ending road out of "self-created immaturity," who uses and tempers the brilliant light of the Enlightenment that both burns and heals? And in this case, what is her relation to the middle piece of the triptych, above which the moon is shining, the moon which is masculine in German (*der Mond*), feminine in Spanish (*la luna*)? A marvelous, enchanting, spellbinding lunar landscape, not just centuries but cultures removed from the magical moonlit night of German romanticism. This moonlight is clear, almost hard, above a plain in which only a few boulders stand and resist it, casting sharp shadows. And then, to the right of this landscape, comes the third piece in the triptych, which shows not the masculine German death (*der Tod*) but *la Muerte,* the woman death of the Spanish-speaking peoples who takes in order to give, who with a gesture that is almost gentle takes the dying into the cycle of life, the same cycle to which the woman with the sun mask belongs.

Looking at the print in which two almost dwarflike forms stand facing each other—"de Sade" and "Kant"—while a great hand reaches down from above, we could say this image is eminently philosophical; whereas in the triptych—drypoint and aquatint—Nuria Quevedo seems to have achieved a synthesis, a summation of all the drafts and exercises she made over so many years. Throughout this time—during which so many have not only been exhausted

Nuria Quevedo, illustration to Karl Mickel's *Kants Affe* (1993).
Courtesy Edition Balance.

but have lost their impulse to work—she has labored on steadfastly.
Amid so many insecurities, she has achieved a security that derives
from the total lack of compromise in her work, a quiet stepping
forward without masks.

➤ 1 9 9 4 ◄

Torn in two, Germany
and at odds outside and in
One part lets the other be
in cold and dark that have no end
It would all be child's play
and you'd have abundant wealth
of fields and towns to make your way
if you could ever trust yourself

BERTOLT BRECHT, 1952

Parting from Phantoms

On Germany

↠ ↞

Everything about Germany has been said. I make this claim
after wearily pushing aside the stacks of recently published
books, the piles of fresh newspaper articles that I have read,
skimmed, or left unread. What a giant gruel Germans have been
cooking up, talking and writing and analyzing and arguing and po-
lemicizing and pontificating and lamenting, even satirizing themselves and Germany, in the past four years. We have stirred this
gruel ourselves, put the pot on the fire, watched it simmer, bubble,
sizzle, boil over; we have tasted it, eaten it up like good little children. But the gruel cannot be consumed, nor can it be held in check
any longer. It is spilling over the stove and kitchen, out from the
messy house onto the road, onto all the streets of our German cities,
apparently bringing no nourishment to the homeless Germans who
huddle there. And if we well-housed Germans want to be honest—
and what do Germans today want more urgently than to be hon-

Lecture given at the Dresden Staatsoper as part of the "Dresden Lectures" series, February 27, 1994. This translation (first published in *PMLA*, May 1966) © 1996 by The
University of Chicago; all rights reserved.

est!—we must admit that we no longer like the taste of this German millet gruel. We are sick of it. We are fed up with it.

"No!" cries the German Suppenkaspar, the Boy Who Won't Eat His Soup, who along with his friend Struwwelpeter is just this year celebrating his 150th birthday in blooming health (that is, their story is still being printed in great numbers): "O take the beastly soup away / I won't eat any soup today!" The question arises how a child raised to be antiauthoritarian can be forced to eat up the soup he has cooked himself, to swallow something he doesn't like. Normally he prefers to stuff himself to the gills with Italian food, he is definitely no anorexic, unlike the earlier soup rebel that the Frankfurt doctor Heinrich Hoffmann gave his little son Karl for Christmas 1844 and who died on the fifth day of his hunger strike.[1]

What can we do but laugh at that, since we know better about practically everything, including hunger strikes? How long did the hunger strikers hold out in the Bischofferode potash plant? Twenty days? Yet they are still alive. And it all happened just because they wouldn't eat the soup that others had cooked for them but that they too in their gullibility had helped to cook for themselves. You must make allowances for them because the party for which the majority of them voted, as Christians, in March 1990 neglected to tell them that their plant would unfortunately have to be closed down as part of achieving the level playing field demanded by a market economy.[2] So we saw on our TV screens the image of faithful Christians,

1. After presenting his cautionary tales to his son in 1844, Heinrich Hoffmann (1809–94), published them in 1845 as *Der Struwwelpeter. Lustige Geschichten und drollige Bilder ...* (Slovenly Peter: Merry tales and funny pictures ...); the book appeared in English translation a few years later. The series of characters mentioned by Christa Wolf—the Suppenkaspar (the Boy Who Won't Eat His Soup), Little Konrad, the Blackamoor, the Wild Huntsman, Little Pauline, Johnny Head-in-Air, Flying Robert—are from the Struwwelpeter tales. The metaphor of eating one's soup, which Christa Wolf uses throughout, also plays on a German idiom, "eating the soup you have made," which corresponds to the English proverb, "If you make your bed, you have to lie on it."

2. A summary of some of the events in the East German revolution will provide background to Wolf's comments throughout her talk. A series of demonstrations against the government of the German Democratic Republic began in Leipzig in September 1989 and spread to other major cities. The largest was a gathering on November 4, 1989, in East Berlin, which drew one million participants. Addressed both by opposition leaders and by members of the governing Socialist Unity Party, this demonstration led directly to the resignation of the Honecker government on November 7, to the legaliza-

some still fasting, giving union speeches in their church, and we heard them singing hymns like battle songs along with their priest, and we saw many of them weeping, men and women both.

Where am I headed? First, I just want to ask what really has become of good old Struwwelpeter, whom the well-known German psychoanalyst Georg Groddeck compared to Goethe's Faust for the depth of his effect on the German psyche. Is he still the same old Shock-Headed Peter, after five changes of government and society—the same whose hair (his creator admits) may have been "wickedly pulled" in the revolution of 1848? And who then, no doubt, cut off his unkempt mop and marched against France wearing a Prussian military haircut; who surely didn't stand in the way of Bismarck's founding of the empire; who has tried out a number of different coiffures since then; and who confronts us today with a managerial fringe or a bald pate? Is he still the same old Peter, adaptable to anything?

And what about his friend Little Konrad? Is he still sucking his thumb or chewing his fingernails down to the quick the minute his mommy turns her back or leaves the house for a bit—for her hus-

---

tion of the opposition group New Forum on November 8, and, on November 9, to the opening of the Berlin Wall and the approval of reforms to end the monopoly of the Socialist Unity Party. In the subsequent effort to define a new relation between the GDR and the Federal Republic, Wolf supported the "For Our Country" petition (see note 3 to "Berlin, Monday, September 27, 1993," above). Opposed to the *Anschluß* that would occur if the eastern states were immediately absorbed into the Federal Republic under Article 23 of the West German constitution, or Basic Law, the more than one million signers of the petition generally wanted the Germanys to unite gradually through close cooperation or favored a federation of the two states. They sought to halt what they considered a destabilizing offensive from the Federal Republic, to build an alternative to capitalism, and to ensure that any new German state was nonaligned and demilitarized rather than a part of NATO. In the elections of March 18, 1990, the Christian protesters of the Bischofferode plant in the GDR would presumably have voted for the Alliance for Germany, a coalition dominated by the East German Christian Democrats. Put together by the chancellor of West Germany, Helmut Kohl, the Alliance for Germany separated the Christian Democrats from left-wing groups with which they had been associated, allying the party with conservatives. This coalition favored rapid monetary union and unification under Article 23 of the Basic Law. Wolf's view is that the FRG government, seeking to facilitate the takeover of the GDR, deliberately destabilized the new political parties and reform groups in the GDR. See Harold James and Marla Stone, eds., *When the Wall Came Down: Reactions to German Unification* (New York: Routledge 1992).

band doesn't dispute her right to a job (he is out of work, incidentally, and hangs out in a bar, so what is she supposed to do at the stove all day?). Then the little boy gets bored, and "Zoom, his thumb's in his mouth!" I would like to know in how many German families children are still told that little boys who suck their thumbs get their thumbs cut off, snip snap snip. The Institute for Applied Social Science fails to give us the dope on this. On the other hand, it does inform us that, as of November 1993, 92 percent of Germans feel they are not a united people. Seventy percent in the East and 60 percent in the West reportedly feel that the divisive factors predominate, so perhaps it is all the more useful to remind ourselves of something we have in common: the book *Struwwelpeter* with its "merry tales" and "funny pictures" that all Germans read as children and that has affected even those who have not read it. This is what distinguishes a true book of popular literature: it springs from the national soul and pours its spirit back into its source, flowing back and forth, and—this is another thing we have learned—is hard to replace with a tradition of rational thought.

Alas, we shake our heads when we read *Struwwelpeter.* Even back in the 1840s, the "coal-black crow-black black-a-moor" could not "stroll past the door" without Ludwig "running over," "waving his little flag"; and when Kaspar and Wilhelm joined him, "they shrieked and laughed all three / As the little moor went by / For black as ink was he!" Those really were the good old days! All they did was shriek and laugh; they didn't throw the nigger off the commuter train, didn't put a knife to his throat, didn't even kick him with their hobnailed boots. How can that be? Dad and Mom actually smile at black people on the street, and at Turks and refugees, too, and think even Jews are human, and they are slightly taken aback if Sonny Boy doesn't share their opinions. But when they are on their own and stir the embers of their piety, they pray, "Dear God, I thank thee that I am not like those people!" Thanks to German unification, they are now free at last to accompany Frederick the Great to his ancestral resting place at Sans Souci in Potsdam, no matter what anyone may think. And Kaiser Wilhelm is being hoisted back up on his high horse, where from the elbow of the Rhine he can now cast his baleful gaze on France—at the very moment when, as it happens, we Germans are once again struggling to find our identity, which after all we must be allowed, at last, mustn't we? And how much nicer it would have been—yes, it would have been *even nicer*—if at Schinkel's New Guard House in Berlin we had been allowed to remember not only the victims of wars caused by Germans and their tyranny but, at the same time, those who have these victims on their conscience.[3] But you can't have everything at once, can you, and isn't moderation a splendid German virtue? But now I remember why I brought up the subject of German history.

Incidentally, a victim sometimes gets to turn the tables, as the folktales of *Struwwelpeter* acknowledge. In the tale of the wild huntsman, the hare grabs the musket from the hunter, sets his spectacles on her own nose, and boldly aims the gun at her persecutor: "And now she makes the gun to fire, / The hunter is in deadly fear."

We ought to be familiar with this kind of fear. I felt it as a refugee at the beginning of May 1945, somewhere on a highway in Mecklenburg, when German prisoners from the Sachsenhausen concentration camp who had been abandoned by their German guards and driven off by the advancing Soviet troops started to arm themselves with the cast-off weapons of the defeated German Wehrmacht—a sight that caused my muted uneasiness to cross the threshold into guilt, though it could not yet cross the far higher barrier into language. That took years to happen. The closer your ties to a guilty system and the greater your share in the guilt, the longer you need before you can express it. And, as we know, many Germans, very many Germans, never acknowledged their guilt or their complicity by a single word or made any apology. On the contrary, first they suppressed any guilt feelings that might have arisen, and then they suppressed the dull underlying discomfort as well. They let it sink down to the dregs of the unclarified and the unexpressed in the German temper, which are cultivated in many German families—in how many? I ask again. And the same people now hear it said that the gas chambers that exterminated the Jews never existed and read in the newspapers that in Berlin the names

3. Schinkel's New Guard House: Karl Friedrich Schinkel was the architect of Die Neue Wache, an 1818 neoclassical building. After the division of Germany it stood in East Berlin, where it was made into a monument to the victims of militarism and fascism.

of Communists murdered by the Nazis are to be removed from street signs. So I shall say their names here: Hans Beimler, Katja Niederkirchner, Heinz Kapelle. And I shall ask what signal the German mind will receive and no doubt is meant to receive from this elimination of history, which confirms us in our innocence. I almost hesitate to say the other names that are now at risk, for I can hardly believe it: Marx, Engels, Rosa Luxemburg, Karl Liebknecht.[4] But Berliners are allowed to keep the names of German fighter pilots on their street signs.

All coincidence, no doubt. Yet the coincidences are beginning to mount up, and coincidentally they all are heading in the same direction: to the right. This is a moment of opportunity, and people are taking advantage of it. The German woman too can be put back in her proper place. In Heinrich Hoffmann's tales she already lacked the power of speech, for "Upon the table all around / The mother looks and makes no sound." But the *Struwwelpeter* book also tells us the story of Little Pauline, who clearly has too good a time when she is left alone at home, jumping around the room "light of heart and full of song," a silly little thing, easily led astray, who can't resist playing with matches and gets her just deserts: she goes up in flames, so that nothing is left of her but the frivolous red shoes she liked to dance around in, no doubt with lewd intentions. Burning up spoils her fun entirely, which may well be the secret message of the auto-da-fé. One little girl in a book among so many little boys, and she is the one who has to burn. That is striking, because setting fires, burning up houses and people, has always been boys' work and still is. In 1845, when Little Pauline appeared on the pages of Hoffmann's book, the last witch burnings lay less than seventy years in the past.

We are in Frankfurt, three years before the first European revolution, which will jump from Paris into southern Germany and will immediately turn Frankfurt into one of its main arenas. The German Michel,[5] depicted in a nightcap by the irreverent German ro-

4. Karl Liebknecht (1871–1919): see note 5 to "Whatever Happened to Your Smile," above.

5. The name "Michel" was used by Heinrich Heine and other German authors of his period to designate the French revolutionary slumbering inside every German.

mantics, seems to be waking up. Before the revolution of March 1848, Heine had urged him to revolt:

> Michel, how long till the scales
> Fall from your eyes and you know
> That the best of your soup never fails
> To be stolen from your bowl?

> *(Michel, fallen dir die Schuppen*
> *Von den Augen? Merkst du itzt,*
> *Dass man dir die besten Suppen*
> *Vor dem Maule wegstibitzt?)*

"Liberty! Unity!" he now cries in the newspapers and even on the streets, which means: A German republic is long due, is overdue. A nation-state. Then the German princes abdicate one after another, or consent to the demands of—shall I call them the revolutionaries?—in more than thirty major German capitals. They have met all our demands! The cry goes out from Munich to Berlin, from Coburg to Hannover. The March 1848 revolution in Berlin is followed by the assembly that meets in Frankfurt at the end of March to draw up a constitution. People think they are dreaming: Metternich's parliament itself is publishing the elections to the National Assembly. They have met all our demands! And August Hoffmann von Fallersleben exults, "You'll never put Michel to sleep again!" He could not imagine that this same Michel, his nightcap concealed under his spiked helmet, would one day sing with deep emotion, "Deutschland, Deutschland über alles!"[6]

The men of the March 1848 revolution who met in the Paulskirche in Frankfurt for a constitutional debate did not imagine how their splendid revolution would be wrested away from them piece by piece, or that in the end, when the people of Frankfurt rebelled

---

6. August Hoffmann von Fallersleben (1798–1877), a patriotic poet who influenced the student movement and paved the way for the revolutionary events of 1848, wrote "Deutschland, Deutschland über Alles" in 1841 to express the desire of German liberals for unity. The poem provided the words for Germany's national anthem after World War I, and its meaning was reversed under Nazi rule. After World War II, the third verse was adopted as the national anthem of West Germany.

against them, they would place themselves under the protection of the Prussian army. For the time being, the German revolutionaries furled their flags. Struwwelpeter's pal Johnny Head-in-Air had been dreaming again and had fallen into the water; his little red pencil case was floating far away in the river. And defiant Robert, who dared to go outside in the rain and storm instead of staying snug at home "like a good little boy," in punishment would be lifted into the air along with his umbrella and blown away, never to be seen again. The second German Victorian Age had dawned. Karl Marx, who uncompromisingly called for a true unification of Germany as a republic, saw that the "powers of the past" were once again becoming the "powers of the present," and he concluded that the proletariat could win only under the governance of a revolutionary party that was independent in its ideology and organization.

A plan that failed, though it once had its reasons. Here, too, we should perhaps resist the temptation to separate cause from effect by obliterating memory. What is happening today has roots that reach far back into history. I think the men and women who patrolled around Berlin's Alexanderplatz in the early morning of November 4, 1989, wearing sashes with the inscription NO VIOLENCE! were aware of this. A remnant of hope still echoed in the slogan, the hope of leading a warped system back to its original ideals. But the main reason for invoking nonviolence was, I believe, a sense of reality. In the nights of October 7 and 8, East Berliners had had a foretaste of what things would be like if the state were to deploy its power against them. And this demonstration was called for the same reason as those in 1848: all demands had been granted. Were the hundreds of thousands of demonstrators nothing more than German Michels taking action when it was no longer dangerous to do so? They were harshly reproached afterward for not having stormed the Central Committee headquarters and the Council of State.

A troop of actors had assembled outside the Palace of the Republic, masquerading as the Politburo. They responded benignly and paternally to the cocky demonstrators who dared to wave at them—a humiliating exercise, often practiced with irony and self-irony so that it reduced the whole thing to the absurd; and that put an end to that maneuver. And what about storming the Central

Committee? What we didn't know at the time, though we suspected it, was that companies of militiamen armed with live ammunition had assembled in official buildings near the Alexanderplatz. *If* blood had flowed, it might have been plentiful, and it would not have been the blood of those who demand action after the fighting is over. No: what we did here was to put to rest the evil tradition of German conformists who relish their subservience. The sovereign, the people, walked the streets and laughed away those who presumed to guide and direct them: "Ciao!" Who ever heard of such a thing in Germany? When were Germans in the mass so un-German? Humorous, cheerful, ungloomy, relaxed, full of joie de vivre and well able to express it, imaginative, ingenious; and, nonetheless, what almost beggars belief, these people were not intoxicated, not would-be revolutionaries, but sober and self-confident. And they were—to apply this rational term to ourselves for once— solid citizens, whose sharp, incisive wit was attested by the multitude of banners and placards that I saw a few months later, rolled up and assembled in a hall in the Unter den Linden historical museum. The woman who opened the room for me told me of the feelings she had when classes of schoolchildren and West and East German visitors to Berlin came to view these evidences of a brief phase of our history that she had helped to shape: she felt it had all been for nothing.

Whichever thread I touch, the whole web stirs. One of the projects we began at the Round Table talks was a draft constitution for a German Democratic Republic worthy of the name, and when the rapid process of unification was under way, a board of trustees developed the draft into a constitution for a "democratically composed federation of German states." This led me, among others, to attend a constitutional debate in the Paulskirche in Frankfurt am Main in June 1991. I mention the date because we seem to be forgetting things at an ever-increasing speed. You would be amazed at how many men and women from East and West met there, and you would be amazed at who these people were who discussed with expertise and passion a new constitution for a new, remodeled Germany. The paper we released to the public bore a motto from Heinrich Böll: "The only way to be realistic is to get involved."

This assembly at the Paulskirche was not dispersed. The board of trustees that coordinated the work at Democracy House on the Friedrichstrasse in Berlin, that processed all suggestions into a mature draft and offered it for debate, dissolved voluntarily on July 30, 1993, suffering from lack of money and influence. Their last letter read, "We are experiencing with shock the devastating results of a constitutional debate held under the de facto rule of an executive interested in its own power." Meanwhile, a different commission, which did have money and influence, had been officially appointed. It ignored the work of the grassroots body and two years later presented the people of the united Germany with a Basic Law that had hardly been changed at all. Thus the commission threw away the chance to involve East Germans in a large-scale constitutional debate that would have allowed them to develop the kind of model patriotism that is based on a constitution. "Establishing a constitution is an expression of collective self-discovery," states the Paulskirche Declaration of June 1991—one more splendidly progressive German document that has ended up in the archives, where it awaits the study and possibly the favorable verdict of historians and may one day help our descendants to understand what in heaven's name the ungrateful East Germans found lacking in the process of German unification and in what manner they experienced democracy.

Those are the snows of yesteryear; let's leave them behind. Our children's children, and their children, will sing, "German women, German loyalty," with gusto,[7] no longer hearing "Deutschland über alles" as its unsung, suppressed subtext. What a consoling thought that is. But they won't know that for a brief time people talked about a different anthem. "And not above and not below other peoples do we wish to be." That would not be the worst of subtexts for us to hear.

Where am I headed? I am talking about forgetfulness. Of how oblivion evens out the differences between the generations. If I did not have such respect for my audience, I would have some fun making you guess who wrote the letter I am about to quote from and when it was written: "We cannot fail to perceive that we are merely living under the rule of force. It is all the more incisive because it

---

7. The first line of the second stanza of "Deutschland, Deutschland über Alles."

comes from those we called upon to help us against the [Danish] power and who now, having helped us to overcome it, treat us like a defeated tribe, throwing overboard our most important institutions without asking us, while forcing other institutions upon us as they see fit ... Germany cannot be united in this way." Theodor Storm was wrong about that, don't you think?[8] (Of course, he's the one who made the statement.) For that's exactly the way Germany has been united, at least since Bismarck, who said to the members of the North German Federation in 1867, "Gentlemen, let us put Germany in the saddle, and it will surely discover how to ride!" A man's comment, using the cavalry-based language of the German Junker. And, indeed, the horn has blown many a time, signaling Germany to mount up and also—although this came later—signaling people to ride for Germany. The first time was against France in 1870–71. The preparation for that war was the work of Bismarck, who led the Prussians to liberate Storm's homeland, Schleswig-Holstein, from the Danes. Storm had been forced to leave his home when it was under Danish occupation, only to see it annexed again by Prussia in 1866—the event of which Storm complains in his letter. But the acquisition of Schleswig-Holstein was just a prologue, a successful coup to outfox the Austrians and provoke the French. Have we forgotten it all? Okay. So this is the way you unite Germany: you proclaim the king of Prussia the emperor of Germany, in the Hall of Mirrors at Versailles. In the land of the enemy. As the fruit of victory in war and as a triumphal gesture to humiliate a conquered people. Germany, the "delayed nation," now makes up for lost time. The profit from the peace treaty that the French signed in Frankfurt am Main after the defeat of the Paris Commune brought German industry its long-desired boom, at least temporarily. The other Germans benefited from having a concrete place in which to install their free-floating sense of nationhood, though some, admittedly, were immediately deprived of their nation once again. As we well know, German Social Democrats, down to the present day, have been turned into "stateless persons" whenever it was deemed necessary. Social division erupts under the cloak of German unity.

In 1941, when Anna Seghers was in exile in Mexico, she wrote

8. Theodor Storm (1817–88) was a German realist essayist and novelist.

that in Germany demands for social justice had never been made conjointly with the demands for nationhood.[9] "On the contrary, they were smothered by those who had appropriated national pride for themselves." She realized how this German national trait, which was the product of German history, forged the chain of misfortune, disaster, and crime that so often dragged the Germans into the ruin they had prepared for other peoples and how it was the schism between social justice and nationalism that so often made German writers homeless in their own country and drove them into exile.

Where am I headed? Do I mean to lose myself in history, as I search for the sources of Germany's division? Where am I going? Secretly, I have known the answer for many days as I leafed through history books and the texts of constitutions, working on these pages, wondering if I would or should quote the words that lie behind all these other words. But now I shall see where it leads me.

Nine months ago, I lived and worked for a time in Santa Monica, California. I was invited to meet a group of Jewish Americans who called themselves members of the "second generation," the generation after the survivors of the Holocaust who were their parents. The president of the group, a physician who had never been to Germany and never wants to go, introduced me as "a voice out of the wilderness." I will give only a brief indication of what happened to me in the hour that followed, when I felt compelled to resist the image of Germany as a "wilderness"; the things I saw in my mind's eye as I talked about Rostock, Mölln, Solingen—the only images of Germany that all Americans had seen flitting across their TV screens—trying not to explain them but to place them in perspective;[10] and the subtext I heard in the long discussion afterward and later, in a café, when I was told more of the many tales of suffering by Jewish families.

What I felt first was a certain defensiveness: What did I have to do with Solingen? I very quickly had to accept the fact that for

---

9. See "The Faces of Anna Seghers," above.

10. The racist violence that increased in both parts of Germany after unification was typified by a 1992 attack in Mölln in which three Turks were burned to death, by several incidents in Solingen, and by the burning of a refugee center inhabited by Gypsies and Vietnamese in Rostock in 1992. Formerly, Mölln and Solingen were in West Germany, and Rostock was in East Germany.

these people I was not East or West German but simply German. The way they looked at me made me that. The doctor was just reading my book *Patterns of Childhood*. I remembered the lines I learned at the age of ten or eleven that I quote in that book and have never been able to forget: "We feel as Germans, are of German mothers / Our thinking's German, has been so from birth / First come our people, then the many others / Our homeland first, then the entire earth!" [11]

The time when I, along with many of my generation, ardently wished that we did not have to be German was already past when I began to write. All the same, I felt glad I was living in the smaller and poorer of the two German states, the one that had to bear the brunt of the war's consequences, had to pay for it much longer than the larger and wealthier Germany, which, moreover, dealt less severely with the remains of our Nazi past. Later, the GDR government became troubled by the reactionary, nationalistic names of institutions. During this period, which lasted several years, the government began to replace the word "German" with "GDR" in all public titles. No doubt this was a sort of defiant reaction to the West Germans' habit of regarding themselves as the only true Germans and designating themselves accordingly. In the end, nothing in the GDR had the name "German" any more except for the German Imperial Railroad, the Free German Union Federation, the Party newspaper *Neues Deutschland*, and the Socialist Unity Party of Germany. GDR citizens were supposed to consider themselves the "people of the GDR." The German Writers' Association and the German Academy of Arts were renamed. We used to joke about it, but I don't think we attached much importance to the adjective "German."

One of the group of American Jews I talked with said that as a result of the German persecution his parents came to feel for the first time that they were Jews. A woman stated her belief that "second-generation" Jews and Germans had something in common—namely, in neither case had the parents talked to their children about the past. It really isn't the same thing, I replied. But the woman stuck to her opinion: the silence of the parents had pro-

---

11. The translation of these lines is quoted from *Patterns of Childhood*, trans. Ursule Molinaro and Hedwig Rappolt (New York: Farrar, Straus & Giroux, 1980), 129.

duced similar effects on the children. That evening I began to get a feeling I couldn't give a name to, at least not for a long time, but which has remained with me ever since.

I began to wonder when and for what reason I had sought refuge in German literature. Why had I retraced a root of the modern, of alienation, of the industrial age—which like everything else was late to arrive in Germany? I became intimate with the mental universe of Karoline von Günderrode, Bettine Brentano, the women of romanticism who, like us, were the offspring of a failed revolution.[12] Their life histories, their lacerating conflicts. The way they were destroyed by the conflicts or made something out of them. I too went through an anxious time when the scales were evenly balanced between those two possibilities. I remember exactly how I felt when I stood by Hölderlin's tower in Tübingen for the first time; when I saw Georg Büchner's grave in Zurich. And now Bertolt Brecht's house on 26th Street in Pacific Palisades. We were shipwrecked like them, knew it for a long time, expressed it, and, remarkably, learned to see our life histories as possible German biographies of this century. I learned to see myself as a German writer. The "true Germans" who still exist, or exist again, now seem to regard this as an act of presumption.

Back in Los Angeles in May 1993, however, I was faced by a different challenge. I had never before had to answer for crimes of the new, united Germany, the large nation that had absorbed me along with the whole of the poorer Germany—crimes for which I did not feel accountable. All of a sudden I was asked to assume responsibility for the neo-Nazi atrocities in Rostock *and* in Mölln, to supply reasons why these young people in East and West had become uprooted, and to vouch that their brutality would not lead to a new German chauvinism. The Jewish Americans listened to me, but they were not sure if they could believe me. At least one young woman told me after the meeting that she doubted what I said and did not intend to go to Germany now. She asked if I wanted to go back. "Of course," I replied. But I couldn't help seeing Germany with different eyes.

What I saw was a country tied up in internal contradictions and

12. See note 1 to "The Faces of Anna Seghers," above.

struggles, a country over which the explanatory slogan "German unity" arched like a rainbow. This unity, which had at last been "fought for and won," or had been negotiated, or restored, or achieved, or brought about—this German unity was now a fact, the highest good, what people in the GDR had been calling for when they cried, "We are one people!" And it had been brought about by the politicians of the Federal Republic without first asking the West German people, some of whom reproach them for it now. But it was all done in an orderly procedure, even with parliamentary sanction. Looking at Germany from the outside, I now saw a nation in flux: great rivers of unemployed young people flowing out of the deindustrialized territories from East to West, some of them "commuters" and some leaving East Germany altogether. And much smaller rivulets of politicians, civil servants, judges, professors, institute directors, head physicians, managers, investors flowing from West to East, frequently commuting back and forth, forming the new upper class in the new eastern states of the Federal Republic and creating the new structures. There is an extremely brisk flow of letters back and forth between established property owners or their attorneys in the West, and the new owners or tenants of houses, apartments, and building lots in the East. And on another level—so it seemed to me, looking from the outside—there still are two distinct systems operating independently of each other: a small loop, which is growing weaker, and a large, high-powered one. Am I mistaken, or are we seeing a sort of allergic defensive reaction growing stronger in the western system against intruders from the East, a reaction first directed at intellectuals and writers, then at other former GDR citizens, including certain clergy members and others in the church, and now finally at the few East German politicians who had advanced into Western political institutions and are being excluded one after another? And isn't joie de vivre steadily vanishing from both systems—or, more accurately, biosystems—even in families, groups, territories that have few or no material worries?

Only gradually have I come to realize that many people in the West, and by no means only members of the establishment, consider East Germans to have occupied and still to occupy a lower level of civilization. The West's sneering at the East has a long tradition. I remember how in the spring of 1945, when we were refugees living in barns and attics, ragged and unkempt, we looked on the victorious Soviet troops as barbarians and enjoyed telling each other that they would flush their potatoes down the toilet to wash them. And this in Mecklenburg of all places, where few villages even had any toilets in 1945!

Thus, viewed from the West, people from "over there" are pouring through the just-opened border in dubious vehicles, which they mistakenly refer to as cars. Crowds of them, clutching plastic bags, are hurrying to the nearest distribution center, where money is eagerly handed out to newcomers and where, as *Bild* magazine has carefully documented, they pass off other people's children as their own to hook an extra hundred marks. They flood the discount stores—the ones they can reach—and leave again with their plunder. Brothers and sisters from a family unfamiliar to us—ill-bred, plebeian, proletarian, and yet demanding. Did they even know what a computer was before now? You feel ashamed to be related to such people. And then, on top of it all, when these East Germans are actually allowed to vote for the first time instead of just folding pieces of paper, they ruin the plans of West German left-wingers who had counted on their vote to support the left's goal of reshaping West German society into a social and economic commonwealth— that is, of reducing the capitalist features and enhancing the democratic features in West Germany's capitalist democracy.

Far be it from me to mock the disillusionment of West Germans on the left. On the contrary, only when I realized what they had hoped for and how their hopes were dashed did I better understand the aggressiveness they displayed toward formerly East German intellectuals who expressed critical views. These West Germans feel not only that East German critics gave an unclear picture of conditions in the GDR (although this allegation could be disputed) but also that they—that is, we—did not stop many GDR citizens from (at first) blindly buying the fantasy that everything was rosy in the West. West and East German intellectuals were separated by their disappointment instead of sharing it and working together to dismantle their self-deceptions.

Where am I headed? I'm in search of a name for a feeling. In Santa Monica, I confronted a compromising phase in my past. I learned how difficult it can be to face the past honestly and adequately when, in Germany, "overcoming the past" on the public level usually takes the form of a chronicle of scandals or a mere skimming of documents—documents that reduce people's personal histories to simple patterns of yes or no, black or white, guilty or innocent, and provide no information beyond that. I thought then and still think that this credulous faith in files is possible only in Germany. I shall not forget, nor do I want to forget, the physical sensation of being replaced, piece by piece and limb by limb, by another person who was built to suit the media, and seeing an empty place arise at the spot where I "really" was. It was an eerie sensation. I then found words for my eerie feeling: the disappearance of reality.

"Unreality" is a word Thomas Mann applied to Germany in 1934, when he was already abroad but not yet in exile. He spoke of the return to unreality. The phrase struck me and preoccupied me. I would often travel up to Mann's house in Pacific Palisades and walk down Amalfi Drive, where he used to walk almost daily when he was writing *Doctor Faustus*, that awe-inspiring self-confrontation of the German intelligentsia in their failure against fascism. Cautioning myself inwardly not to make pat comparisons, I wondered, Have we Germans now come together in a polity that at last is proof against the temptation to think "tragically, mythically, heroically," the kind of thinking Thomas Mann attributed in 1934 to those dear compatriots of his who had succumbed to German myth? Aren't we at last thinking "economically," "politically"—that is, realistically—in what Mann said then was not the German way? Yes, if thinking economically means thinking that the maximization of profit is the highest of all values and if thinking politically means putting the interests of one's own party above everything else.

Am I being unjust? Partisan? Four and a half years of German unity, and myths and legends abound—some circulated intentionally, some necessarily arising from the way German unity is being pursued. The large-scale attempt to reduce the GDR to the status of an "unconstitutional state," to assign it to the realm of evil and thus to block historical thinking about it, has proved useful in the equally large-scale title challenges and mass expropriation of the property of GDR citizens. But above all it has helped hide the fact—from our West German fellow citizens, among others—that history is once again sailing in the direction favored by those who have enough clout to determine which way the wind blows. (All the same: the impressive total of West German claims for the recovery of property in East Germany—2.1 million!—involves a territory several times larger than the entire area of the GDR, which retroactively legitimizes an old joke we used to tell in the GDR, satirizing the hubris of the authorities: "We are the biggest GDR ever.")

Joking aside, the Federal Republic has always regarded itself as the normative case for postwar German history, while the GDR is treated as an accident of history—a view that ignores the historical situation that produced the GDR and ignores the phases of its development, which, by the way, were always related to circumstances in the Federal Republic. The GDR is painted as nothing but a repellent monotony of oppression and scarcity. Everyone who lived in this state or came into contact with it is tainted (a thesis now backfiring against West German politicians of every hue, with the result that it may be withdrawn from circulation). No one in the eastern provinces has anything to be proud of: that has been the message for a long time. Nor did those in the West see any cause to be sensitive in the way they treated the personal histories of East Germans, to ask the motives for actions and omissions, or to find out how people changed. Except for a few, who were allowed to call themselves victims and often really were victims, all East Germans were to be considered Stasi accomplices, government supporters, or collaborators. When I try to put myself in the place of a West German who has never been in the GDR, who never plans to visit the new federal states, and who has been asked to pay a solidarity tax on behalf of the dubious folk who live there—the disappearance of reality turns out to have some undesirable practical results. Only very generous and very enlightened minds in the West have struggled through to the realization that they could not guarantee, given the same circumstances, that they would not have ended up like "those people." I finally understood why the Federal Republic of Germany had turned as if by magic from an object of critical reflection into almost an object of desire for many West Germans on the left: if the other German state lost value, the value of their own state could not remain the same. To trade a past unreality for a new unreality seems to me questionable on either hand. Am I partisan? I believe that a clearer and more differentiated picture of conditions in the GDR would be useful to West Germans as well as to us. Should we not be struck by the fact that the East Germans who were critical of the GDR—citizen activists, literati, young protesters—are now the very ones who are warning against a demonization of the GDR? I have heard a number of them complain about the unquestioning assumption that they got the worse deal because they had to grow up in the GDR. Meanwhile, East Germans who went along with the status quo in the past now know which side their bread is buttered and are once again taking care not to voice any protest.

I think this is normal, and Germans in the western states of the Federal Republic should not be at all surprised by it, although it may hurt their feelings. Indeed, it's hurtful for both sides, especially when they find out how similar they are after all in many respects. The differences in mentality still experienced by many people as very noticeable and disturbing are determined if not by differences in region, at least by differences in social order. Even though the Federal Republic and the GDR both represented developments of industrial society, even though both strove for efficiency, profit, productivity, and growth, nevertheless West Germany, which was able to pursue a market economy without ideological hindrance, implanted in its people a catalog of values different from those in the East. I believe that what separates us most clearly is our relation both to property—because, like it or not, people in the GDR dealt with property in a different, looser way, regarding its value as lying merely in its use—and also, sad to say, to money, the pivot around which thoughts and circumstances revolve in a free-market economy. It must be offensive to West Germans if East Germans still betray by a glance or by a smirk that they consider the role of money in the West abnormal. Of course, they are eager to learn the new ways, sometimes too eager. They worry about their money; they too are always talking about it now; they fill out the dozens of forms required for them to get the money they have coming to them. But in their heart of hearts, I'm afraid, they don't yet see their society as being divinely appointed to produce more and more superrich people at one end and more and more poor people at the other—and I'm not talking of material poverty alone.

Here I pause and ponder. My West German friends, in fact most West Germans I know, have exactly the same concerns we do: they worry that the model of the market economy in a crude form has been elevated to a new dogma following the collapse of state socialism. Moreover, by a wicked irony of history, the fundamental flaws in the market economy are becoming increasingly apparent, faster than anticipated, so that it is losing its powers of integration even in its Western core nations and is now driving more and more people into the margins here, having already done so in large areas of other continents. Of course, this is not exclusively a German problem. An attempt is still being made to present it as a consequence of unification, or at least as something temporary, a valley from which we will emerge in an upswing, with increased sales, expanded production, and progress. But what if this doesn't happen? What if the limits of growth have nearly been reached? Isn't it possible that people who have just endured the collapse of their economic system after engaging in hopeless competition with a free-market economy may now be particularly alert to the symptoms of another collapse? Isn't it possible that they could help speed up the demystification of the free-market model, so successful in the past? And that on this level, the level of identical social interests, those who belong together will gradually come together after all?

But if this is the case, we East Germans too should say goodbye to our own denials of reality, with speed and determination. On the economic plane, unification admittedly developed into a struggle over the distribution of wealth in which most East Germans had no chance. And, admittedly, East German territory is being colonized by West German administrators, who get extra "jungle pay" for their laudable service in an underdeveloped country. But one day somebody should sing the praises of those many West Germans at every level of the economy, administration, and culture who do not gloss over the problems but are working together with their East German colleagues, selflessly and without arrogance, with tact and expertise. Moreover, colonization becomes a fact only if the "natives" behave like a colonized people, either slavishly ingratiating themselves with the new bosses or exhibiting childish defiance. Even in a parliamentary democracy, recognition as an adult is something you don't get for free, especially in times of unemployment and recession. Now the price has changed.

I was speaking of the loss of reality. We can't say goodbye to our past as easily and cheerfully as we thought we could at the Alexanderplatz on November 4, 1989. I have the impression that many former GDR citizens, experiencing a new alienation and finding that if they are candid with others their openness is used against them, are employing this experience as a pretext to avoid any critical self-questioning and are even revising their life histories. I am sometimes amazed to hear normal, well-adjusted acquaintances of mine reveal what brave resistance fighters they have been all along. I know how hard it is to work yourself out of feelings of injury, hurt, helpless rage, depression, and paralyzing guilt and soberly to confront the events or phases in your life when you would prefer to have been braver, more intelligent, more honest. Of course, you can always, or usually, find people who need self-examination even more than you do. I expect you realize I am not talking about criminal acts. Nor can I believe, unfortunately, that the majority of those who cooperated informally with the Stasi will search out the people they had under surveillance and confess their misdeeds to them. To believe that would be Protestant wishful thinking. They would probably rather go on living with the burden on their souls, or they will try to relieve the burden by defending what they did, or they will cling to the ideological suppositions that made them prone to such activity in the first place. No, the people I am talking about do not have especially burdened consciences; they are not especially heroic but are "ordinary" people who, I think, could gain more freedom and a greater sense of reality from a sober examination of their personal history—and gain more pleasure, too, by coming to understand what is happening in the present and even learn to recognize and endure the paradox of our lives. Or am I hoping for too much?

Even though it's a myth that GDR citizens chose their current fate—when they chose unification and parliamentary democracy, they thought they were choosing prosperity and naively believed that fraternity came along with liberty and equality—the choice offered to them clearly made the GDR a special case among the nations under state socialism with their protracted, socially costly, and to some degree fruitless efforts to convert to market economies. In eastern Germany, too, the cost of not sinking into the condition of a so-called third world country is very high, especially for many people over fifty. They must come to terms with the fact that, given the distribution of political power in Germany in 1990 and given the high status of property and possessions in a capitalist economy, they stood no chance of having their modest share of property legally recognized—for example, by a one-time reversal of a central law, allowing compensation before restoration—though such a step would have avoided an enormous amount of sorrow and rage in the new federal states as well as friction, hatred, and envy between East and West Germans (more than a few of whom, incidentally, find themselves thrust into roles that don't suit them). But the restoration of old property relations took precedence over relaxed and friendly relations among Germans. The reality of these straightforward political, social, and legal facts of life is being denied, swept under the rug of unification, or raised to a "higher plane" of morality and kept there as long as possible because people are less likely to rebel when they are put in the wrong. Unless one day they just strike out blindly in all directions.

Where am I headed? I think that in East and West Germany it's time to part from the phantom that each was to the other for so long and thus to part from the phantom of our own land, too. Get real, Germany! And why not? We know what happens to denied, repressed reality: it disappears into the blind spot in our consciousness, where it engulfs activity and creativity and generates myths, aggressiveness, delusion. The spreading sense of emptiness and disappointment also produces social maladies and anomalies in which groups of young people "suddenly" drop out of civilization, cancel what seemed abiding social contracts, and turn into young zombies without compassion, even for themselves.

At a secondhand bookstore in Santa Monica, I found a story by Friedrich Torberg, *Mein ist die Rache* (Vengeance is mine).[13] The author describes the sadistic practices of a concentration-camp com-

13. "Mein ist die Rache" In *Golems Wiederkehr und andere Erzählungen* (Frankfurt/Main: S. Fischer, 1968), vol. 6 of Torberg's *Gesammelte Werke*.

mandant in 1943 who drives a group of Jewish prisoners to commit suicide one after another. It is almost unbearable to read. One reader, apparently an émigré German Jew, added some bitter marginal notes after World War II. On the last page this reader penciled in: "America is full of Jews who love Germany and yearn for it."

The night after I read this book, a question occurred to me that has stayed on my mind ever since and that I want to pass on to you: What would we all give, each one of us, each individual German, for this not to have happened? It's a "pan-German" question. Perhaps we shall know something more about ourselves if each one of us tries to answer it individually, as honestly and, above all, as concretely as possible. And doesn't it lead to three other questions that are worrying us: What was? What remains? What will be?

An English clergyman told us recently that the Germans must make up their minds about themselves, must learn to affirm themselves and the positive sides of their history; otherwise the young people will drift farther and farther away. My family thought about what we Germans could be proud of, what we have that is particularly good, and my fourteen-year-old grandson, who had just spent two weeks in the United States, said: "The bread we bake in Germany." We laughed, and the more I thought about it, the more satisfied I was with that answer. Bread as an ancient symbol and as everyday materiality, as *the* food par excellence, a sensual pleasure you never tire of, simple and at the same time delicious. It fills you, it has aroma, it has flavor, and with its color and manifold shapes it is also a feast for the eyes. Along with wine, it stimulates conversation, friendship, hospitality. What I would like to see—and it's already happening—are Germans from different points of the compass working together, developing projects, and then sitting down around the table to talk, even to argue, and to eat in common the soup they have cooked for themselves. To set on the table the bread they have brought from their various regions, offering it to each other and sharing it gladly and generously.

Index

➤➤ ◄◄